FORBIDDEN RELIGION

Suppressed Heresies of the West

Edited by J. Douglas Kenyon

Bear & Company
Rochester, Vermont

Bear & Company
One Park Street
Rochester, Vermont 05767
www.BearandCompanyBooks.com

Bear & Company is a division of Inner Traditions International

Library of Congress Cataloging-in-Publication Data

Forbidden religion : suppressed heresies of the West / edited by J. Douglas Kenyon.
p. cm.

Summary: "Reveals the thread that unites the spiritual paths that have opposed orthodox religion over the centuries and the challenge they provide the status quo"—Provided by publisher.

Includes bibliographical references.

ISBN-13: 978-1-59143-067-4 (pbk.)

ISBN-10: 1-59143-067-4 (pbk.)

1. Jesus Christ—Miscellanea. 2. Christianity—Miscellanea. 3. Secret societies—Religious aspects—Christianity. 4. Christianity—Controversial literature. 5. Freemasonry—Religious aspects—Christianity. I. Kenyon, J. Douglas.

BT304.93.F67 2006
273—dc22

2006018075

Printed and bound in the United States by Lake Book Manufacturing

10 9 8 7 6 5 4 3 2 1

Text design and layout by Jon Desautels
This book was typeset in Sabon with Avant Garde and Rubber Stamp used as display typefaces

All pictures are reprinted from *Atlantis Rising* magazine unless otherwise noted

FORBIDDEN RELIGION

Contents

Acknowledgments

To all of those to whom I directed special credit in *Forbidden History*—our previous volume—once again I claim an extra measure of gratitude for making *Forbidden Religion* possible. Included, of course, are my wife, my parents, my original financial supporters, and many others who made *Atlantis Rising* magazine—as well as this latest project—possible.

This time, though, I would like to make an important addition to the list of those to whom I am deeply indebted.

I speak of the founders of the United States and of the protections they bequeathed to us all through the Constitution. These days, when so many of us feel free to challenge entrenched authority wherever we find it, it is worth remembering that such challenges have not always been easy, a fact that remains true in much of the world today. Indeed, as we chronicle in these pages, many of our forebears paid with their lives for attempting to express sentiments much like those written here.

However, the fact that our freedom of religion—no small matter in a book called *Forbidden Religion*—and the freedom of the press, so dear to all of us in the publishing business, are now taken for granted may be both a wonderful thing and something to worry about. If we forget how fortunate we are, can we expect to continue so? In a time when so many feel threatened by the freedoms of others—especially freedom of conscience—and they seek the means to deny such rights to those with whom they differ, we must not forget the importance of vigilance.

That these liberties, at least as spelled out in the Constitution, may now be commonplace does not mean they are insignificant. Without them, we suspect that some would try very hard to prevent publications such as ours from seeing the light of day. We are forever grateful to be free of their oppression, and to be able to discuss our issues openly, without fear of the consequences.

Introduction

J. Douglas Kenyon

The history of the world, some allege, is the history of a war between secret societies. And religion, they argue, is but the public tip of a secret iceberg by which human activity can be directed for good or ill. Just as leaders may have kept their real agendas secret, so have the true purposes of many religions been hidden from public view.

But, as with the wind, invisibility does not mean an absence of force, direction, or intensity that, to a careful observer, can reveal the ultimate goal. Just as approved religions may advance the hidden purposes of powers that be, virtually *forbidden* religions exist that do not, and their followers must gather in secrecy.

If religion is defined as a set of beliefs and practices maintained by the faithful that assert the nature of divinity and his (or her, or its) relationship to humanity, then, in fact, many people are religious who do not think they are. Indeed, even those who deny the existence of a deity are themselves religious, in that they espouse a belief in the nature of deity (i.e., that it does *not* exist) that they cannot prove and that they maintain by something very much like faith.

In the meantime, many have come to believe that behind the veil, strings are pulled and preachers of every persuasion—including the secular, the scientific, and the political—proclaim visions that have been revealed to them, while an ancient and invisible chess match among hidden elites has shaped our entire history and continues doing so to this very day. This great struggle is focused on the true dimensions of man's inner being, and at stake may be the survival of the human soul itself.

On the one hand are those who see the human race as little more than consumers of artificially manufactured stuff—religious and academic doctrines included. According to this line of thinking, we are all products of the Darwinian struggle and nothing more. Whatever claim we have to worth and dignity is due solely to our collective advancement since leaving the caves a mere few millennia ago, from which, we are told, we set forth on a heroic ascent to our present "lofty" height. Notions of immortality and transcendent individual possibilities are said to be illusions born of social conditioning—nothing more.

Those who support another view, however, see unlimited capacities in each of us—not excluding personal immortality. Never mind that the human psyche of today clearly suffers from ancient wounds. The evolutionary scheme is seen by these optimists as far grander, more subtle, and, indeed, more sublime than mere survival of the fittest.

And yet, in this age, so many people are enslaved by a shriveled concept of their own identity. Programmed to accept the authority of the dominant scientific/secular/humanist establishment, we have given up on the more exalted possibilities that lie within us. The ruling—academically rooted—edifice has convinced most of us that its formulations are settled matters, well beyond challenge. We are left to play our assigned parts—nothing more.

The writers of this book argue that the underlying logic or rationale on which the ruling establishment—whether Church, state, or academia—bases its authority is fallacious, if not corrupt, and has been so for a long, long time.

At the heart of the matter remains the old dispute over how one can know the truth of anything—and which is better, science or religion? Let's not forget that the distinction between science and religion, so fundamental to our twenty-first-century point of view, is an entirely modern one born out of the alienation of Western civilization. Only a society that sees a great gulf between what is within and what is without is capable of drawing such a sharp distinction between the two. Even quantum physics has demonstrated the lack of separation between the observer and that which is observed, yet we stubbornly cling to our cherished—albeit artificial—distinctions.

The ancients did not divide the world in this way. For them, science and religion were one. What mattered was ultimate truth, not category. If their enlightened understanding of the soul was actual knowledge and not entirely based on faith—as we have learned to believe today—who can say what kind of science and technology may or may not have developed?

Could the study of subjects like electricity, magnetism, gravity, and energy have grown out of experience with the soul in search of immortality? For us, the natural world as currently conceptualized is subject to scientific study; but if we can't conceptualize it, we call it supernatural and consider it—if not hallucination—simply beyond human understanding.

Perhaps the ancients were not so constrained. If, as we encounter their legacy, our arrogant attempt to pigeonhole their handiwork falls short, the fault is more likely ours than theirs.

Knowledge, it has been said, is power. We have also heard that a little knowledge is a dangerous thing (emphasis on *little*). We think the important question is: What is knowledge anyway? Or—to take a cue from neurotic contemporary thought—does knowledge even exist?

In many great and ancient spiritual traditions, gnosis or knowledge of some sort—self-knowing, truth-knowing, love-knowing—is *a* goal, if not *the* goal, of life. And yet we see Western culture questioning the very possibility of knowing anything with certainty, least of all the answers to ultimate questions of truth: Who are we? Where did we come from? What is our purpose?

The issue, of course, is not whether there is such a thing as truth, but how capable are we of apprehending whatever it may be. From *Slaughterhouse Five* to *A Clockwork Orange,* from *Catcher in the Rye* to *Rebel Without a Cause,* countless contemporary myths make disputing the capacity of humankind to understand truth into a kind of heroism. From psychoanalysis to existentialism, from situation ethics to political correctness, today's thought has undermined the authority that goes with true knowledge. Hamlet-like, we are left to wonder if we should *be* or *not be.*

On such issues, science—at least the kind of science that dominates civilization today—does us little good. The best an honest empirical method can hope to achieve is an indication of probabilities. Nowhere in the halls of academia is pure knowing found, the kind that comes with what philosopher Theodore Roszak called "rhapsodic declaration." Present in copious quantities, though, is despair.

When, a few centuries ago, we decided to free ourselves from the corrupt priesthood of the Dark Ages and turn to what we thought was a more enlightened way of deciding things, we believed we were getting closer to true knowing. Ironically, what we got in the bargain was *doubt,* and in place of old superstitions came a new kind of fear. Instead of hellfire, we got the void. It has taken awhile for the full implications to sink in, but who can question that a widespread hunger for certitude now threatens to overwhelm civilization?

Sadly, that unrequited longing has already carried many beyond the brink of madness and into the abyss. Into the knowledge vacuum created by our corrupt scientific priesthood has rushed a multitude of false priests and charlatans promising the true wine of spiritual knowledge while delivering a plethora of poisons—from genocide to jihad. Whether Adolf Hitler or Osama bin Laden, the pied pipers of hell, by exploiting the legitimate human desire for ultimate answers, continue to ensnare the unwary masses.

Ironically, at the dawn of the twenty-first century, one relic of nineteenth-century thinking maintains a grip on modern thought. Still dancing its strange Kabuki ritual on the public stage is something that may reasonably be called the cult of reductionism.

This archaic philosophy—also known, ironically, as logical positivism—promoted materialism and doctrines such as social Darwinism, behaviorism, Marxism, and even phrenology (a system claiming that human character can be understood by measuring skulls). Logical positivism promoted many other discredited notions, once insisting that the universe could be explained in simple terms fully transparent to conventional science.

To the logical positivists, the cosmos worked something like a giant pinball machine with objects colliding and careening about in ways that were inherently compatible with the science of the day. They had little use for metaphysics, spirituality, or invisible forces in general, and they certainly would not have cared much for quantum physics. Long written off by more discriminating minds as naive at best, the reductionist conceit was largely replaced by deeper and more subtle notions promoted by thinkers such as Jung and Einstein. Nevertheless, like Count Dracula, militant reductionist thinking clings stubbornly to its twilight existence.

Today it maintains considerable influence over much thinking in academia, politics, and the media. The bolder of the breed even set themselves up as a virtual priestcraft of professional "debunkery," pretending to expose the so-called fallacies and quackery that threaten their most cherished assumptions—weirdly echoing the Dominican inquisitors of an even darker time. The reductionist's task is aided, in no small measure, by widespread public ignorance of relevant facts. Subtle preachings of this primitive belief system can be found in current science news. Here, findings of the research community are offered to explain away evidence for concepts that are anathema to materialist reductionists—for example, belief in the paranormal is said to arise out of genetic predisposition; near-death experience is a brain anomaly; God is a subatomic particle; and so on.

Self-styled skeptic Michael Shermer, author of *Why People Believe Weird Things,* argues in an article in *Scientific American* that "smart people believe weird things because they are skilled at defending beliefs they arrived at for non-smart reasons." By "weird," Mr. Shermer refers to notions he rejects or cannot understand, and since he admits smart people espouse them, he is forced either to trash these notions or to own up to his own failings. Not surprisingly, he has chosen the former.

Like a slow-witted child, the unrepentant reductionist has deduced that the cart propels the horse—not the other way around.

But hopeful signs emerge. Indeed, something in our collective psyche may have shaken loose in the shock of 9/11 and its aftermath, forcing us to think about things we had set aside or forgotten for too long. In the face of looming threats to life itself, the search for meaning and the real purpose in our existence has taken on new urgency for many of us; consequently, we are less tolerant of the shams and scams that, in less turbulent times, could be foisted upon us with impunity. Such changes do not bode well for the merchants of illusion who have flourished in the twilight.

Philosophies and scientific paradigms that limit the possibilities of the human soul clearly reflect the corruption at the top of the idea establishment. From this quarter has come a multitude of cheats and ploys calculated to align us with discredited worldviews—or what might be called false religions.

"Scientifically" derived doctrines declaring that we are mere animals—accidents of nature for whom destiny is a meaningless illusion—seem no longer to awe the people or to empower these self-anointed custodians of ultimate truth. Notwithstanding frantic efforts to prolong their tenure at the top, a corrupt "scientific" priesthood—out of touch with its own divinity—finds the emptiness of its official pronouncements becoming clear to all, and its departure from the dais of authority inevitable.

The recent best-selling novel Dan Brown's *The Da Vinci Code* brought massive and—from the orthodox viewpoint—unwelcome attention to several topics seldom considered by the general public. To the extent that it may result in some sorely needed education, we applaud. We are well past the day when the most crucial aspects of Western civilization's suppressed history should be shouted from the housetops. Any secret agenda of Leonardo da Vinci or his brethren is well worth unraveling. However, to the extent that Brown has, in our view, misrepresented many of the matters he reveals, we are not so happy. How unfortunate that the multitudes discovering this esoteric realm for the first time are, in our opinion, poorly served.

To suggest, for example, that the Holy Grail is a specific person or even a bloodline seems an inadequate and shallow interpretation of a truly profound mystery. At the least, it is reductionist and materialistic, if not idolatrous, and it misses the sublime point made by great sages and saints of East and West that "the kingdom of Heaven is within you" (read: "in all of us"). Certainly Parsifal and his fellow knights were required to learn that lesson well or fall short in their quest for the Grail. Buddhists have a saying: "If you meet the Buddha on the road, kill him." The point being: Don't identify your liberation with an external physical being—look within.

We have no doubt that, in the pursuit of power, corrupt institutions on this planet have played the games that Brown describes (this book itself details many of them). Fortunately, their games do not include what some call the "ultimate game," and that—for those who have ears to hear and eyes to see—is written between the lines of our sacred, albeit forgotten, texts.

An important point to grasp is that in the development of our civilization, the divine feminine was rejected and trampled underfoot. We think it equally important to understand that the means to her rescue are within us all, not confined to a secret elite. The divine feminine within us must be brought into harmony with our masculine aspects, where it can be raised well beyond the rudimentary stage. When this elevation is ardently and honestly pursued, the ancient wisdom teachings say that life energies will rise like sap in spring up the spinal stalk. This uniting of masculine and feminine polarities at every level causes the chakras to blossom, culminating in the unfolding of the thousand-petaled lotus in the crown, with a new birth in the new earth of infinity—a world unlimited by mortal constraints.

This, we suspect, is the nature of enlightenment and the goal of evolution. And yet, like the seven blind men and the elephant—where each attempts to use his own limited experience to describe something virtually indescribable—we tend to interpret according to our individual lights. If we've lost sight of our immortality, simple procreation may seem like the best thing we have going.

The quest for truth cannot and should not be abandoned—far from it. We are convinced, however, that the goal should be pursued more sanely, wisely, and less fanatically.

For those lost in the sea of meaningless contemporary life who yet seek to navigate past the pirate coves and into the safe harbor of true gnosis, remember that anyone claiming special knowledge of such things—seeking the authority that goes with such knowledge—is subject to challenge and must be required, among other things, to show his real fruits.

To put it another way, when evaluating truth, the proof is in the pudding. Nothing else has quite the flavor of the real thing.

PART ONE

CHRISTIANITY: THE TRUTH BEHIND THE ORTHODOX VEIL

1 The Mystery of the Christ

Is There More to This Story Than Even Hollywood Imagines?

J. Douglas Kenyon

As millions have flocked to see Mel Gibson's *The Passion of the Christ,* a multitude of controversies have also arisen. For some the issue is: Can such graphic violence serve a spiritual purpose? For others, questions of anti-Semitism are crucial, while still others see advancement of a religious agenda. Hollywood's moguls, however, look to clone the formula, create a franchise, and perhaps develop a holy cash cow.

Everyone agrees on at least one thing: The movie has been a phenomenon, breaking most box office records. *Passion,* it seems, may have benefited from the same power source that brought the world the Christian religion in the first place. Certainly the story of a hero unjustly sacrificed for the crimes of the multitude has been the stuff of countless tales from many cultures, and the catharsis that comes from frequent retelling has, over the centuries, provided no small measure of cultural uplift.

In *Hero with a Thousand Faces* and other books, the mythologist Joseph Campbell has suggested that the solitary journey of the universal Hero—East or West—is fundamental to the survival of the human tribe, even though that tribe may persecute and even kill its benefactor. Others, such as Sir James Frazer in *The Golden Bough,* make similar arguments. Indeed, echoes of this theme undergird many of Hollywood's best efforts, from *Lord Jim* to *The Man Who Would Be King.*

Unfortunately, Mel Gibson seems little interested in such stuff. As in his previous blockbuster *Braveheart,* he appears fixated on the graphic details of physical torture. *Passion* spends an interminable ten minutes on the actual flaying of Jesus by Roman guards, and it dwells in excruciating detail on the most violent aspects of the story. In *Braveheart*'s climactic scene, Gibson's Scottish hero William Wallace is vividly executed. Such imagery, Gibson has argued, serves to move his audience emotionally. Indeed it may, but whether it serves any higher purpose is debatable.

Passion relies for its narrative in large measure on the gospels and on familiar Catholic tradition. The fourteen Stations of the Cross are clearly depicted, including the wiping of Jesus's face by Veronica. Though the scene is probably unfamiliar to most evangelical Protestants, they have embraced the film nonetheless. Regarding the actual events of Jesus's last hours, Gibson veers little from orthodoxy, thus doubtless endearing himself to conservative Christians bitterly opposed to less conventional Hollywood versions of recent distribution (e.g., *The Last Temptation of Christ*).

Opinions divide largely along believer/nonbeliever lines. On one side is mainstream Christianity—represented by Catholics and Protestants—and on the other, the secular humanist establishment. Ironically, both sides base their reaction on literal biblical interpretation. Christians who read the Bible literally and believe accordingly are opposed by secularists who object to a literal reading of the Bible and maintain their *dis*belief accordingly.

The charge, for example, that *The Passion of the Christ* is anti-Semitic is based on a fear that blame for the crucifixion will fall on Jews, whose first-century elite priesthood provides the villain of the story. A more enlightened view—that sees the antagonist as a perennially corrupt power elite present in every generation—is lost in the argument. We fail to notice the "Scribes and Pharisees" all around us, who appear in our modern culture in entirely different guise—perhaps as college professors or intellectuals preaching new, more subtle doctrines of intolerance.

Both camps attempt to apply an essentially materialistic standard to subject matter usually considered spiritual. Almost unheard in the tumult is a third point of view, one that looks for meaning in symbolic terms, along some of the less traveled byways of history. Often stereotyped as "New Age," its adherents can actually claim a pedigree far older than that of most popular religions, including Christianity and even Judaism. At times called the perennial wisdom or an esoteric or mystical brand of Christianity, the general outlines of this view are accepted by authorities as diverse as Edgar Cayce,

Fig. 1.1. The Head of Christ, *a traditional representation of Jesus, as painted by Rembrandt van Rijn in 1655.*

Mary Baker Eddy, Paramahansa Yogananda, and Helena Petrovna Blavatsky.

According to this thinking, the real power of Christ's message to bestow eternal life has been stolen from Christianity by a corrupt elite. In an attempt to frustrate the natural aspirations of "God's children" on Earth—namely, to return to their creator/parent—the true wine of an ancient wisdom tradition represented by Jesus has been returned to mere water by Earth's powers and principalities.

Advocates for esoteric Christianity point out that the Bible, as currently constituted, is the product of church councils convened to address early controversies. The Council of Nicaea, for instance, was assembled in A.D. 325 by Constantine I, the newly converted Christian emperor of Byzantium. At the top of the council's agenda was the so-called Arian heresy. This argument centered on the divinity of Jesus was waged between the Gnostics (or Arians) and the Nicaeans. The Gnostics sought direct personal knowledge of God (gnosis) and took seriously such statements by Jesus as "Know ye not that ye are gods?" and "The kingdom of heaven is within you." The Nicaeans, on the other hand, saw Jesus as the absolutely essential mediator between God and man. The Gnostics were outvoted and their teachings were thereafter forcibly removed from Church doctrine.

Some researchers, including Michael Baigent, Richard Leigh, and Henry Lincoln in *The Messianic Legacy*, have argued that fourth-century Gnostics inherited the mantle of the apostle James, brother of Jesus and leader of the first-century Church. Few people realize that the Church's early years produced many gospels and books purported to have been authored by direct associates of Jesus (e.g., The Gospel of Thomas and The Gospel of Mary Magdalen, as well as the recently discovered Gospel of Judas). Most of these gospels and books were destroyed by order of the Church, which wanted no interference with its designs. Recently, however, some have been rediscovered near Nag Hammadi, Egypt. Author Elaine Pagels has included many excerpts from these writings in her best seller, *The Gnostic Gospels*.

The Gnostic texts appear to fill in gaps exposed by the so-called Dead Sea Scrolls, which were discovered near Qumran in Palestine in the 1950s. Despite bitter resistance from orthodox scholars, many respected researchers believe the scrolls were created by a sect known as the Essenes, a group that likely included Jesus and his followers among its members. Many common elements between the Dead Sea Scrolls and the teachings of Jesus are easily recognized.

Norman Golb, author of *Who Wrote the Dead Sea Scrolls?* says handwriting analysis indicates that at least 500 scribes were involved. To the reasonable

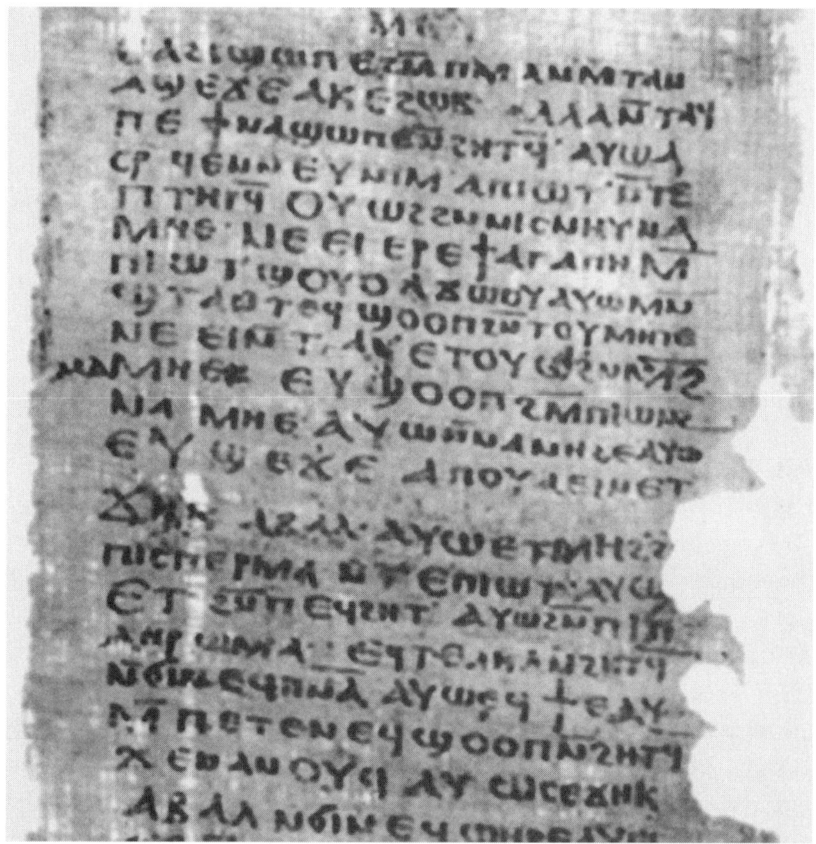

Fig. 1.2. A fragment of a Gnostic gospel. These gospels were suppressed by the early Christian Church.

mind, this suggests that the texts were produced by a broad movement that encompassed Palestine and Judaea, not by some tiny, isolated sect. This view is supported by the influential scholar Robert Eisenman.

Baigent and Leigh, in their book *The Dead Sea Scrolls Deception,* draw on Eisenman but go even further by contending that the Qumranians and early Christians not only were one and the same, but also were nationalist militants trying to install their priest/king, Jesus, on the throne of Israel, and possibly his brother James after him. They cite Jesus's lineage from King David, as does Matthew's gospel. In their view, Jesus becomes a literal king of the Jews, perhaps a freedom fighter against the Roman occupation. Ensuing elements of this story line, as it may have impacted European history, figure prominently in Baigent, Leigh, and Lincoln's *Holy Blood, Holy Grail* and, most recently, in Dan Brown's best-selling novel *The Da Vinci Code.*

In the past few years, such revelations emanating from alternative scholarship have offered compelling insight into Christian origins. Emerging from the mists of antiquity is a picture of intrigue and treachery in which Jesus's original teachings were codified as laws and doctrines enforced by a priestly elite in collusion with secular princes determined to preserve their authority. The hidden agenda was to deflect the people's attention away from troublesome notions of personal immortality and substitute the specter of sin and guilt, requiring the intercession and vicarious atonement of Jesus. This doctrine mandated actual worship of Jesus as the wholly unique Son of God with the burden for all human error borne on his shoulders alone.

Thus diverted from accepting responsibility for their own sowings, the people were robbed of the power to address personal challenges and, ultimately, to transcend their circumstances—prevented, in other words, from endangering their rulers' supremacy.

Seen in this light, the current campaign—epitomized by Mel Gibson's movie—to emphasize Jesus's suffering and focus on the guilt associated with it appears aimed at reenergizing a formula for control that—though successful for centuries—now seems in danger of losing its grip.

Many mysteries remain concerning the actual life of Jesus, and esoteric Christianity seeks to supply answers. Rumors have circulated for years that the Vatican suppressed material relating to the life of Jesus. Indeed, some argue that Jesus lived for a time in India; this notion is strengthened by strong links between material found in the Gnostic gospels and some tenets of Eastern spirituality. Another compelling theory draws comparisons between the ancient Egyptian god Osiris and Jesus, and suggests that certain aspects of Christian tradition regarding Jesus were modeled on this unique Egyptian figure.

Esoteric Christianity presents the life and teachings of Jesus primarily as a path of initiation on which the Christ, acting more as a priest than a king, guides disciples—those with "eyes to see and ears to hear"—through various rituals of purification, culminating in their illumination and liberation. (This might constitute at least one source of hostility from an ignorant high priest—jealousy.) In this sense, Christ's role as the anointed revealer of sacred mysteries harmonizes with the purest and most ancient temple wisdom and practice.

To initiates seeking gnosis, Jesus's every step takes on rich symbolic significance. Striving—spiritually speaking—to assimilate their master's very body and blood (his example and teachings), the initiates' resulting illumination ultimately unlocks the mystery of communion with the master. This sacred communion is symbolized by the cup at the Last Supper—otherwise known as the Holy

Grail—and leads to unity with their master and eternal life, or immortality.

Ironically, the makers of *The Passion of the Christ,* whatever their conscious intentions, may have participated in a much greater process than they realized, and one they may have been powerless to escape—one in which both they and their audience may have been led unwittingly upward.

In one variation of Masonic practice, the initiate is invited to climb "the 33 steps of the spinal altar to the place of the skull, where the Christ is crucified between the two thieves of the anterior and posterior lobes." The concept is that as consciousness evolves—spiraling upward through the various centers aligned with the spine (also known as chakras) toward liberation—it must pass through stages symbolized by the crucifixion. Those who focus their attention on that process may benefit, whether or not they understand what they are doing.

2 The Osiris Connection

Hints of Christian Imagery in Ancient Egyptian Artifacts

Richard Russell Cassaro

Why did the Egyptians bury their dead with a headdress on the head, a beard on the chin, and shepherd's staff in the hand?

There is no universally accepted theory in Egyptology providing a logical explanation for these funerary vestures. A new study reveals they form an image of the Christian savior—a bearded shepherd with long hair. The headdress, beard, and shepherd's staff have symbolic meaning. They were used to transform the outward appearance of the deceased into an image of the god Osiris, the single most important Egyptian deity and the first on record to have risen from the dead.

RELIGION OF RESURRECTION

"The central figure of the ancient Egyptian religion was Osiris," wrote the late Egyptologist Sir E. A. Wallis Budge, "and the chief fundamentals of his cult were the belief in his divinity, death, resurrection, and absolute control of the destinies of the bodies and souls of men. The central point of each Osirian's religion was his hope of resurrection in a transformed body and of immortality, which could only be realized by him through the death and resurrection of Osiris."

Early in Egyptian history, religious custom called for burying dead kings in the image of Osiris. Later the upper classes, and eventually the common masses, were given an Osirian burial. The custom reflects the Egyptian quest to follow in the god's resurrection.

Henri Frankfort, once a professor of pre-classical antiquity at the University of London, underscored this idea: "It may be well to emphasize that the identification of the dead with Osiris was a means to an end, that is, to reach resurrection in the Hereafter."

Hieroglyphics for the name Osiris (Ausar) include the silhouette of a bearded man with long hair. This same image was engraved on the anthropomorphic coffins. The *nemes* headdress, beginning at the forehead of the deceased and resting upon the shoulders, is symbolic of long hair, and was tied into a ponytail in the back of the head, as is often done with long hair. The plaited beard on the chin represents a long beard.

This burial pattern presents us with a fascinating mystery: For thousands of years before the rise of Christianity, Egyptians strove to share in the resurrection of a bearded man with long hair and acquire life after death!

Coffins depicting the image of Osiris also display a shepherd's staff in the left hand, a distinctly Christian symbol—Jesus described himself as the Good Shepherd of the human flock and portraits of Christ show him holding a shepherd's staff. Egyptian artworks include a shepherd's staff in the hands of Osiris. In literature, his epithets *sa* and *Asar-sa* mean "shepherd" and "Osiris the shepherd."

The term *shepherd* seems an appropriate title for a beloved spiritual leader whose religion of resurrection ensured a promise of life after death.

CROSS OF LIFE

Remarkably, the continuation of the life of the soul life after death was represented by the ankh cross, another symbol with a counterpart in Christianity. The ankh was the most revered and prolific emblem in Egyption lore; it was inscribed on tombs and temples and was depicted in the hands of gods, kings, priests, viziers, ordinary citizens, and their children. Its origins are unknown, but its significance is strikingly similar to the meaning of Christ's crucifix, also symbolic of life after death. Jesus's Doctrine of Eternal Life is a recurring theme in Christian scriptures—in John 11:25 Jesus says: "I am the resurrection, and the life: he that believeth in me, though he were dead yet shall he live: And whosoever liveth and believeth in me shall never die."

Notably, symbolists see in the ankh the outline of a crucified man: The circle represents his head, the horizontal line his two arms, and the vertical line his legs nailed to the cross as one.

DAY OF JUDGMENT

After Osiris's resurrection, he became judge of the souls of the dead, wielding the power to grant life in heaven to those who behaved righteously on Earth. Wallis Budge explained: "The belief that Osiris was the impartial judge of men's deeds and words, who rewarded the righteous, and punished the wicked, and ruled over a heaven which contained only sinless beings, and that he possessed the power to do these things because he had lived on Earth, and suffered death, and risen from the dead, is as old as dynastic civilization in Egypt."

Fig. 2.1. Michelangelo's painting The Last Judgment *(left) has much in common with the image depicting the Day of Judgment (below) as found on Egyptian tomb walls. In the Egyptian ceremony the heart of the deceased—symbolic of his virtue, moral character, and earthly deeds—was laid on a set of scales before Osiris and weighed against a single feather representing* maat, *the divine law. If the scales balanced, the deceased was allowed to pass into heaven.*

Similarly, the Day of Judgment is a central tenet of the Christian religion. Souls of the deceased shall stand before the judgment seat of Christ. Those who have followed his teachings during their lives shall be deemed righteous and be admitted to heaven. In 11 Corinthians 5:10, the scriptures state: "For we must all appear before the *judgment seat* [emphasis added] of Christ; that every one may receive the things done in his body, according to that he hath done, whether it be good or bad."

Depictions of Christ and Osiris as judge are remarkably similar.

Michelangelo's *The Last Judgment* has many features in common with the Day of Judgment etched on Egyptian papyri and carved on tomb walls. In the Egyptian judgment ceremony, the heart of the deceased—symbolic of the individual's virtue, moral character, and earthly deeds—was laid on a set of scales and weighed against a single feather representing *maat,* the divine law. If the scales balanced, the deceased was allowed to pass into heaven. As judge, Osiris was portrayed in the seated position, a posture that parallels the Christian scriptures' characterization of the judgment seat of Christ.

What are we to make of these striking similarities? Did Christian scholars simply borrow images and symbols of Osiris from the Egyptian religion? Or does this evidence reveal a profound and hitherto unheralded phenomenon that has influenced the course of human civilization? By revealing the similarities common to the Egyptian and Christian religions, are we in fact rediscovering the sacred blueprints of an ancient Messianic tradition that has accelerated human cultural and spiritual development since the beginning of history?

MYTH VERSUS FACT

Because the story of Osiris was so well known in Egypt, it was never set down in writing. As a result, modern researchers cannot accurately determine the events surrounding his life, death, and resurrection. The first written accounts of Osiris come down to us from sources outside of Egypt by way of ancient historians such as Diodorus Siculus (first century B.C.), Herodotus (fifth century B.C.), and Plutarch (first century A.D.).

These classical writers describe Osiris as a semi-divine king who abolished cannibalism, taught men and women to live according to the law of maat, advanced their morality, and—filled with love for mankind—set out on a quest to travel the world and bring the benefits of civilization to other cultures. Their commentaries continue with mythological descriptions of the murder of Osiris by his jealous brother, Seth; his rebirth, accomplished by the magic of his sister/wife, Isis; and his second death, caused again by Seth, who dismembered his body and scattered the pieces up and down the Nile. After the utter destruction of Osiris, his son Horus defeated Seth in an epochal battle, thereby vindicating his murdered father.

The myth of Osiris unfolds half in our world and half in an enchanted world of magic and make-believe. This element of fiction is responsible, in part, for the misconception that Osiris was a fictional being. The facts left among the ruins of ancient Egypt tell a different story. The Osirian religion sparked a renaissance among ancient Nile-dwellers, the effects of which touched on every facet of their primitive society. It instilled in them a high moral code, a sense of good and evil, and an inclination toward brotherly love and admiration that was unprecedented in human history and unparalleled by other ancient nations.

The Osirian religion also fostered a highly advanced philosophy. Osiris worshippers realized the human body was neither perfect nor permanent. Given this, they were also convinced that death was not the end of their being. An eternal, spiritual element dwelled within them that would rise—resurrect—from the body and exist in a higher spiritual realm, provided their behavior was in accordance with a high moral code—maat. For these reasons, they avoided becoming too attached to the things of this world. This is the same philosophy expressed in Christianity, sparked by the life, death, and resurrection of the Christian savior.

PHOENIX IN THE EAST

The Egyptians likened the spirit of Osiris to a heavenly bird much as Christianity portrays the soul of Jesus as a white and shining dove. The Egyptians called the bird Benu; the Greeks called it the phoenix. According to legend, this magnificent creature miraculously appears in the eastern sky during fixed points in history to announce the start of a new world age. When it appears, the bird mysteriously sets itself ablaze and is consumed by fire, leaving only ashes. And yet it arises triumphantly from death, renewed and rejuvenated.

Scholars agree that the phoenix was a symbol of Osiris. German philologist Adolf Erman explained: "The soul of Osiris dwells in the bird Benu, the phoenix . . ." A passage from the Coffin Texts (ancient magical funerary texts) supports this observation: "I am that great Phoenix which is in On. Who is he? He is Osiris. The supervisor of what exists. Who is he? He is Osiris."

The attributes of Osiris as phoenix are the same attributes associated with the Christian Messiah. Both the phoenix and signs of the Messiah appear in the eastern sky (the star of Bethlehem arose in the east heralding the newborn King). Both rise from the dead. Both embody the theme of life after death through resurrection. Both herald the start of a new age. (Christ's appearance initiated the current age: B.C./A.D.) Finally—and perhaps most importantly—both are associated with a destined reappearance (Christians await Christ's imminent return: i.e., the Doctrine of the Second Coming).

What significance lies behind these parallels common to the phoenix and the Messiah? Does the phoenix myth enshrine the wisdom of a recurring savior appearing throughout human history, a savior whose life, death, and resurrection were purposely designed to accelerate the development of human culture? Is there a powerful and well-guarded tradition expressed in the myth of Egypt's enigmatic phoenix? And is it a tradition now on the verge of being rediscovered?

THE "FIRST TIME" OF OSIRIS

The Egyptians associated the first appearance of the phoenix with a golden age in their history known as Zep Tepi, the First Time. They were convinced the foundations of their civilization were established during this remote and glorious epoch. R. T. Rundle Clark, former professor of Egyptology at Manchester University in England, commented on the ancients' conception of the First Time:

> Anything whose existence or authority had to be justified or explained must be referred to the First Time. This was true for natural phenomena, rituals, royal insignia, the plans of temples, magical or medical formulae, the hieroglyphic system of writing, the calendar—the whole paraphernalia of the civilization. . . . All that was good or efficacious was established on the principles laid down in the First Time—which was, therefore, a golden age of absolute perfection.

The First Time appears to have been the period during which Osiris reigned as foremost king of Egypt. During this era he established law (maat) and initiated worship of Ra, Egypt's monotheistic god. Rundle Clark explained: "The reign of Osiris was a golden age, the model for subsequent generations. Maat and monotheism, the 'model for subsequent generations' set forth by Osiris, was the driving force behind Egyptian culture for thousands of years."

What exactly does the phrase "the First Time" mean? Is it a reference to the first appearance—the first coming—of the Christian savior on Earth? Was there a guiding force behind the rise of Egyptian culture? And did this same guiding force inaugurate the empire of Christendom? Was the First Time an era during which an ancient Messianic tradition was first established? Was it a tradition aimed at revealing cultural wisdom, law, and spiritual truth to mankind during different historical epochs?

In the past decade, extensive research has been undertaken—by authors Graham Hancock, Robert Bauval, and Adrian Gilbert—to link the events of the First Time with the god Osiris and the constellation Orion. They believe the three Great Pyramids at Giza were constructed to form a mirror image of the three stars of Orion's belt (Orion was perceived as the celestial counterpart of Osiris).

Using computer imagery, these authors demonstrate that the best fit for the Orion/pyramids correlation was the year 10,500 B.C. One of the so-called air shafts inside the Great Pyramid points directly to the stars of Orion's belt during the 10,500-B.C. epoch—further evidence, according to the authors, of a connection among the First Time of Osiris, the Giza pyramids, and the three stars of Orion's belt.

What is the significance of the 10,500-B.C. era? Could Osiris's life, death, and resurrection have occurred during this remote epoch? By establishing a date for the First Time of Osiris, have Hancock, Bauval, and Gilbert unwittingly discovered the date of the first appearance of the phoenix (Christian Messiah) on Earth?

Interestingly, 10,500 B.C. is an important date to the Ammonites, a hidden community of about 27,000 members who still practice the ancient Egyptian religion. Though the Ammonites are said to have been destroyed by the Israelites thousands of years ago, they have lived in hiding throughout the Middle East for centuries, settling for a time in Iran, Iraq, Pakistan, and Afghanistan. Their history can be traced back to the era of the first Ammonite kingdoms in Jordan, outside Egypt. The Ammonite Foundation is said to have been established by King Tutankhamun after the reign of the heretic Akhenaten, its purpose being to protect the sacred Egyptian texts from corruption.

Ammonite tradition asserts that the appearance of Osiris, known by his ancient Egyptian name Ausar, occurred in circa 10,500 B.C. Jonathan Cott, author of *Isis and Osiris: Exploring the Myth,* conducted an interview with Her Grace Sekhmet Montu, a spiritual leader of the Ammonites. She described the birth of the Ammonite tradition: "We didn't start counting ourselves as followers until the death of Ausar [Osiris], and the date of his ascension into the other world marks the first day of the Ammonite calendar—12,453 years ago from this June 21, 1991!"

Here again the mysterious date 10,500 B.C. arises in connection to the First Time of Osiris.

Interestingly, the twentieth-century American psychic Edgar Cayce also spoke of the year 10,500 B.C. According to his readings, during this era the primitive Nile-dwellers came in contact with beings of a more ancient and advanced civilization who accelerated their culture and sense of spirituality by laying down the fundamentals of Egyptian civilization.

3 East of Qumran

Searching for the Roots of Western Faith

David Lewis

In 1947, near the banks of the Dead Sea, Bedouin tribesmen found seven crumbling scrolls hidden in caves since the time of Christ. From then through 1956, archaeologists discovered a total of eight hundred scrolls in the same area, the desolate Judaean wilderness near the ruins of Qumran. In biblical times, a mysterious religious sect lived there, twenty miles east of Jerusalem. While the exact nature of the sect is uncertain, historians say they were the Essenes and that they authored the scrolls. But authorship of the scrolls has become a matter of fierce debate. Renegade scholars contend the site was not home to a sect at all, but instead to the fortification of a militant nationalist movement. They say these militants who wrote the scrolls were none other than the early Christians themselves.

If so, the ship of religion, even Western civilization, begins to rock in high seas. The Judeo-Christian world may have to take another look at itself and where it comes from. But a veil has settled upon the Dead Sea, upon the scrolls and their meaning, keeping them hidden still. Clues link them to other texts found as far away as Tibet. And Dominican priests, said to be fearful of the scrolls' import, kept them secret for decades while tenaciously denying their relevance to early Christianity. Found near the ruins of Khirbet Qumran, deemed by historians as both a monastery and a fortress, the scrolls remain one of the most controversial and puzzling discoveries of our time.

From the beginning, a veil of intrigue fell over the scrolls. Early on, an agent of the newly formed Central Intelligence Agency examined one of the manuscripts in Damascus. However, any possible role that the CIA might have played in the subsequent drama remains unclear. In the political turmoil surrounding the formation of the state of Israel, it was uncertain which nation owned the scrolls, never mind who wrote them.

The scrolls changed hands on the black market, passing from Bedouins to shady antique merchants. Years passed. The world, it seemed, would fail to recognize the discovery's significance, as if a sinister force had cast some spell upon the scrolls. But in 1954, an intriguing advertisement ran in the *Wall*

Street Journal. It described biblical manuscripts for sale. Incredibly, these were the Dead Sea Scrolls searching for a buyer. The scrolls, already enigmatic, then fell behind another veil of secrecy, the Vatican.

The Ecole Biblique et Archéologique, a Dominican body created by the pope in the nineteenth century, took possession of the scrolls under the lax auspices of the Israeli Antiquities Department, which had painstakingly acquired the scrolls from black market and other sources. While slowly translating and publishing copies of biblical and apocryphal texts, the Ecole kept another category of scrolls secret. Until the 1990s, one-fourth of the entire corpus dealing with the political, cultural, and mystical nature of the mysterious Qumranians remained unpublished. Some scholars suggest that the Dominicans, in keeping the scrolls secret for so long, acted on the Vatican's behalf because the texts threaten beliefs about Christian origins. And their suggestion, it turns out, has a historical basis.

In the nineteenth century, the Vatican assembled the Ecole Biblique to deal with archaeological discoveries and scientific theories pertaining to biblical history, just as science took up the empirical method. With newfound authority, archaeologists showed the world the truth or falsity of religious myths—Heinrich Schliemann's discovery of ancient Troy being a notable example. As archaeologists dug beneath the ruins of the Temple at Jerusalem, the Vatican shuddered, recognizing the threat to religious doctrine posed by modern science. In the old days, heretics would simply be burned at the stake.

But this was the 1800s; an inquistion wouldn't do. So the Vatican created an intellectual Guardian of the Faith, the Ecole Biblique et Archéologique Française de Jérusalem. Today the Ecole, though financed in part by the French government, is still composed largely of Dominican priests.

To deal with the Dead Sea Scrolls, the Ecole worked in semi-secrecy through an international team composed mostly of Dominicans. The Ecole's team, while monopolizing the texts, meticulously pieced them together, translating from Aramaic and ancient Hebrew. The Ecole's Father de Vaux promised publishing dates as early as 1970, already quite late. In 1989, a publishing date of 1997 was suggested, an incredible fifty years after the initial discovery.

Scholars trying to gain access to the scrolls protested, having been refused access for decades. In the press, the Ecole's delaying tactics provoked charges of scandal. Herschel Shanks, editor of the prestigious *Biblical Archaeological Review* in Washington, D.C., charged that piecing together and decoding thousands of crumbling fragments written in ancient Hebrew and Aramaic—an ancient jigsaw puzzle—was too great a task for the team. He said they would never publish the scrolls because the team was too small. Shanks, as we shall see, was right. The scrolls went public through an independent source, with possible CIA connections.

Everything changed in the fall of 1991. The Huntington Library in California announced, magically, that it had a set of photographs of all the Dead Sea Scrolls. Back in 1961, Elizabeth Bechtel, wife of Kenneth Bechtel, of the megalithic but shadowy Bechtel Corporation, somehow acquired the photos and entrusted them to the Huntington Library. How Mrs. Bechtel came into possession of the photos is unclear—perhaps through her husband's connections with Middle Eastern governments or the CIA (Bechtel Corporation built the huge military complex in Riyadh, Saudi Arabia, which was the staging ground for forces in Operation Desert Storm; Bechtel is often linked with the Central Intelligence Agency). The Ecole team and the Israeli government demanded the photos from the Huntington. The Israeli Antiquities Department even charged the library with theft—without a legal basis, it turned out, for Israel had taken the scrolls as a kind of war bounty.

Undaunted by these threats, the Huntington Library responded by offering scholars access to the photographs for a mere ten dollars. The veil had parted, at least to a degree.

So, what do the scrolls say?

Interpretations vary. But language in the scrolls suggests the Qumranians were involved with the early Church. The language used gives the scrolls weight—the Bible and Jesus speak in Qumran-like phrases and cadences, using terms such as *zeal, liar,* and *law* that renegade scholars Robert Eisenman and Michael Wise, in their book *The Dead Sea Scrolls Uncovered,* associate with militant Zealots who challenged the Roman domination of Palestine. Jesus's fierce denunciation of the Pharisees, too, imitates the tone and character of certain scrolls, specifically *The Community Council Curses the Sons of Belial,* as translated by Eisenman, an execration of *The Angel of the Pit and the Sons of Belial.*

John the Baptist too speaks and acts much like a zealous Qumranian. And travel to the Jordan River, where John baptized Jesus, requires a route that passes very near the ruins of Khirbet Qumran—Jesus and his followers would at least have known of the settlement. Moreover, the gospels, the Beatitudes, and the Sermon on the Mount repeat key words and concepts from the scrolls as if the terminology and context were second nature to Jesus and the early Christians. In short, because the scrolls predate the Bible, which was written after A.D. 60, early Christianity may derive from the sect at Khirbet Qumran.

The scrolls, therefore, may be as relevant to early Christianity as the Bible, though most scholars squeamishly reject this. But looking at the Christian scriptures, the renegade scholars identify specific passages that suggest not only a connection to Qumran, but an origin there as well. Some texts refer to Qumranians as followers of the Way, using the same phrasing found in the Christian scriptures. The Bible, in fact, is rife with Qumranianisms that when put in context give those phrases a revolutionary meaning. Especially revealing is the use of the Hebrew "Ebionim," meaning "the Poor," found in the "Hymns of the Poor," in other Qumran texts, and in the Christian scriptures. Synonyms appear as well—"the meek," "the downtrodden": terms familiar to Christians. In the Dead Sea Scrolls, however, Qumranians use these terms as self-designating.

Eusebius, the fourth-century Church historian, speaks of these Ebionites as sectarian, of Palestinian origin, and responsible for the Christian takeover of Rome. Once the bishop of Caesarea, he writes about this group derisively, since the Ebionites did not regard Jesus as divine. Revealingly, a Christian tradition tells us that the descendants of the early Church, the Jerusalem community of James the Just, the brother of Jesus, went by the name of "the Poor" as well. This suggests that the Ebionites and early Christians were the same people, and that James, as leader of the early Jerusalem Church, did not view Jesus as divine—a problem for the Vatican, and in fact for all of Christianity.

Steven Feldman, also with the *Biblical Archaeological Review* in Washington, asserts that the common phraseology of the scrolls and the Christian scriptures was simply that—the talk of the times—and that linkage of Qumranians with early Christians springs from the fringe of biblical scholarship. Yet traditional scholarship, as we have seen, often prefers a path of least resistance over findings that threaten the status quo, and a wide array of evidence supports the "fringe" point of view.

Ancient copies of the scrolls turned up at Masada, the Jewish fortress besieged by Rome in the first century. Jewish Zealots there apparently revered the scrolls, presumably as they were adherents to the Qumranian form of Judaism. Outnumbered and starving, the rebels committed mass suicide rather than succumb to Rome's suppression of their spiritual and national identity. That some historians see Khirbet Qumran as a fortress, not a monastery—and draw connections between it and the Maccabean Revolt of the first century A.D.—contradicts the long-held notion of a pacifist Essene community on the banks of the Dead Sea. With Christian scripture linked to the scrolls, and scrolls turning up at Masada, the early Christians look more like the rebels in *Star Wars* fighting the Darth Vader of Roman hegemony than the passive sheep of tradition.

Michael Baigent and Richard Leigh, authors of *The Dead Sea Scrolls Deception* (and coauthors with Henry Lincoln of *Holy Blood, Holy Grail,* a source book for the fictional *The Da Vinci Code*), portray a pacifistic Jesus as equally unlikely. As the authors point out, Qumranian phrases flowed from his lips, sometimes word for word. These were phrases of the same Qumranians who eschewed the world outside of Judaea and Palestine while possibly linked with, or identical to, Zealots fighting and dying for their national cause.

Traditionally, scholars concede that at least some Zealots were within Jesus's inner circle. The Bible itself reveals Jesus acting in a Zealot-like way, driving moneychangers out of the Temple, violently overturning their tables. He states in the gospels: "I am come not to bring peace, but a sword." In the same vein, when a cohort of Roman soldiers come for Jesus in Gethsemane, Peter raises his sword against them, hardly the act of a meek Christian. Equally revealing is the number of soldiers in a Roman cohort—six hundred, according to Baigent and Leigh. Why send 600 soldiers except in anticipation of armed resistance? And crucifixion, as we might well recall, was the designated method of execution for rebels, not rabbis. These biblical events, in conflict with Christian tradition, do not conflict with the Qumran context of the renegades. To the contrary, they fit within it.

Norman Golb's book *Who Wrote the Dead Sea Scrolls?* points out that, based on handwriting analysis, at least 500 scribes worked on the scrolls. To reasonable minds, this disproves the small-sect theory of Qumran. Instead, the texts must have come from a broad movement spread across Palestine and Judaea.

Eisenman supports this view. Baigent and Leigh draw on Eisenman's work but then go further. They contend that the Qumranians and early Christians not only were one and the same, but also were nationalist militants trying to install their priest/king Jesus on the throne of Israel, and possibly his brother James after him. They cite Jesus's lineage from King David, as does tradition. Jesus becomes, in their view, someone other than the traditional Jesus—a would-be king of the Jews in the literal sense, perhaps a freedom fighter against the Roman occupation. You can almost hear the Vatican rumbling.

Through gleanings from the gospels, however, and from more obscure sources that we shall explore, Jesus remains a revolutionary, but a deeply mystical one, a warrior of the spirit drawing on traditions from a far broader geographic and spiritual context than even the renegades of modern scholarship dare reveal. Was he far from Palestine, as one tradition claims, during the lost years of the Bible? Could he have been in India, or Tibet, and returned to a politically chaotic Palestine? The Bible itself supplies some initial clues.

While the Bible provides little historical information, the writings of the apostle Paul help explain how early Christianity may have evolved from a fervent nationalistic Judaism to a purely spiritual movement that swept the Western world. Also, Paul's experience on the road to Damascus may provide us with a missing piece in the 2,000-year-old puzzle—that of mystical communion.

After the death of Jesus, Paul traveled and preached a doctrine beyond Judaea and Palestine, actions inconsistent with the religious nationalism of the Qumranians (and of Judaism). Was he a Roman agent infiltrating the Jewish rebels, co-opting the movement, as Baigent and Leigh suggest? Or was he a mystic teacher inspired by progressive revelation?

After being struck by his vision of Jesus on the road to Damascus, Paul sets out for Rome, Greece, and Asia Minor, spreading a new religion that extols faith in Christ, while the scrolls—the writings of James's Jerusalem Church, we are told—extol Jewish law and works over faith. Keeping in mind that the Christian scriptures did not yet exist, that formal Christian doctrine did not manifest until the Council of Nicaea in A.D. 325, we see Paul creating a new religion.

Paul makes Jesus into an Eastern-style avatar, like Krishna, capable of leading his followers into a divine state, a mystical promised land. He preaches joint heirship with Christ, oneness through inner contact, a blend of Eastern mysticism and Judaic dualism that defies orthodoxy to this day (where spiritual parity with Jesus is blasphemy).

Paul speaks of an "inner man of the heart," much in the way the Vedas of ancient India speak of an inner spiritual identity united with Brahman, the All. The Dead Sea Scrolls also speak of this identity, as does the Kabbalah, suggesting ties, or at least shared knowledge, between Eastern mystics and the Jews of the Hebrew and Christian scriptures.

Eisenman offers the following revealing translation from a Dead Sea text, called the Beatitudes for its similarity to the biblical passage of the same name. His translation reads: "Bring forth the knowledge of your inner self." This phrase (among others in Western scripture) appears to derive from the Vedas of India, just as Jesus referring to himself as the "Light of the World" resembles Krishna's language in the Bhagavad Gita. Implicit in Eisenman's translation is that this "self" (Atman in the Sanskrit) is the divine identity residing mysteriously within each individual. This heretical teaching is not Christian in the orthodox sense. But do the traditions of East and West have a common origin in Eastern mystical experience?

Other evidence tells us that Jesus taught the initiatic mysteries, the science of immortality, like the great Eastern mystics. In 1958, at a Greek Orthodox monastery in the Judaean desert, Morton Smith discovered a letter written in A.D. 200 by Clement of Alexandria—the same Morton Smith who suggests that the writings of Jesus himself were suppressed. The letter speaks of a secret gospel of Mark, "[a] more spiritual gospel," Clement writes ". . . read only to those who are being initiated into the great mysteries."

This intriguing letter, written long before Eusebius, tells of a secret mystical tradition without nationalistic borders. That Jesus taught and participated in this tradition is more than likely. In so doing, in all probability, he was no slave to regional agendas—beyond symbols of relative good and evil, Jew and Gentile—while fiercely opposed to spiritual evil embodied in corrupt priests.

Paul also speaks of hidden truths for the "mature," or initiated, that he would have learned from Jesus through some paranormal exchange. And Paul frequently uses the word *mystery,* which in the context of ancient religious tradition had to do with initiatic cults and secret doctrine. In this context, the Ecole Biblique, and scholarship at large, falls short when tracing Christian origins. Neither considers the likelihood that Jesus was an adept in the Secret Mysteries, which draw upon Eastern mystical tradition—or that Christianity sprang from this tradition.

Could it be that Paul seized the kernel of Christian and Vedic wisdom, leaving behind the rind of local politics; that as a mystical initiate, he tried to bring Eastern wisdom to the Western world? The teachings of "joint heirship" and the "inner man of the heart" seem to do precisely that by suggesting parity with a divine identity within, stated in the Dead Sea Scrolls as "Bring forth the knowledge of your inner self." Could this be the real threat the scrolls present—spiritual freedom, individual enlightenment, as opposed to subservience to rigid orthodoxy? Going a step further, was this pursuit of mystical oneness at the heart of early Christianity?

Texts from a Tibetan monastery provide some clues.

For many years rumors have circulated that the Vatican holds exotic texts about the life of Jesus Christ, texts that would drastically alter traditional beliefs about Christian origins. In 1887, a Russian traveler, Dr. Nicolas Notovitch, claimed to have discovered these texts in a monastery at Himis, Tibet. Returning to Russia, he wrote *The Unknown Life of Jesus Christ,* a book about Jesus's journey eastward as a young man—his lost years. Another book detailing Notovitch's Tibetan adventures, *The Life of Saint Issa,* describes Jesus studying and teaching the Vedas in India.

Taking up with a caravan at an early age, the story goes, Jesus traveled the Silk Road, then on to Kapilavastu, the birthplace of Buddha. While in India, Jesus denounced the Hindu priest class, the Brahmins, in much the same way he denounced the Pharisees in Matthew's gospel, which resembles the tone of the Dead Sea texts. An Indian swami, Abhedananda, published a Bengali translation of the Buddhist texts in 1929. The same year, Nicholas Roerich, the painter and explorer, quoted from those texts in his travel diary. Roerich's transcription reveals a mystical teaching on the Divine Feminine given by Jesus in India—again, with similarity to teachings in the scrolls, a decidedly different take on reality than that of the Vatican.

If it seems a stretch that Jesus traveled to India and studied the Vedas, and that Vatican clerics stashed away Buddhist accounts of his journey, remember the Vatican-founded Ecole Biblique and the Ecole's handling of the Dead Sea Scrolls. Consider that Thomas, the follower of Christ, journeyed to and built a mission in India, and that faithful Christians worship there to this day. Consider this opening verse from the Gospel of John: "In the beginning was the Word, and the Word was with God, and the Word was God."

And this verse from the more ancient Rig Veda of India: "In the beginning was Brahman, with whom was the Word, and the Word is Brahman" (Vak being translated from the Sanskrit as "Word").

The original texts discovered by Notovitch disappeared though stories of secret vaults in the Vatican persist. If the stories are valid, as the Buddhist texts seem to be, then the Vatican, and perhaps the Ecole Biblique, found itself facing another challenge to its authority. This challenge may have been evidence that Jesus pursued and taught the wisdom of the East, that he searched for and found his divinity through mystical practices at the feet of Eastern sages. And if he pursued that tradition, he almost certainly found a teacher, through whom he contacted Brahman, the All.

So would it be any wonder that Paul extolled spiritual communion with his teacher above all else, or that he, like Jesus, set out around the world preaching a message of inner illumination?

If Jesus spent much of his short life in India and Persia as the texts say, far from the din of Palestine, the alleged militancy of early Christianity becomes less of an issue. On his return, Jesus would have found himself in the midst of zealotry and rebellion—which he most likely honored in principle. He may even have introduced to the Western world the Buddhist teaching of Metta or the Hindu Ahimsa, kindness and harmlessness.

Reciprocally, Notovitch tells us he challenged a corrupt priesthood in India, as he did in Palestine, fulfilling perhaps the christic role of standing up for the little guy everywhere. But if he was God, he was also man, as the gospels bear out, telling us he wept and got angry, that he was passionate, much like the rest of us. So why should we deny him the right to be caught up in the struggle of his people? Yet during his pursuit of the Great Mysteries throughout his life, in India, in Egypt, and in Palestine, Jesus would have evolved from a Palestinian Jew into a spiritual adept—a divine man. The Bible says at the age of twelve, he preached the Hebrew scriptures on the Temple steps. At thirty, he may have preached the Vedas, only to have the record lost.

Pieces of this puzzle, scattered across time, tell us there is more to early Christianity and more to ourselves than Western tradition reveals. The truth reaches from crumbling texts, barren landscapes, into the most inward part of us, prompting us to solve the mystery from within. The battle over the nature of Christian origins rages nevertheless, like the battle over the Holy Land itself, as if the most sacred treasure stands to be won or lost—and this is more than likely the truth: the treasure being, as a veil parts above the Dead Sea, that of our own history, our origin, our soul.

4 New Light on Christian Origins

A Closer Look at the Role of James, the Brother of Jesus

Cynthia Logan

The scene beamed around the world was stunning: People of every faith filled Saint Peter's Basilica to mark the passing of Pope John Paul II. Interspersed among the traditional black worn by mourners and the scarlet-and-white robes of the priests, bishops, and cardinals appeared the white turbans and orange robes of Muslims and Hindus. John Paul's enormous charisma and popularity aside, interest in the Vatican and fascination with the origins of Christianity are clearly piqued now, as we investigate the abuse scandal, seek out books on some aspect of the history and secrets of the Church, and enjoy the movie version of *The Da Vinci Code*.

Perhaps we're ready for a massive conversion to Catholicism—in the larger sense of the word. The 265th pontiff of the Roman Catholic Church, built on the Rock of Peter, cracked open the door to tolerance. But will his successor(s) embrace increasing evidence indicating that the very foundation of Christendom was flawed? According to Lutheran minister Jeffrey J. Bütz, the Rock of the Church was really James, and the scene described above should have taken place in Jerusalem. And, by the way, the James we're talking about is James the Just—blood brother of Jesus Christ, second son of Mary and Joseph.

It's a sensational concept—one that Bütz, admittedly on the "liberal" end of the Lutheran spectrum, carefully researched for his S.T.M. (master of sacred theology) degree at Lutheran Theological Seminary in Philadelphia. The year he finished his thesis (2002) coincided with the controversial discovery of an ancient Middle Eastern ossuary (a burial box) bearing a startling inscription in Aramaic, the dialect of Hebrew spoken by the Palestinians at the time of Jesus: "James, son of Joseph, brother of Jesus." Intrigued, and already convinced that an understanding of James's true role in Jesus's mission could help breach the ever-widening gap among Christians, Jews, and Muslims, Bütz expanded his research into a recently published book, *The Brother of Jesus and the Lost Teachings of Christianity.*

"James has been the subject of controversy since the founding of Christianity," said Bütz in an interview with this author. In speaking with him, it is clear that Bütz is openly proud of his presentation of scholarly evidence, both for its accessibility to a layperson and for its adherence to the facts. He suggests that "bringing others' findings together to allow a bigger picture to emerge" may facilitate "an emerging paradigm shift in the field of Christian scriptures studies," and says he approached the task "with the eye of a forensic scientist searching for clues at the scene of a crime." Using the canonical gospels and letters of Paul, the writings of the Church Fathers, and apocryphal and Gnostic texts, Bütz argues that Jesus's core teachings are firmly rooted in Jewish tradition, and that early Christianity was not a separate, distinct religion, but rather a sect of Judaism. "Remember," he says, "Jesus was a Jewish rabbi; he probably wasn't interested in starting a new religion called Christianity. He followed the law of Moses, as did his brother, James."

For Bütz as well as for an increasing number of scholars, researchers, and the Protestant Church as a body, the question of whether or not Jesus had siblings is a non-issue. "There are numerous references to Jesus's four brothers and [at least] two sisters in the Bible itself," he maintains. If Jesus had siblings, then obviously his mother did not remain a virgin (whether Jesus was conceived "immaculately" or by more human means isn't something Bütz spends much time worrying about), which poses a massive problem for the Roman Catholic Church, whose orthodoxy is heavily invested in a perpetually virgin Mary.

An adjunct professor of world religions at Penn State University's Berks-Lehigh Valley College, Bütz tells students what he doesn't tell his parishioners at Grace Lutheran Church in Belfast, Pennsylvania—that Jesus Christ was the promised Messiah and is Lord and Savior—but was not God Incarnate. This same belief is held by Muslims as well as by Jews and, according to Bütz, was held by James and many early Christian sects.

As a researcher and scholar (Bütz also holds a master of divinity degree—magna cum laude—from Moravian Theological Seminary), Bütz is comfortable with the belief that Christ wasn't the embodiment of Divinity. As an ordained Lutheran pastor, however, he sticks to the traditional Christian gospel: "I would never preach from the pulpit that Jesus wasn't the Divine Son of God," he said, "but now that my book has come out, I'm surprised to find my 'flock' much more open-minded than I thought they would be."

That he preaches as well as teaches is something of a miracle. Raised in the Lutheran faith with five older half sisters, Bütz became a self-styled "post-confirmation dropout. . . . By the time I was in the middle of high school, I began to have doubts about my faith," he says, "and by the time I graduated I'd declared myself an atheist." Not the quiet, keep-it-to-yourself kind, either. Bütz was evangelical about atheism and went about trying to convince Christian friends that they had been deceived.

About ten years later—in the late 1980s—he had an overnight conversion. "I'd just finished the last page of *Holy Blood, Holy Grail,* and was hoping to use some of its evidence in arguments with my Christian friends," Bütz recalls. "It was two or three in the morning and I could feel the spirit of Christ in my room. I didn't see anything or hear any voice, but I was convinced that Christ had appeared to me. It was a powerful, overwhelming conviction of the heart."

Though Bütz's conversion was nearly as instantaneous as that of Saint Paul (albeit not as dramatic), the Protestant minister-to-be had become less than enamored of the man who brought Jesus to the Gentiles. "Paul argued with James and Peter about whether or not Gentiles should have to adhere to the Law of Moses in order to follow Jesus," explains Bütz. "He didn't think they should have to be circumcised" (and understandably so, he remarks). Paul, whose message focused on faith rather than on works, became enormously popular. His version of the gospel was embraced by the Roman state. He then became the point man of Protestantism, eventually driving Judaic-based Jamesian Christianity underground.

All branches of Christianity have believed that Peter was the leader of the apostles, yet research shows that to be a misunderstanding, according to Bütz. "James was the leader of the apostles after Jesus's resurrection. That leadership naturally would have passed to the next of kin." He points out that Peter is subservient to James in an incident recorded in the fifteenth chapter of the Book of Acts. "At the Jerusalem Council, the first Apostolic Council, all the early Church leaders came together to discuss how much of the Law of Moses Gentiles would have to adhere to in order to be considered followers of Christ. James settled the issue, stating that Gentiles wouldn't have to be circumcised, but would have to follow a bare minimum of the Torah," recounts Bütz, who also mentions the "Antioch incident," described in Paul's letter to the Galatians.

"Jewish and Gentile populations were eating together, a violation of the Law of Moses. James learns that Peter is having 'table fellowship' with the Gentiles in Antioch and tells him he's going overboard." Again in subservience to James—whom Bütz believes was probably a member of the Nazarites, a strict, ascetic Jewish sect—Peter ceases the fellowship. "If anybody deserves the title of First Pope of the Church, it's James, not Peter," insists Bütz, who points out that, though he was a stickler for the law, it was James who enabled Paul to continue his mission. "He put the official stamp of approval on the mission to the Gentiles, but didn't expect Paul would go so far as to say that you don't need to follow the Law of Moses, the Torah, but just believe in Jesus Christ. This is really the split that caused Christianity to become a separate religion."

Bütz wonders how differently the history of Western civilization might have played out had the seat of Christendom remained in Jerusalem. He finds it fascinating that the ancient city is again at the epicenter of religious evolution, a paradigm shift foreseen by the prophet Isaiah. He also finds it no accident that after 2,000 years of obscurity, James the Just gained sudden international prominence shortly after September 11, 2001, through the ossuary discovery in early 2002. "He may be the one figure who can today bring peace to the Middle East and reunite the divided family of Abraham," Bütz postulates. "In James there is a potential bridge over severely troubled water. James believed in the Hebrew scriptures's prophecies that one day all people, all nations of the world, would worship the One God of Israel and be united through Jesus as Messiah. Through Jesus's brother James, God seems to be calling us to a common *jihad*—to a holy struggle to bring reconciliation and healing to His splintered, wounded family."

Bütz teaches that the rise of Islam was greatly influenced by Jewish/Christian sects—such as the Ebionites, who claimed to be descendants of original apostles—surviving around the northwestern perimeter of the Arabian Peninsula where Muhammad lived and worked. "Syria was a great center for Jewish Christianity at that time," he notes. "They believed that Jesus was the promised Messiah, a descendant of King David, but not that he was divine, the same theology that Muhammad held. There are many teachings and writings about Jesus in the Qur'an. Muslims believe Jesus was the last prophet God sent before contacting Muhammad. They don't believe in the Holy Trinity and the Incarnation, nor did James."

Fig. 4.1. Pastor, professor, and author Jeffrey Bütz.

Reverend Bütz says he's learned to be humble with his theology and with what he claims to be absolutely true, "because I've gone through so many theological changes in my life—from being a standard Christian to being a firm atheist, back to being a staunch

Christian. When I first reconverted, I retreated into a very fundamentalist Christianity. Thankfully, I attended a more liberal seminary, which opened my eyes to the dangers of fundamentalism, and I slowly evolved to become more open-minded. I'm very tolerant of different views. Jesus is my Lord and Savior, but I believe that God has provided many paths up the mountain and I believe that God has given revelation to all cultures on Earth at various times in history. I believe He's sent Hindu and Muslim prophets. I find truth in all religions and I've become a student of all religions."

In his younger years, Bütz was a member of rock bands and still joins his wife Katherine, son David, and daughter Rachael in a yearly local theater performance "rocking out" behind the drum set. In addition to his love of reading, writing, and researching, he enjoys fishing, the outdoors, and playing chess. His keen interest in science yielded a bachelor's degree in earth science, but second only to his theological leanings, his deepest passion lies heavenward. An amateur astronomer, Bütz says he loves to "set up my telescopes on a clear night and look up into God's universe—that's the most spiritual experience for me."

While a fan of Dan Brown's book *The Da Vinci Code,* Bütz has a problem with Mel Gibson's movie *The Passion of the Christ.* "Students and parishioners are always asking me about it, but other than the excessive gore, what bothers me is that it's not at all factually based. Gibson has admitted he based it on *The Dolorous Passion of Our Lord Jesus Christ,* written by a nineteenth-century Roman Catholic nun, Anne Catherine Emmerich, who claimed to have had visions of Christ's crucifixion. Gibson is an ultra-orthodox Roman Catholic that would make the new pope seem liberal!" exclaims Bütz, who says he heard Gibson say in an interview that he wrestles daily with the fact that he won't be in heaven with his wife, since she's Episcopalian and not Roman Catholic.

Working on his second book—tentatively entitled *The Underground Stream,* about Jesus's bloodline Bütz reports finding abundant evidence for descendants of Jesus's family. Though he suspects Christ was probably married, he's neither assuming nor ruling out the possibility that Jesus and his wife had children. "The descendants are most likely nieces and nephews, but perhaps children and grandchildren," he says. "I'm also doing historical research on the original Jerusalem Church (so-called heretical sects such as the Nazarenes, Ebionites, and Elkesaites), all of which, despite being a persecuted minority, hung on in Syria and Arabia and influenced Muhammad and the rise of Islam, the Knights Templar, and Freemasonry."

In the meantime, he's hoping that his current book will bring about a new appreciation for James, whom he says has been whitewashed, hidden, and suppressed. "He's a historical figure who has suffered more injustice than anyone else. As the brother and successor to Jesus, most Christians don't even know he existed. Once the role of James is realized, once we realize the Jewishness of Jesus, there will be more understanding between Christians, Jews, and Muslims."

That would be a very, very good thing indeed.

5 Spreading the Goddess Gospel

Thanks to *The Da Vinci Code,* Margaret Starbird Finds Herself with a Worldwide Audience

Cynthia Logan

After *The Da Vinci Code* topped the best-seller list, author Dan Brown picked up the phone and called Margaret Starbird. He wanted to acknowledge the primary concept he had gleaned from her work: the idea that Jesus Christ was married to Mary Magdalen. Starbird's books *The Woman with the Alabaster Jar* and *The Goddess in the Gospels* had given him ample research to back the material in his page-turning thriller.

Starbird, in turn, got her food for thought from *Holy Blood, Holy Grail,* the premise of which is not only that was Christ married, but that his wife and bloodline had survived in Western Europe—something Starbird, a practicing Roman Catholic and Vanderbilt Divinity scholar, had found disturbing. She couldn't bring herself to buy the book, but borrowed it from the library. Reading the back cover, she was appalled. In an insightful interview, she recounted the experience: "I almost threw it down, almost fled from the building," she says of her first encounter with a hypothesis she knew would challenge her beliefs to the core. "I was not merely shocked by the idea, I was shattered." But open-mindedness and a desire to know the truth guided her, and, as she pondered, she had to admit the theory was provocative and that the compilation of evidence strongly suggested the truth had been ruthlessly suppressed by the orthodox Catholic hierarchy and the Inquisition.

With the support of her prayer group, she began what would become a seven-year journey to debunk what she still considered blasphemy, investigating it through a study of history, symbolism, medieval art, Freemasonry, mythology, psychology, and the Bible. The result was a radical restructuring of her faith and the birth of her first book. "It was a labor both long and difficult," she remembers. "At times, I thought it would turn me inside out. Doctrines I had believed on faith had to be uprooted . . . the entire framework of my childhood had to be dismantled to uncover the dangerous fault in the foundation, and the belief system carefully rebuilt when the fissure had been sealed."

But even as a former Fulbright fellow at Christian Albrechts Universitat in Kiel, Germany, with an M.A. in comparative literature (University of Maryland), Starbird never intended to write a book—"I was just researching this because I was passionate to know Christ better." Without industry contacts, she didn't expect the book to be published, but she queried a single publisher anyway. She was advised to send the full manuscript with enough postage for return after rejection, but two months later she received a letter saying that hers would be among the twelve out of 7,000 manuscripts received that would be published that year. She was astonished to read: "Yours is a book we've been looking for all over the world!" *The Woman with the Alabaster Jar* is now available in twelve languages and has become a quiet best seller in its own genre.

Starbird's theory of the Magdalen stands on two "pillars": the ancient science of gematria (ancient Greek and Hebrew numbers contained within the letters of the alphabet) and myths dating back to neolithic matriarchal cultures. In particular, she cites the myth of the "Bridegroom/King," who is first anointed by the highest representative of the Goddess, joined to her in marriage, then tortured, killed, and "planted" to ensure that the crops will flourish and the people will prosper. (This was a physical rite in some cultures; in others, the King was symbolically sacrificed.)

Starbird notes that this ritual was part of the cultures of Sumer, Babylon, and Canaan, among others. In many versions of this story, the couple are reunited in a garden. In Greek mythology, this rite is known as the *heiros gamos* or Sacred Marriage. Since Israel was under Greek influence for nearly three hundred years following the conquests of Alexander the Great, it is logical that the Hebrews were aware of such a rite. "Its mythological content would have been understood by the Hellenized community of Christians who heard the gospel preached in the cities of the Roman Empire, where the cults of the love goddesses were not completely extinguished until the end of the fifth century A.D.," writes Starbird, who thinks there is abundant evidence that it was Mary Magdalen who anointed Jesus with spikenard as a marriage ritual and that the anointing was recognized as such by those in attendance.

For starters, "It should have been scandalous for a woman—any woman—to touch a Jewish man in public, but there's barely a hint that Jesus's friends were scandalized by her action," she writes. She points out that the Hebrew scriptures' Song of Songs, widely popular in Palestine during the time of Christ, was the wedding song of the Shepherd/King and his Bride, and that identical lines are found in a liturgical poem from the cult of the Egyptian goddess Isis. Starbird provides further parallels, stating that the frequent allusions to Jesus as the Bridegroom of the fertility myth could be "the creation of the Hellenized authors of the gospels" (none of whom actually knew Christ!), but she thinks it far more likely that these allusions originated with Jesus himself. In the Hebrew tradition, prophets had proclaimed Yahweh as the heavenly Bridegroom of the community and the king of Israel as his faithful son, the anointed Messiah—terms also found in Sumerian and Canaanite mythologies.

Which leads to the question: Was Jesus a real person or a mythological being? "I personally think that somebody named Jesus or Yeshua lived in the first century and actually embodied the myth," says Starbird. "People noticed that, and recognized him as the Messiah. I think Christ came to embody that myth, but I think it was the myth of sacred partnership that He and Magdalen embodied together."

This is the crux of her message—that Jesus and Mary Magdalen were representatives of a unified masculine and feminine principle as old as the cosmos itself. She explains the "fire" (pyramidal apex on top) and "water" (apex pointing downward) triangles as symbols of these principles, noting that the hexagram formed when joining them is the "star of partnership." Interestingly, it has been a universal symbol for union since prehistoric times—in the east Indian tradition of Shiva and Shakti embracing, in Plato's harmonic fusion of opposites, in the Seal of Solomon, inside the Ark of the Covenant, and in the Great Seal of the United States, placed by the founding fathers in the mandala of the thirteen stars that represent the first colonies.

Fig. 5.1. Margaret Starbird, scholar and proponent of the Goddess gospel.

Starbird is the first to admit that her theory isn't provable ("What I have is a huge case of circumstantial evidence"), but she is frustrated by Christian fundamentalist writers who dismiss her theory because she doesn't have a Ph.D. after her name. For a quiet-spoken, rational woman, her opinions can be mighty strong. For instance, she feels that although "Roman Catholic fundamentalist Christian clergy apologists for the Church are trying to mainstream everybody," they're only following the tradition they've learned and are holding one another up the best they know how.

"One of the things I'm really irritated about in the wake of *The Da Vinci Code* is that so many people are trying to debunk it, and they don't go back and look at my stuff. It's infuriating, because I had my Ph.D. except for the dissertation. I was working in Maryland and my husband [the man who gave her a "New Age" last name is a retired Army engineer] was transferred to North Carolina. I married and raised five college graduates. I sacrificed my Ph.D. for my family and now I'm written off—they won't even look at the evidence I bring. I can't prove that the tenets of the 'Grail heresy' are true. I can't even prove that Mary Magdalen was the woman with the alabaster jar who anointed Jesus at Bethany. But I *can* verify that these are tenets of a heresy widely believed in the Middle Ages, that fossils of it can be found in numerous works of art and literature, that it was vehemently attacked by the hierarchy of the established Church of Rome, and that it survived in spite of relentless persecution."

This so-called heresy has a number of variations, from the Gnostics to the Cathars to the Rosicrucians. However, its central tenet, that Mary Magdalen (Starbird stresses the importance of the final "e" in her name, following the original Greek gematria and distancing her from a town called Magdala) wasn't a prostitute, but the Bride of Christ and the embodiment of the Holy Grail, has incurred the wrath of Catholic orthodoxy for centuries. Starbird can't resist a comparison: "I just watched *The Godfather* again and I think the Mafia is built on the same model as the Vatican: 'Protect each other at all costs and get rid of anyone who is against you.' We'll never prove anything against the Vatican, because they won't let anyone into their archives. They'll protect their power . . . that's what the masculine principle does. Like the Enron people. When will we see them in jail? We got Martha Stewart in jail, but not those guys."

She says these things without anger—she simply sees evidence of the "lost feminine" everywhere. "It's playing out in the desert right now; the unbalanced masculine principle warps the whole psychology of Western civilization. Because we have so much power, we're trying to impose it on the whole world." Starbird feels the only way to heal the planet is to reclaim the feminine principle: "We can't hear the voices of wives and children anymore, because we've written them out of our story."

Wryly, she sums up the family model provided by the orthodox Church: a patriarchal father divorced from the virgin mother of a perpetual bachelor. She's surprised that, with all the questioning of whether "the Code" is fact or fiction, the focus isn't on—in her case—the child Magdalen is said to have borne: a daughter known as Sara Kali. "Of all the things in my book, she's the most speculative, and she's never questioned," laughs Starbird. "There's no proof of the bloodline and I don't think God wanted that to be the issue.

People in the Middle Ages latched on to these promises of the Davidic bloodline, but genealogies don't hold up through the Dark Ages; they just don't have the documentation." Besides, she and Brown agree, the message is Sacred Marriage, not royal-blood elitists running around saying, "I'm it." She also wonders if chasing historical facts is a waste of time when the real issue is how we live our lives. "The idea was to learn to love the essence of the gospels in service to others," she says.

Starbird may be the perfect vessel for voicing what many feminist forces have been saying for centuries. "If someone as conservative as I am can buy this, anyone can," she quips. Her views support the "and/both" paradigm of the feminine principle rather than the "either/or" paradigm of the masculine: She remembers expressing her support of the Equal Rights Amendment at Vanderbilt University and the surprise she generated when that support didn't extend to abortion rights.

Starbird is a bridge, an example of someone who practices the love Christ taught, not judging people and issues. Gay marriage, for example, doesn't rankle her: "I always ask myself, 'What would Jesus and Mary do?' I think they would embrace the gay community." Many married priests support her work; in fact, she says that her own priest and most people in her parish agree with her—quietly. "I'm a Roman Catholic, but I don't go [to church]," she says, sighing. Partly it's her travel schedule. Starbird leads retreats and gives lectures and keynote speeches that keep her from mass. But it's also an ethical issue: "I put my money where my mouth is. . . . I don't really feel comfortable supporting a Church that has so many problems it won't address."

She hasn't seen Mel Gibson's *The Passion of the Christ* and doesn't plan to ("*Ben-Hur* works for me and I think Gibson's a little off with this"). She's disappointed that, once again, Gibson portrays Mary Magdalen as a prostitute or an adulteress: "That's fifty years too old; now we know better than that."

Starbird is appreciative of female clergy, historians, and academics who are willing to see Magdalen raised as an apostle equal to Peter, but thinks they're still missing the mark: "This does not 'heal the desert,' " she says firmly. "All it does is restore a model for power in the Church that's equal to Peter (the 'rock' of Christ's church), but it's not like the yin/yang symbiosis of Christ and Magdalen together—they model the spirit manifest in the flesh. Thank God Dan Brown caught on to this!" Starbird considers Brown's book an answer to her prayer about getting her work to a wider audience. "Yes, the book is fiction, but the story behind it isn't—there's a ninety-nine percent chance that Christ was married."

After nearly two thousand years, writes Starbird, "[i]t's time to set the record straight, to revise and complete the gospel story of Jesus to include his wife. Our ravaged environment, our abused children, our maimed veterans, our self-destructing families, and abandoned spouses are all crying for the restoration of the Bride of Christ." She points out that the scriptures never said Jesus wasn't married; they only omitted specific mention of his wife—and the danger to her life seems to have been reason enough to have blotted it from the written record. Amazed at the rapid and growing interest in this subject, Starbird is waiting to see what the Catholic establishment will do: "It is possible that the Vatican will continue to deny that Jesus was married. But it is also possible, when faced with the evidence, that the fathers will decide it is time to receive the Bride . . . perhaps they will allow the church bells to ring out across the land to announce her safe return and welcome her home."

6 Searching for the Real Star of Bethlehem

Who Were the "Wise Men" and What Were They Up To?

Peter Novak

Holding official governmental positions as imperial counselors to the Parthian emperor, the Zoroastrian priests known as Magi were renowned for their expertise in religious arts such as prophecy and astrology. Herodotus attested to their astrological prowess. Like it or not, all we know about the Star of Bethlehem rests on what these peculiar stargazing ecclesiastics had to say about it, and, perhaps more importantly, how they reacted to it. They seem to have been the only ones who witnessed this star at all. Contrary to popular imagination, it apparently didn't stand out in the sky, and must not have been very impressive to look at. No one in Jerusalem seems to have known anything about this star before the Magi brought it to their attention, and when it was, the whole city seems to have been caught off guard by the news:

> After Jesus was born in Bethlehem in Judea, during the time of King Herod, Magi from the East came to Jerusalem and asked, "Where is the one who has been born king of the Jews? We saw his star in the East and have come to worship him." When King Herod heard this he was disturbed, and all Jerusalem with him. (Matthew 2:1–3)

This passage is all we have to go on. Fortunately, it tells us quite a lot. It tells us that the star didn't attract the attention of anyone but astrologers. When the Magi first saw it, it was rising in the East at sunset. Matthew reports that it was rising "*en te anatole*"—a Greek phrase normally translated as "in the East," but which, in fact, refers to a specific astronomical event: the acronychal eastern rising of a star, a relatively rare occurrence, when a star rises in the East just as the Sun is setting in the West. And the passage tells us that this star seemed so important to these priests that they decided to make a long and difficult journey to look for a newborn baby; and when they found this infant, they intended to worship it like a god.

Most theories about the Star of Bethlehem don't take any of this into account. The legend of this celestial event has grown to such proportions that one assumes the star must have been an awesome spectacle, even though the written record describes it as something most people never even heard about. Virtually all theories about the star begin by asking "What could have made such a striking star appear in the sky at that time in history?" The proper question, "What could have made the Magi get so excited over such an insignificant-looking star in the sky?" is virtually never asked.

Also, no theory explains how the star could have been seen rising on one horizon as the Sun was setting on the other (the Sun, Earth, and Star of Bethlehem being in a perfectly straight line), nor why the Magi (and later, the author of the Gospel of Matthew) felt it was so important to pass along this curious detail. And, of course, no theory attempts to explain why the Magi had their unique reaction to this star, concluding from it that a baby—who deserved to be idolized and worshipped—had been born.

DATELINE INDIA: SEPTEMBER 16, 1 B.C.

Yet this is all exactly what would have occurred if the Star of Bethlehem had been the planet Uranus. There is an excellent chance that Magi living near India's Indus River discovered the planet Uranus during the New Moon of September 16, 1 B.C. They would have been looking in the right place at the right time, and if they did spot Uranus then, they could have reacted exactly as the Bible describes.

Numbers of Magi did live in India, and they would have had particularly compelling reasons to monitor this New Moon. It was an unusual lunation, a rare lineup by anyone's standards: The Sun, the Moon, Jupiter, and Pluto were all tightly grouped together on one side of the sky, with Mars and Uranus close together on the exact opposite side of the sky.

In effect, Pluto, Jupiter, the Sun, the Earth, the Moon, Mars, and Uranus were all in a straight line from one side of the solar system to the other. Any New Moon that close to Jupiter (less than one degree away) would have been considered noteworthy by astrologers of that era, since such tight New Moon/Jupiter conjunctions only occur about once every 27 years. But to have this Jupiter/Sun/Moon conjunction oppose Mars at the same time would have made this a definite must-see event for ancient skywatchers.

Observers in India, however, would have seen something more, something that would have made the whole alignment take on a far greater personal urgency: The alignment straddled both their eastern and western horizons at the precise instant that the New Moon became exact. Such an unusual angular alignment, the Magi would have known, occurs only once in many thousands of years. *Parans,* or near-simultaneous angle crossings such as these, were considered extremely important in ancient astrology.

Of course, *risings* were held to be of far greater importance than *settings;* risings were the future, while settings were the past. This simple fact might have caused those imperial counselors concern, for the glorious (Jupiter) New Moon alignment setting precisely on their western horizon would have carried the uncomfortable suggestion that their own civilization might be about to fall, while some other martial force (indicated by Mars rising at the same time on the opposite horizon) might be poised to appear.

Would those Magi have been confident that this was the correct interpretation of the alignment? Surely not; experience would have likely taught them to be wary of jumping to extreme conclusions. But some concern probably would have crossed their minds, and they would have made a point of watching this alignment closely, measuring it as best they could. On that dark New Moon evening, India's Magi would have been paying close attention to this alignment in their skies, and after they watched the Sun set on their western horizon, they would have naturally turned to observe Mars rising like clockwork in the east.

And as they carefully monitored its slow upward progress into the night sky, they would have been in a perfect position to see a strange new star they'd never noticed before. Uranus was just below Mars in the sky that night, and though Uranus is commonly assumed to be invisible to the naked eye, this is not entirely true. Objects with an apparent visual magnitude of 6, such as Uranus, can be seen with the naked eye when conditions are right.

The Magi had a long-standing reputation as excellent astrologers and believed themselves to be thoroughly familiar with all the visible stars in the zodiac. If they happened to notice Uranus rising up beneath Mars that night, they would immediately have realized that it didn't belong, that it hadn't been there before, at least not according to their records. And just as the Bible recorded, they would indeed have first spotted this new star "en te anatole," rising in the east just as the Sun was setting in the west.

AND THE STAR MOVED!

What would have been the Magi's reaction if they had spotted Uranus? They probably would have done just what the Bible reports. At first, they'd have studied it carefully, and after some months of observation (Uranus moves slowly), they would have realized—to their astonishment—that it was not just another fixed star at all, but instead a whole new planet, another moving star—another god!

Two things conspired to keep Uranus invisible to them before that night: Its visibility comes and goes, and it moves around from place to place in the sky. It is the only planet in our solar system that has both these qualities. The rest of the known planets also move around, of course, but their visibility remains relatively constant. The visibility of many low-magnitude stars also comes and goes, but since they always stay in the same place, it remains a simple matter to confirm their existence and exact position.

The ancient Magi would have been able to return again and again to re-study and remeasure and reexamine all the other visible stars, and over the centuries, every last star could have been verified and re-verified, even those

Fig. 6.1. Eastern astronomers studying the night sky at the time of Jesus's birth.

whose light fluctuated on the edges of visibility. But Uranus not only appeared and disappeared depending on the viewing conditions, but it moved around as well. But eventually—Uranus is, after all, visible to the naked eye at least some of the time—one might reasonably assume that the Magi would have noticed it sooner or later.

Their reaction suggests they did just that.

Do we know where the Magi were when they made their famous sighting? The Bible only says "in the East," but we may be able to narrow that down a bit. Any Magi living near the Indus River in India would have monitored the event closely enough to spot the elusive Uranus. Legends about the biblical Magi support this possibility, identifying at least one of those travelers as indeed being from India. Hindu tradition also supports this theory. Not only has astrology been respected and studied in India for ages, but Vedic scriptures suggest that Uranus was, in actual fact, discovered millennia ago by Indian stargazers. And according to Israel's records, Magi from the East saw a strange new moving star in the sky sometime around 1 B.C., and concluded from what they saw that a new god had just been born. Coincidence?

JOURNEY TO SEE A GOD

It would have taken months of observation to be sure that Uranus was really moving, and by that time winter's rains would have arrived, requiring any travel plans to be postponed until spring. The long, arduous, and dangerous overland route from India to Israel would have been unimaginably unpleasant.

That the Magi were willing to undertake such a journey at all speaks volumes about how confident they were about their interpretation of the star's meaning and its urgency. According to T. E. Lawrence (the famous British liaison officer during the Arab Revolt of 1916 to 1918), an inexperienced person riding a camel can cover about thirty miles per day. Departing from India in the spring, the Magi would have arrived in Israel sometime in late summer or early fall. Convinced the divine child had been born the instant they first saw the star, the Magi would have expected him to be slightly over a year old by then.

When Herod became privy to what the Magi knew, he was furious. He gave orders to kill all the boys in Bethlehem and its vicinity who were two years old and under (Matthew 2:16). (According to Jewish reckoning at the time, a child of one year and one month was considered two years old.)

The only real evidence for the Star of Bethlehem is the Magi's reaction: their sojourn in search of a newborn god. The possibility that they spotted an unfa-

Fig. 6.2. The Wise Men follow the auspicious star, which may have been the planet Uranus, to Bethlehem. (Illustration by Gustav Doré)

miliar new planet fits their response better than any other natural phenomenon they could have witnessed. Planetary conjunctions, comets, and so on were all relatively familiar sights, especially for a caste of priests that had been carefully monitoring the heavens for over 500 years. The discovery of a new planet would have been unprecedented. So far as we know, this was the only time the Magi ever took a road trip to go and worship an unknown newborn.

THE MONTH AND DATE

Were the Magi correct in assuming that Jesus had been born at the exact instant of the New Moon of September 16, 1 B.C.? There does appear to be some evidence that Jesus was born in September. For instance, the report that "shepherds were watching their flocks by night" (Luke 2: 8–12) fits a September birthdate far better than one in December. Shepherds were not out in the fields in winter (Song of Solomon 2:11; Ezra 10:9, 13). The ancient custom among Jews was to send their sheep out to fields and deserts in early spring and bring them home at the commencement of the first rain, generally no later than October 15. Still, that only narrows down the likely date of the nativity to half a year.

However, a curious early Christian practice specifically suggests a September nativity. In the earliest years of the Church, during the September Jewish feast of Rosh Hashanah, Christians seem to have carried on their own mysterious celebrations behind closed doors, which some have suggested were the first Christmas festivities.

Remarkably, some evidence even supports the actual date of September 16, 1 B.C. This happens to have been the first day of Rosh Hashanah for that year, when the population of Jerusalem would have swelled from about 100,000 people to over 1,000,000. With all those people, there would have been little room at the inns of Jerusalem and the surrounding towns, just as the Bible reported. Rosh Hashanah is the Jewish New Year, a symbolically appropriate date for the birth of their Messiah.

Was Jesus born on September 16, 1 B.C.? Curiously, the astrological chart for this New Moon appears not only to correspond with the biblical account of Jesus's person and history, but also to match the subsequent history of the Christian Church. The Magi, of course, would have seen this as appropriate, since the birth of Jesus Christ was also the birth of Christianity. More curious is the fact that this ancient birth chart appears, despite all reason, to reflect many of the most significant secular developments of the last 2,000 years as well.

PART TWO

FOLLOW THE GOLDEN THREAD: TEMPLARS AND FREEMASONRY

7 Hidden History

What Are Movies Like *Braveheart* Not Telling Us?

David Lewis

Commenting on his book *The Return of Merlin,* Deepak Chopra once observed that history exists in the eye of the beholder. Chopra spoke of the "history of the soul," versus the textbook variety. And though the author didn't bother to cite examples, it's safe to say that historical accuracy has often taken a back seat to political correctness—the old Soviet Union comes to mind. In the days of Galileo, the Church defined reality. She even rearranged the heavens, declaring that the Sun revolves around the Earth, not the other way around. When heresy ran afoul of her, she obliterated not only the infidels but also their written testimony, as was the case with the Cathars in southern France.

Seven centuries later, a standard textbook definition of the Cathars reflects the Church's geocentricism, as if all revolves around Rome. Yet the last time we checked, the Earth revolves around the Sun, which in turn spins in the arm of a spiral galaxy reeling into infinity. And the truth behind medieval heresies may have a similar trajectory to the one discovered on the path of the neverending quest for absolute knowledge, a path traversed by mystics, Templars, and Cathars alike. That quest, relegated by skeptics to quixotic fancy, has little to do with textbook history, yet everything to do with secret history, the history of the soul.

Braveheart, the twice-released film about the Scottish freedom fighter Sir William Wallace, opened a chapter in this book of secret history. The film deals with the war for Scottish independence in the late thirteenth century, but neglects a rarely discussed element in that struggle that has influenced human events up to the present. Like a golden thread, that key element runs through Scottish and American history. It runs through the Middle Ages and the Inquisition to ancient Israel, the Temple of Solomon, even to ancient Egypt. It links all of the above, winding farther, deeper, and in a more clandestine way than politically correct chroniclers dare conceive. It is the thread that the Vatican armies tried to destroy—the Order of the Ancient Mysteries and their progeny, the Knights Templar.

BRAVEHEART AND BEYOND— THE TEXTBOOK ACCOUNT

In the final years of the thirteenth century, William Wallace rallied Scotland against the English Crown. As he did, many Scottish nobles lent only half-hearted support to the cause, and at times none at all. Even so, Wallace defeated the English governor John de Warenne near Stirling in 1297. As *Braveheart* poignantly shows, Robert the Bruce eventually championed Wallace's cause. But in 1305, Edward II got the better of Wallace. He captured the charismatic rebel and tried him for treason before seeing to it that Wallace was hideously tortured and executed.

But the story continues. By the time of the Battle of Bannockburn, in June 1314, the Scots had all but driven the king's forces back to England. Sterling Castle, the gateway to the Highlands, King Edward's last stronghold in Scotland, was under siege. The castle's weary governor vowed to surrender if the king's army did not relieve him by midsummer. Meeting the challenge, Edward assembled a heavily armored fighting force, possibly as large as 100,000 men but probably closer to 20,000.

He did so, most likely, not only to save Sterling but also to annihilate Robert the Bruce and to occupy Scotland. To intercept the English army, Robert assembled a smaller force of only 8,000 men who were less heavily armed. The two armies met at Bannockburn, where, despite overwhelming odds, the Scots defeated the English. That dramatic victory paved the way for a free Scotland with Robert the Bruce as her king.

WHAT ABOUT THE SECRET HISTORY?

The Battle of Bannockburn took place on Saint John's Day, June 24, a day of particular importance to the Knights Templar, the enigmatic warrior-monks of the Middle Ages. But accounts of the battle leave much to be desired. Even its location stands in question. Historians agree, though, that the English vastly outnumbered the Scots, and that the Scottish army consisted mostly of pikemen, with relatively few horsemen. Furthermore, those horsemen could have been no match for Edward's heavily armored knights. The amazing Scottish victory, then, rests on a mysterious event.

During the battle, with all Scottish units engaged between Bannockburn (*burn* means stream) and the river Forth, something strange happened. A fierce charge erupted, with banners flying, from the Scottish rear. Historians describe the charge as consisting of camp followers, even children—noncombatants whom the English somehow mistook for a ferocious fighting unit. The charge, history tells us, arose spontaneously from the camp followers, who made banners from sheets and gathered weapons from the dead and wounded. Incredibly, this charge—which by necessity would have been launched on foot—inspired such fear among the armored English knights, who were mounted, that they fled en masse.

This almost romantic history appeals to Scottish patriotism. It is the stuff of legends, or of *Braveheart II.* The idea, however, of unmounted peasants driving off a massive English army does not appeal to common sense. That the charge swept panic through the English ranks, though, seems clear. King Edward and five hundred of his knights fled the battlefield, followed soon thereafter by the English foot soldiers. And although some accounts speak of slaughter, chronicled English losses were slight; the rout appears to have resulted from sheer panic alone.

In *The Temple and the Lodge,* authors Michael Baigent and Richard Leigh demonstrate that when the Inquisition began to hunt down Templars all over Europe, many Templars fled to Scotland. Baigent and Leigh point convincingly to the mysterious attackers at Bannockburn as having been the Knights Templar, easily recognized by their banners and splayed crosses, the only fighting force of the time that could have inspired such fear and confusion. At Bannockburn, where a *mounted* Scottish charge is known to have occurred, the victorious Scots marched behind an ark-shaped receptacle known as the Monymusk Reliquary, a model of the Temple of Solomon that figures prominently in the Templar tradition.

A rich and powerful brotherhood, the Templars proved difficult for the Church and the king of France to destroy. King Philip the Fair, allied with Avignonese Pope Clement V, ruthlessly suppressed the order throughout Europe, medieval-style, with arrests, torture, and executions. As noted, many Templars evaded capture and found refuge abroad. The order's entire fleet, in fact, escaped with a vast fortune, the fate of which remains a mystery to this day.

Refugee Templars, evidence shows, found sanctuary in Scotland, where Templar graves bear witness to their having lived and died in the fourteenth century. King Robert the Bruce apparently had no interest in persecuting the order, in spite of a papal bull ordering him to do so. To the contrary, he must have taken advantage of their fugitive status, offering them asylum if they would help him fight his war against England.

WHO WERE THE KNIGHTS TEMPLAR, REALLY?

Hughes de Payns and eight other knights took vows on June 12, 1118, at Arginy Castle near Lyons, France. The nine founders of the order pledged themselves to Christ and to the protection of pilgrims traveling in the Holy Land, the textbooks tell us. King Baudouin of Jerusalem, whose brother, Godfroi de Bouillon, had captured the holy city for Christendom nineteen years prior, received them with open arms as knights, a precedent that was to be repeated by kings all over the world.

According to tradition, the knights built quarters over the ruins of Solomon's Temple, which some modern commentators believe says something about the order's secret purpose. In 1126, the immensely influential Saint Bernard of Clairvaux won ecclesiastical legitimacy for the Templars at the Council of Troyes. From then on, the order's ranks swelled at an extraordinary rate, as did their treasury and holdings. In short time, the Templars held lands in England, France, Spain, Portugal, and Scotland. By the mid-twelfth century they had established themselves second only to the papacy in wealth, power, and prestige, an indication that their success hinged, as tradition suggests, on some secret knowledge.

The Templars proved themselves extraordinarily influential and, despite abuses in the later years, consistently idealistic. Kings who were well aware of their power, and at times subscribed to their ideals, aligned themselves with the knights. The order in turn influenced kings, occupying themselves, for instance, with trying to reconcile England's King Henry II with Thomas à Becket. And Henry's son Richard Coeur de Lion was likely an honorary Templar. He kept company with the knights, resided in their preceptories, sailed in their ships, and sold the island of Cyprus to them, which became the order's official seat for a time.

Richard's brother and rival, King John had, as his trusted adviser, Aymeric de St. Maur, master of the order in England. Owing to Aymeric's counsel, King John, no champion of liberty, reluctantly signed the Magna Carta in 1215, a document that is cited—along with the Declaration of Independence and the Constitution of the United States—as being foundational to the rights of man.

Having grown astonishingly powerful, the Templars accomplished almost anything they desired on a scale and of a nature suggesting an all but supernatural capacity. Their role in designing and building the great Gothic cathedrals of Europe, for instance—a role often not credited to them—testifies to an

Fig. 7.1. An early Templar church, which employs the round architecture typical of Templar buildings.

esoteric knowledge of architecture that transcended anything in Western civilization save the pyramids of Egypt.

As with the pyramids, the Gothic cathedrals baffle historians, as they have no historical technical precedent. Gothic architecture sprang, in fact, from the Templars and their dedication to sacred geometry, the mystical science of number and proportion frequently identified with the Egyptian pyramids and the Temple of Solomon.

WHAT WAS THE TEMPLARS' SECRET PURPOSE?

The order's official raison d'être, as protectors of pilgrims, remains an open question. Judging by their endeavors and associations, the Templars had more profound goals than the textbooks reveal, creating, for instance, material receptacles—Grails, if you will—for the spiritual essence revered within their Mystery tradition: preceptories, cathedrals, churches, even nations—a universal brotherhood.

To this end, the original nine knights excavated the Temple of Solomon, possibly hoping to find the lost Ark of the Covenant (see Graham Hancock's

The Sign and the Seal for a further discussion of this). In so doing, the Templars would have wielded authority that transcended even the pope's, paving the way for a Templar state adorned with structures of mystically oriented design. It is alleged, in this regard, that the original nine knights secured secrets of design and proportion encoded in the Temple of Solomon itself—secret geometry that may date to the building of the Egyptian pyramids.

The Knights Templar, though, like any of us, can best be known by their fruit, which Baigent and Leigh tell us includes writing the medieval Grail romances. The quest for the Holy Grail, then, and the import of that quest, comes down to us from devotees of the Mysteries, those who actually quested. And therein we find Chopra's "history of the soul," the search for divinity (the most politically incorrect heresy of all, the modern age notwithstanding), which in various guises has animated societies since the dawn of time.

We may deduce that the Templars encoded the true nature—that of their order and of their souls—within the famous Grail legends (they were well aware of the consequences of doing so openly). Thus they established the ideal of the search for immortality in the popular psyche, the "history of the soul," which, although being a reliable history, is also an unorthodox one, in Chopra's terms.

We may add this accomplishment, then, to the list of fruits by which the Templars can be known. We also applaud them for trying to syncretize—for the purpose of creating a golden-age kingdom—the Christian, Judaic, Islamic, and Celtic Mysteries, centered at Carcassonne in southern France, where prior to the Inquisition a golden age had already begun to blossom under Cathar and Templar influence.

Tracing our golden thread one step further, Wolfram von Eschenbach (said to have been a Templar himself) wrote the medieval Grail romance *Parzival*. In that epic story, he dubs the Templars "Protectors of the Grail and the Grail Family." In this context, another book by Baigent and Leigh, *Holy Blood, Holy Grail,* presents a cogent theory for the Templars having pledged themselves to this cause, not in fiction, but in reality. It is alleged that the Grail Family is composed of the actual descendants of Jesus Christ and Mary Magdalen, who, legend says, migrated to France, possibly as founders of the Merovingian dynasty.

This extraordinary theory (recently popularized in Dan Brown's novel *The Da Vinci Code*) suggests that in A.D. 679, after the assassination of the last Merovingian monarch, Dagobert II, protectors of the royal lineage formed a secret society, the Priory of Sion, around the *sang real,* the royal blood, of the descendants of Jesus and Mary Magdalen. This may be the true meaning of *sangraal,* Baigent and Leigh suggest, the Holy Grail of medieval romancers.

The Knights Templar, the authors say, may have had much to do with this Priory of Sion, the foundations of which may hearken back to the House of David, to Jesus and Solomon: the lineage of the Israelite kings. The Templars may have secretly dedicated themselves to this very special bloodline, believing the wisdom-legacy of Solomon and Jesus to be their own. Enthroning this lineage during the Middle Ages, the Templars would have set their golden age in motion.

HOW DOES THE LOST ARK OF THE COVENANT FIT IN TO THE PUZZLE?

In *Raiders of the Lost Ark,* Steven Spielberg acquainted the viewing public with one of the great mysteries of all time, the fate of the Lost Ark of the Covenant, the ancient Israelite repository of divine authority. While Spielberg portrays Hitler's Reich lusting after the Ark in fiction, the Templars probably attempted to find the Ark in reality.

Graham Hancock's *The Sign and the Seal* points convincingly to the Templars having pursued the Lost Ark from Jerusalem to its alleged final resting place in Ethiopia. Hancock argues that the Ark itself may have been the enigmatic Holy Grail, and that romancers encoded within their texts the Templars' secret mission to find and harness the Ark's holy power.

Bearing in mind that, in the Middle Ages, possessing the Ark would have meant wielding the power of God, doing so would have established the Knights Templar as the dominant force on Earth, the pope notwithstanding. With evidence of the Templars having excavated the Temple of Solomon, and then of their presence in Ethiopia (a country that figures in Eschenbach's *Parzival*), where the Ark is believed to reside to this day, a case exists for the knights having searched for the famous artifact, probably to further their mystical/political goals of establishing a golden age.

SECRET HISTORY AFTER BANNOCKBURN

Tracing our golden thread to more recent centuries, the quest of the Knights Templar reveals itself long after the period of their official existence. Driven underground during the Inquisition, refugee knights, a specific Masonic tradition claims, gave birth to Scottish Freemasonry. That tradition traces its origins directly to the order and to King Robert the Bruce. Robert, the tradition specifically states, founded the first Scottish Masonic lodge after the battle of Bannockburn to receive Templars fleeing persecution in France.

By the seventeenth century, the tradition had splintered into a variety of forms. The Jacobite variety, the most intensely political and mystically devoted, claimed the Templar tradition as its own. The Jacobites failed to restore the Scottish Stuarts to the English throne, even with the help of powerful Masonic allies in France, but by that time the Enlightenment was under way. The Templar ideal of a free society founded on religious and political liberty had taken root, philosophically at least. Scottish, English, and French Masons had begun to dramatically change the way the world thought.

Locke, Montesquieu, Voltaire—all Masons—preached the philosophy of Liberty, a natural consequence of both Templar experience and the suppression of their ideals. As if by providence, then, the tradition sprouted on distant shores, the threads, now luminous strands, of which united the philosopher/revolutionaries of the New World.

On August 28, 1769, Saint Andrew's Masonic Lodge in Boston conferred a Freemasonic degree named after the Knights Templar. By 1773, the lodge had assumed a highly significant role in the American Revolution. The Grand Lodge of Scotland made the colonial physician and patriot Joseph Warren grand master of the American continent. Other members were Paul Revere and John Hancock. And the lodge's membership overlapped with the most catalytic secret society of the day, the Sons of Liberty, with at least twelve members of the lodge participating in the Boston Tea Party.

But the story does not end in Boston. Freemasons played major roles in the Revolutionary War itself and in the signing of the Constitution. These members included George Washington, many of his generals, Benjamin Franklin, Patrick Henry, and the Marquis de Lafayette. Franklin was a member of a mysterious French society called the Royal Lodge of Commanders of the Temple West of Carcassonne, a mouthful in more ways than one.

That our golden thread links Benjamin Franklin to the medieval city of Carcassonne connects him with some of the most secret history of all. The area around the fortress at Carcassonne, a medieval center for Cathars and Templars, houses a network of profound and mysterious symbols having to do with sacred geometry, symbols that surface in ritual garments worn by Franklin and Washington during Masonic ceremonies. And as if designed by the forces of creation, an uncanny arrangement of mountain peaks forms a perfect Masonic five-pointed star around Rennes-le-Château in the Carcassonne area.

A series of medieval churches, towers, and ancient Celtic sites expand upon the design, creating Masonic triangles in the precise proportions of the golden mean of sacred geometry, an overall pattern that stretches from Rennes-le-Château to the island of Bornholm in the Baltic Sea—where evidence of a

Templar presence exists—to Jerusalem and the Temple of Solomon. The vast geometric design and the symbols carved in stone at the sites have been traced to the Priory of Sion and to the Templars, secret societies working in ways that transcend culture, religion, and mundane history.

Our golden thread represents only a portion of the whole cloth. The greater tapestry suggests that though the mystery is even more profound, even more elusive, it is also as apparent as the Great Seal of the United States or the Masonic symbol found on the dollar bill. That the full story has been kept from us should not be surprising, however.

That which we perceive merely as subtle and continuous manifests as a raging current at the auspicious hour, a deluge that threatens the tyrants of orthodoxy, the guardians of politically correct history. That current rages still, for those who have ears to hear the roaring of the waters. But don't expect to find the secret story in a history textbook.

Instead, follow the golden thread.

8 The Templars and the Vatican

The Forbidden Johannite Heresy

Mark Amaru Pinkham

According to one esoteric tradition, after excavating the foundations of Solomon's Temple for nine years, the Templar Knights left the Middle East with five "caskets" or cases full of treasures they had collected in the Holy Land. These cases, the story goes, were eventually deposited in Kilwinning, the Mother Lodge of Scottish Freemasonry, before being transported to Rosslyn Castle, ancient home of the Sinclair barons of Rosslyn, where they were kept safe until a fire broke out in the building. The cases were then quickly removed from the castle, and very soon afterward the construction of Rosslyn Chapel officially began. Thus, it appears that the chapel may have been built specifically to hold the five cases.

This notion was apparently corroborated in the 1990s by Andrew Sinclair, who conducted ground scans at Rosslyn and discovered five rectangular objects, or boxes, in the crypt underneath the chapel. Sinclair's discovery has fueled speculation about what might be in the cases, including notions of artifacts associated with Solomon's Temple or Herod's Temple and possibly some ancient scrolls.

Conjecture has it that some of the imagined artifacts in the cases were discovered by the knights via clues they found while studying obscure Essene texts, a theory recently corroborated by the discovery of the Copper Scroll, one of the Dead Sea Scrolls. Clues found in the Copper Scroll have led archaeologists to some empty pits that are in close proximity to Templar symbols and weapons, thus apparently revealing that the knights had overseen the secret excavations and then absconded with whatever treasure they found.

The hypothetical scrolls that may exist within the five cases have been theorized to include genealogical information regarding a family spawned by Jesus and Mary Magdalen or, assert authors Christopher Knight and Robert Lomas in *The Hiram Key,* they possibly contain Essene information regarding the origins of Freemasonry. But at present, all that is known for certain about the scrolls is that one of them contains a diagram with symbols recalling the mysterious Johannite Heresy, a Gnostic belief system into which the Templars may have been initiated in the Holy Land.

Copied by Lambert de St. Omer, a retired schoolmaster, when the Templar Knights passed through Flanders as they moved through northern Europe, this diagram—today entitled the "Heavenly Jerusalem"—hangs on a wall in a museum in Ghent, Belgium. It is a map of the New Jerusalem as described in

Fig. 8.1. The diagram of the "Heavenly Jerusalem" in Ghent, Belgium, by Lambert de St. Omer.

the Book of Revelation. Johannite heretical wisdom is evident in the design via the identification of a Messiah—the figure prophesied to found the holy city of the future—as being not Jesus but John the Baptist.

Such a designation is consistent with the ancient Johannite heresy, which stated that John was both Messiah and founder of the Gnostic Johannite path that leads to the intuitive vision of the Heavenly Jerusalem. According to this heretical tradition, there were two Messiahs or Chosen Ones—with John, the Priest Messiah, one rung above Jesus, the incarnated King Messiah.

If the Johannite Heresy is truly the key to understanding the Templar scroll now in Belgium, it must be allowed that the knights were Johannites and embraced a greater veneration for John the Baptist than for Jesus. Furthermore, if they *were* Johannites, then they practiced a Gnostic path composed of heretical rites that culminated in an inner revelation regarding the nature of the universe and the goal of human existence. This would explain why the five cases with their Johannite scrolls ended up in Rosslyn Chapel. The Sinclair builder of the chapel considered himself to be a caretaker and preserver of the Templars' Gnostic wisdom.

Earl William Sinclair was a Grand Master Freemason of the developing Scottish Rite, an order that had descended directly from the Templars who fled France and later made their home in Scotland. According to Niven Sinclair, a contemporary patriarch of Clan Sinclair, rather than risk death by exposing the Gnostic secrets in his possession, Earl William embedded them within his stone edifice. Perhaps he knew at the time that the secrets he was hiding for posterity —secrets that would prove that the Templars were Johannite Gnostics and heretics—were indeed the Templars' greatest secret.

THE DISBELIEF OF POPE CLEMENT V

According to conventional history, the first intimation that the Vatican had regarding the Templars' Gnostic and Johannite predilections came to the surface during the knights' depositions for allegations of heresy in 1307. Then, in 1308, Pope Clement V disbanded the ruthless Inquisition so that he could privately interview the Templar Knights himself. At stake was his own private bodyguard of knights, which since the time of Pope Honorius II and the Council of Troyes in 1128 had been the Holy See's personal militia.

The knights had been accused of a litany of heretical offenses, any one of which could have been reason enough to cast them into the holy fires of the Inquisition, but since many of the knights' confessions had been extracted under extreme torture, their credibility had been compromised. Therefore, having never fully believed the damning allegations against his beloved Templars, Clement V confidently called for seventy-two knights to be transported from Paris to his villa in Poitiers, in southern France, where he was sure they would recant their previous testimonies.

Imagine his surprise when, after assuring the knights that they were safe in his home no matter how damning their confessions might be, the Templars refused to discredit the confessions previously extracted from them in the dark and dank torture chambers of Paris. Pope Clement, who was essentially a pawn put into office by King Philip, could only scratch his head in disbelief and lament that his knights had somehow strayed from the straight and narrow.

To his dismay, he had found out conclusively that the vile allegations against the Templars were indeed true. The pope was forced to accept the fact that he had lost his knights. Later, within the silence of his quarters, the distraught pope must have wondered whether the Templars had ever truly been a Christian army of the Church.

WHAT THE VATICAN REALLY KNEW

Since the time of the Templars' private audience with Clement V, a body of evidence has been forming to prove that—although the pope was blind to the knights' heretical activities—other informed Church officials within the Vatican had known about their heretical propensities. For example, according to testimony given by one Father Antonio Sicci during the Templar trials, some of the knights' Gnostic activities had been witnessed by Vatican spies in Palestine well before 1307.

The fact also became clear during the Templar trials that both the Vatican and King Philip of France had sent their spies to oversee the knights' activities in Europe before 1307; some of the spies were later chosen as witnesses for the prosecution. It was because of the evidence uncovered by these early spies that months before the Templars' mass arrest, King Philip knew exactly what heretical activities to instruct his twelve specially selected spies to look for when he had them infiltrate certain Templar preceptories.

The monarch may also have known what heresies to look for from studying information contained within a secret Templar document. This document, entitled *Baptism of Fire of the Brothers-Consulate* and often referred to by Templar historians as the "Secret Rule of the Templars," was discovered in 1780 in the Vatican Library by a Danish bishop.

Said to have been written in A.D. 1240 by a French Templar Master named Roncelinus, it appears to give a green light to all the heretical offenses that the knights were accused of in the fourteenth century. Permission to indulge in all manner of Templar heresy can be found in this document, including defilement of the Cross, denial of Christ as the Savior, sexual liaison, and the worship of an idolic head known as Baphomet. There is even a passage within the document that gives the knights permission to initiate other Gnostics—including Cathars, Bogomils, and even Assassins—into their order. If the *Baptism of Fire of the Brothers-Consulate* was indeed in circulation beginning in A.D. 1240, it would have been an easy task for Church or royal spies to procure a copy for their employers.

THE KNIGHTS OF ST. JOHN

A more substantial bit of evidence in support of the notion that the Vatican was aware of the Templars' heretical Johannite affiliations came in the mid-1800s when Pope Pius IX gave his famous "*Allocution of Pio Nono*" against the Freemasons. In fact, this address implies that the Vatican may have known all along about a heretical Templar-Johannite relationship.

At the time of his momentous address, the pope was under immense pressure to take a stand against the uprising of numerous heretical Gnostic sects forming in France, one of which was the Johannite Church of Primitive Christians. This sect claimed to be a direct descendant of the early Knights Templar, and the chief of the sect, Bernard Fabre-Palaprat, claimed to be a Templar Grand Master in line from both Hughes de Payns and John the Apostle. Pope Pius's subsequent denigration of the sect during his address proved that the Church had ostensibly known for hundreds of years about an intimate Templar-Johannite association:

> The Johannites ascribed to Saint John [the Baptist] the foundation of their Secret Church, and the Grand Pontiffs of the Sect assumed the title of Christos, Anointed, or Consecrated, and claimed to have succeeded one another from Saint John by an uninterrupted succession of pontifical powers. He, who, at the period of the foundation of the Order of the Temple, claimed these imaginary prerogatives, was named *Theoclet;* he knew *Hugues de Payens,* [sic] he installed him into the Mysteries and hopes of his pretended church, he seduced him by the notions of Sovereign Priesthood and Supreme royalty, and finally designated him as his successor.

Fig. 8.2. Salome contemplates the severed head of John the Baptist. Could it have been the "Baphomet" that the Tempars were accused of worshipping?

Pope Pius's address was soon corroborated by some highly respected esoteric historians of the nineteenth century. In *Isis Unveiled,* Madame Blavatsky revealed: "They (the Knights Templar) were at first the true Knights of John the Baptist, crying in the wilderness and living on wild honey and locusts," while her contemporary, the self-styled Templar descendant and Kabbalist Eliphas Levi, volunteered in *The History of Magic:* "The Templars had two doctrines: one was concealed and reserved to the leaders, being that of Johannism, the other was public, being Roman Catholic doctrine. . . . The chiefs alone knew the aim of the Order the Subalterns followed without distrust."

Thus, Levi confirmed the Templars' affiliation with the Gnostic Johannites, but he went one step further in pointing out that it was principally the Grand Masters and chiefs of the Order who were aware of the knights' heretical activities. This notion has been corroborated by transcripts compiled by the Papal Council during the Templar trials that show that when the knights were questioned regarding one of their most important Johannite rites—that of worshipping the idolic head called Baphomet—only the chiefs of the Order knew anything about it. The caretaker of the head was, at the time, Hughes de Peraud, the second in command under Templar Grand Master Jacques de Molay, who secretly carried the head from one preceptory to the next whenever an initiation or ceremony called for its presence.

WHAT WAS THE BAPHOMET?

Who or what was the Baphomet and how did it connect the Templars to the Johannites? The contemporary Johannites, who became separated from mainstream Templarism in the mid-nineteenth century, claim to know. Supposedly their church, the Apostolic Johannite Church, is in possession of secret wisdom descended directly from the chiefs of the Knights Templar.

According to James Foster, former primate of the Johannite Church, the Baphomet of the Templars was the decapitated head of John the Baptist, the Messiah of Johannite tradition. This would explain the extreme sanctity the Templars ascribed to the head and why it was in the sole possession of the Order's second in command. According to the Templars at their trial, the head possessed special power and could make "trees blossom and the land to produce."

Legend has it that when John's head was found by the Templars in the Boukoleon Palace in Constantinople during the Fourth Crusade, the head had been used to keep an eleventh-century emperor of the Eastern Roman

Empire vibrant and alive by moving the head into close proximity to the emporer's body on a daily basis. This power, known as the Holy Spirit in the West and Kundalini in the East, is the same power John was saturated with during his lifetime in the Holy Land. It is this power that can awaken itself as a normally dormant evolutionary energy at the base of the spine and culminate in Gnostic awareness.

9 The Lost Templar Fleet and the Jolly Roger

Did the Pirates of the Caribbean Have a Covert Vendetta?

David H. Childress

In 1307 King Philip IV of France traveled to Rome to convince Pope Clement V that the Knights Templar were not holy defenders of the Catholic faith, but were instead seeking to destroy it. He succeeded.

On October 13, King Philip ordered simultaneous raids on all the Templar priories in his country. Within weeks, hundreds of knights were captured, including their grand master, Jacques de Molay. The official day of the suppression of the Templars was a Friday—the origin of popular belief that Friday the 13th is unlucky.

Templars throughout Europe were arrested and harassed in an effort to extract confessions of heresy. All those captured were tortured, sometimes for months and years, to make them divulge the secret of the Holy Grail and its whereabouts. Jacques de Molay was given special attention and suffered years of agony. But, it is said, none of the Templars revealed the desired information. In 1312—even though the Templars had effectively been crushed in France—Philip pressured Pope Clement V into disbanding the order throughout Europe. A papal bull suppressing the order everywhere was issued.

At this time, the king's men entering Templar castles found that many of them were abandoned. The few men discovered were arrested, tried, and found guilty of sins against God. In 1314, de Molay, who had suffered in Philip's dungeons for seven years—blinded by red-hot irons, his genitals boiled in oil and pulled off with cords, and most of his bones broken or dislocated on the rack—faced, by order of king and pope, his last torment: roasting alive over a slow fire. This barbarous destruction of a human life was never to be forgotten, and today, seven hundred years later, de Molay's name lives on as the title of a Masonic youth group.

The Knights Templar, now hunted men, dispersed all over Europe. Yet these refugee knights still commanded immense respect from Europe's fighting men. In many places they were welcomed and given sanctuary as heroes. Some joined the Teutonic Knights and fought against Mongol and Tartar incursions in Eastern Europe; some went to Hungary and fought against Turkish expansion; some went to Scotland, others to Portugal.

THE LOST TEMPLAR FLEET

The mysterious Knights Templar had an extensive sea network and may even have inherited some of the maps and other secrets of the Phoenicians. Their great fleet is discussed in Michael Baigent and Richard Leigh's book *The Temple and the Lodge.* The authors point out that the Templars had a huge fleet at their disposal, a fleet operating out of ports in Mediterranean France and Italy as well as northern France, Flanders, and Portugal.

When King Philip ordered the raids on October 13, 1307, the Templar fleet based at La Rochelle somehow got advance warning. The entire fleet set sail, escaped Philip's net, and has never been heard from since.

The disappearance of the Templar fleet has become one of the great mysteries of history. What happened to it? Was it scattered on the seven seas or did it secretly regroup?

Baigent and Leigh claim that the fleet escaped en masse and sailed for a mysterious destination offering political asylum and safety: Scotland.

To get there, the Mediterranean fleet had to sail through the dangerous Straits of Gibraltar, and it probably stopped at various friendly Portuguese ports such as Almourol Castle. Portugal was one of the few places where the knights could find asylum—a country that, unlike Spain, was largely sympathetic to their cause.

In Portugal, the Knights Templar retained something of a cohesive organization, merely changing their name to the Order of the Knights of Christ. Here they found royal support to which the Church could only turn a blind eye. First, King Alfonso IV became the Grand Master of the "new" Knights of Christ, and began to send Portuguese ships into the Atlantic. Later, his son Prince Henry the Navigator also became a Grand Master of the Templars and continued his father's tradition of Atlantic exploration.

The curious history of Portugal, and later Brazil, is tied to the Templars and their lost fleet. Even the name Portugal is curious. It has been suggested that it is a Templar name—Port-O-Gral—meaning Port of the Grail.

Portugal has always had close ties with England, and one wonders if this does not have something to do with the Templars and their fleet in Portugal. And how was small Portugal to remain independent on the Iberian Peninsula?

Was it because of this strong connection to the Templars and ancient seafarers? Later, Portugal's transatlantic colony Brazil was set up in much the same way as the United States, as a union of independent states; and, significantly, it was set up by a series of Masonic lodges—just as in North America.

THE TEMPLARS' LAST STAND

Baigent and Leigh go on to say that the Templar fleet sailed from Portugal and up the west coast of Ireland to safe ports in Donegal and Ulster, where Templar properties were located and arms smuggling to Argyll was common.

The fleet reached Argyll by sailing to the south of the islands of Islay and Jura into the Sound of Jura, unloading men and cargo at the Scottish Templar strongholds of Kilmory, Castle Sweet, and Kilmartin.

Robert the Bruce controlled portions of Scotland, but not all of it. Significant portions of the northern and southern highlands were controlled by clans allied with England. Robert had been excommunicated by the pope in 1306, one year before the Templar persecution began. Essentially, the papal decree that outlawed the Templars was not applicable in Scotland, or at least in the parts of Scotland that were controlled by Robert the Bruce.

The turning of the tide for Robert the Bruce, Scotland, and (perhaps) the Knights Templar was the famous Battle of Bannockburn. Although the actual site of the battle remains undetermined, it is known to have taken place within two and a half miles of Stirling Castle, just south of Edinburgh.

On June 24, 1314, Robert the Bruce, together with 6,000 Scots, miraculously defeated 20,000 English soldiers. Exactly what took place that day has never been fully recorded. It is believed by some that the battle was won with help from a special force of Knights Templar.

PIRATES—GUARDIANS OF THE SANGREAL

But what became of the missing Templar fleet? Was it grounded in Scotland? Did it sail across the Atlantic a hundred years before Columbus? Did it become one of the great fleets of the Portuguese and Scottish kings? Did it become a fleet of pirates that attacked ships loyal to the pope and the Vatican? Perhaps all of the above!

According to Michael Bradley, author of *Holy Grail Across the Atlantic,* the Templars were guardians of the Holy Grail, in the sense that it comprised the "Sangreal" or "Holy Blood." The story goes that descendants of Jesus living in southern France were evacuated from Montségur during a terrible siege in March of 1244. They probably hid, as some troubadour poetry suggests, in numerous secret Pyrenees caverns for months or even years.

But for the long-term safety of the Templars and the Holy Blood, the order and the Grail had to be taken out of France, and, ultimately, out of Europe. Bradley says the Garonne River was the obvious route of eventual escape, as it extends from deep in the Pyrenees across southern France to the Garonne Estuary on the west coast.

La Rochelle, home of the Templar fleet, is situated on the estuary. A sanctuary at the town and fortress of Angouleme along the way may have been used as a haven for two or three generations. As long as the Templars remained a cohesive and independent order, there was hope that the lineage could secretly hide in Europe and begin recouping its fortunes.

Bradley believes at least some Templar vessels that disappeared in 1307 carried the Holy Grail. This may have included not only individual members of the former Merovingian royal family, but also a large assortment of physical treasures, including a fortune in gold coins, crosses, jewelry, and possibly even the famous Cup of the Last Supper (Grail Chalice) or, incredibly, the Ark of the Covenant. Both the Cup and the Ark were rumored to be in the possession of the Templars, though most historians consider this—like most of the Holy Grail material—to be mere fantasy.

Bradley agrees with Baigent and Leigh that the Templar fleet sailed north through the Irish Sea to their final destination, the western fiords of Scotland, carefully avoiding the Irish coast because of pro-Vatican control of the ports.

The fleet landed in various areas north of present-day Glasgow, in the environs of Oban. Here Templar graves were marked with the familiar Templar symbol of skull-and-crossbones.

In Scotland the Templars apparently chose not to organize themselves into a new order of knighthood but elected instead to spread their secret doctrine more widely by creating Freemasonry under the leadership of the powerful Saint-Clairs (Sinclairs) of Roslin. At this point, the naval war with the Vatican began in earnest.

Says Bradley, "An upsurge in European piracy begins from this time, and the pattern of it suggests that many pirates were not mere freebooters who would attack anyone, but very curious 'pirates' who confined their attentions to Vatican and loyal Catholic shipping."

The Templar fleet was to be split into two parts. One would anchor in the Orkneys and prepare for Sinclair's ambitious journeys to North America. The other was to sail the Atlantic and Mediterranean as a naval force attacking ships associated with the Vatican and their allies. Some of the Templar fleet would go on to be absorbed into the Portuguese navy and fly the Portuguese flag, while other ships—usually commanded by French or English captains—flew a black flag with a skull-and-crossbones, a symbol that would become known worldwide as the Jolly Roger.

THE KINGDOM OF THE JOLLY ROGER

The skull-and-crossbones symbol on the flags of early pirates originated because the Templars and their fleet could not safely fly their true flag—a red cross on a white background. This was the mystique of the early pirates: They were essentially a secret navy that was not supposed to exist. (This navy even traveled to the New World nearly a century before the Spanish.)

Authors such as Baigent, Lincoln, and Bradley maintain that the skull-and-crossbones imagery that the Templars employed is nothing but the old Templar "cross pattee" rendered in human skeletal material, with the knobs of the leg bones being the pattees of the Templar cross. The message of the skull-and-crossbones is abundantly clear, says Bradley: It was a "neo-Templar" vow to oppose the Roman Church to the death, and thus the symbolism of human bones on both the flag and Templar gravestones.

The term Jolly Roger itself was an homage to Roger II of Sicily (1095–1154). Roger had reputedly been associated with the Templars during the Crusades, and conquered Apulia and Salerno in A.D. 1127 despite opposition from Pope Innocent II. He was crowned king of Sicily by Antipope Anacletus II in A.D. 1130. Innocent eventually yielded and invested Roger with the lands he already possessed.

Roger established a strong central administration, largely free of Rome, and his brilliant court at Palermo was a center of arts, letters, and sciences. His court was full of dancers, music, and entertainers, and he was known as Jolly Roger. In many ways, the Renaissance began at Roger's court. His fight with the pope was well known, especially to seafarers and traders.

Roger also established a navigational school on Sicily, one isolated from the Vatican by both the sea and his fleet, which invited Jewish and Islamic geographers as consultants. The Arabic geographer, Ibn Idrisi, was attracted to Roger's court and produced a "celestial disc" and a "terrestrial disc," both in silver, which represented respectively all the astronomical and geographic knowledge of the day. Idrisi and Roger also produced the important navigational treatise, called *Al Rojari*. Roger was fond of Islamic and ancient Hebrew love poetry, with a taste for beautiful women to match the allusions in it.

Roger, through the Arab geographers in his court, also began to obtain important maps that the Muslims had acquired from libraries such as the one at Alexandria in Egypt.

THE RISE OF PIRACY ON THE OPEN SEAS

When the Spanish Inquisition was established in the New World after 1492, the Templar "pirates" spread their attacks to the Caribbean. Later British seamen—such as Francis Drake in the sixteenth century—would elevate piracy to big business. Once the Inquisition had been installed in Spain, Drake preyed only upon Spanish Catholic ships.

Eventually the pirates would journey on to Pacific ports in Peru and Mexico—all in the name of an ongoing naval war that had had its genesis many years earlier with the Knights Templar.

10 The Mystery of the Battle of Bannockburn

Is It Revealed in the Ancient Maxim "As Above, So Below"?

Jeff Nisbet

Perhaps no battle in history has been written about more passionately and at greater length than the 1314 Battle of Bannockburn. Without that great battle, Scotland may never have managed to shake off the yoke of English domination, may therefore never have established a true national identity, and so may never have birthed the stirring Declaration of Arbroath, which was, in the opinion of many, the model for America's own Declaration of Independence.

No fewer than seven accounts were written within sixty-three years of the battle, and countless others since. Two were published in the last year alone.

Why all the talk? Because at the heart of that battle has always lain a great mystery: how the enormously outnumbered Scots could have won the day against a force described as the greatest army that a king of England had ever commanded.

To solve that mystery, researchers have studied the site's topography, the political climate, each side's leadership—even the height of the tides—to explain how the underdog could have prevailed against such overwhelming odds. Yet still the mystery remains. Introduce a possible eleventh-hour intervention of the shadowy Knights Templar into the mix and the mystery only deepens.

But was Scotland *really* the underdog, or was it only meant to appear so? Working under the credo that what looks too good to be true usually isn't, I looked someplace new—at the sky *above* the battlefield—and saw what had perhaps been hidden there, in broad daylight, almost seven hundred years ago.

Let's go back.

It's 1286. With the death of Alexander III, Scotland is suddenly without a king. Alexander's infant granddaughter, Margaret, the daughter of King Eric II of Norway, is the only heir to the throne, and the Scots quickly swear fealty to her. It doesn't take long for Alexander's brother-in-law, England's crafty King

Edward I, to arrange Margaret's betrothal to his own son. But his plan fails when the little queen dies en route. The Scottish throne stands vacant.

Two powerful Scottish nobles, each related by blood to Alexander, vie for the prize. One is Lord John Balliol of Galloway and the other Lord Robert Bruce of Annandale, grandfather of the man who eventually wins victory at Bannockburn. Civil war seems inevitable. Whom to choose?

Incredibly, Scotland asks the king of England to choose. Edward, true to form, picks the weaker of the two, John Balliol, and is himself declared superior lord of both realms in the bargain. With Balliol under his thumb, Edward garrisons Scotland's castles with his own men. Although not the crowned king of Scotland, Edward is the next best thing.

But a hero soon steps forward who captures the hearts and minds of the downtrodden. That hero is William Wallace, whose exploits, romanticized in Hollywood's *Braveheart,* are now widely known. Edward eventually has Wallace castrated, drawn, and quartered, sending the pieces of Wallace's body north as a gentle warning against future mischief.

Fig. 10.1. England's King Edward II, son of Edward "Longshanks," who fought Robert the Bruce at the Battle of Bannockburn, Scotland.

Enter Annandale's grandson, Robert the Bruce, who systematically recaptures Scottish strongholds, the exception being Stirling Castle, near Bannockburn.

The Scots lay siege.

Edward's son, by then King Edward II, is given an ultimatum: Arrive with an army by midsummer day, 24 June 1314, or Sir Philip de Mowbray will surrender the fortress. Edward accepts the challenge and arrives one day early, with a mighty beast of an army that outnumbers Robert's by at least three to one.

The Scots' situation seems hopeless.

Let's now look up.

At dawn, Taurus the bull stands on the horizon, facing north in a sky already too bright to see him. The uppermost stars of Orion the Hunter have just risen. Venus, a planet long associated with the pre-Christian Goddess, shines just north of Orion's weapon, in a direct line with the bull's lower horn. The Sun rises in Gemini, the heavenly twins, followed by Jupiter, Mercury, and the Moon. Bringing up the rear is Leo the lion, with the war planet Mars below its breast. Accompanying Orion are his two hunting companions, Canis Major and Canis Minor, the Big Dog and the Little Dog.

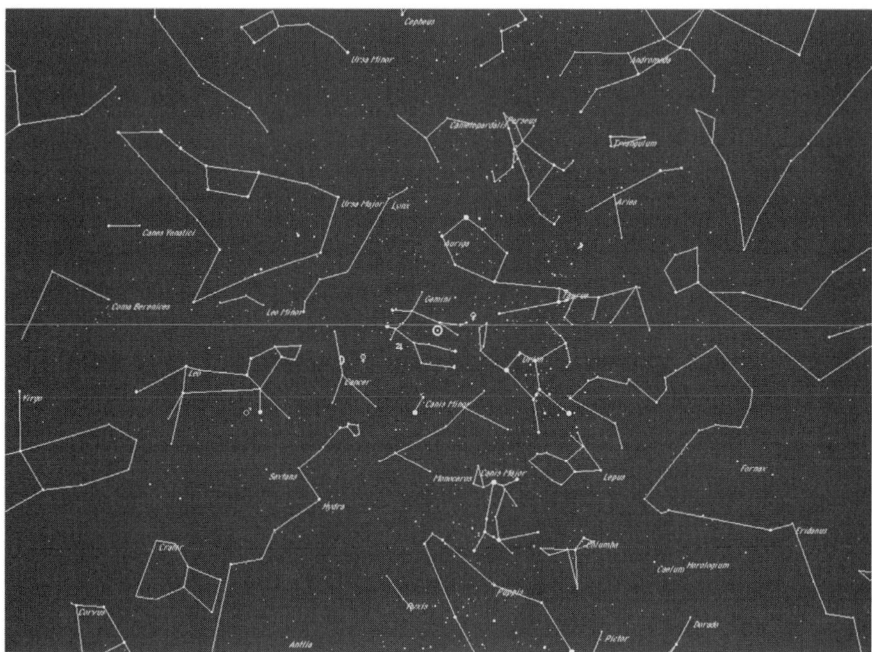

Fig. 10.2. The sky at dawn above Bannockburn, Scotland, as it appeared at the time of the famous fourteenth-century battle between the British and the outnumbered Scots.

Throughout the day, this celestial group moves westward. Taurus reaches his zenith at midday, and begins to descend. As evening falls, Orion drives Taurus below the horizon. The Sun sets, and night returns. Short as a midsummer night is, at that latitude, for those who must fight at dawn it must seem all too long. Many will never see another.

Let's now consider events at Bannockburn over that same period, keeping in mind the Hermetic dictum "As above, so below." The parallels are striking.

First, an event at midday that becomes the single most memorable of the entire two-day engagement: first blood.

Due to a leadership dispute, Edward's army is split into two great horns as it thunders near. Earl Gilbert de Clare of Gloucester commands one horn. Earl Humphrey de Bohun of Hereford commands the other.

Some fifty yards ahead of Hereford's column rides his nephew, Henry de Bohun, clad in full armor, on a powerful warhorse, with his spear in his hand. Henry spots the king of Scots, armed only with a battle-ax and shield, sitting on a small gray horse, inspecting some of his troops at the forest's edge. De Bohun sees the chance to singlehandedly win the battle before it begins, and takes the shot.

He couches his lance and charges, full-tilt, toward Robert, but Robert is ready. A split second before Henry's lance can pierce him through, Robert sidesteps his horse and, standing in his stirrups, delivers Henry a mighty blow that cuts through helmet, skull, and brain.

It is a tidy tale stirring enough to survive down through time, as was perhaps intended.

Etymological research reveals that de Bohun relates to both Taurus and the word *boun,* the name given to cakes traditionally offered to the Goddess in pre-Christian times. Interestingly enough, bannocks, as in Bannockburn, are Scottish cakes that were similarly used. In John Barbour's fourteenth-century biography of King Robert, Barbour specifically refers to de Bohun and Robert as "the Boun" and "the Brus." I suggest that "Brus" may derive from the Middle English word *brusen,* meaning to crush or mangle.

Is it possible that John Barbour intended de Bohun's single combat with Robert to symbolize the simultaneous struggle between Taurus and Orion in the sky above? Was he secretly pointing up?

First let's consider two so-called myths about Scotland that refuse to die.

The Egyptian Connection: The fifteenth-century *Scotichronicon* claims that the Scots derive their name from Scota, daughter of the pharaoh who pursued the children of Israel out of Egypt. Scota and her followers left Egypt shortly thereafter and, after many years, her people eventually settled in a land they call Scotia.

Recently the claim is made in Keith Laidler's *The Head of God* that Scota's father was Akhenaten, the pharaoh who tried to establish monotheism in Egypt using the Sun to represent the one true god who should otherwise have no image. Most astonishingly, Laurence Gardner, author of *Bloodline of the Holy Grail,* recently claimed that Akhenaten was in fact Moses, the man who led the Israelites out of Egypt.

The Jesus Connection: In 1982's *Holy Blood, Holy Grail,* by Michael Baigent, Richard Leigh, and Henry Lincoln, the authors argued that Jesus Christ and Mary Magdalen—contrary to Christian dogma—were married and had children, founding a holy bloodline that continued to thrive through some of the highest and mightiest families of Europe. Evidence of that bloodline may have been uncovered by the Knights Templar while excavating beneath the ruins of King Solomon's Temple in Jerusalem in the early twelfth century. Upon that order's barbaric 1307 dissolution, it's thought that many of its members escaped from France to Scotland just in time to help Robert the Bruce—a man whose parentage may have united *both* bloodlines, the Egyptian and the holy—in his struggle with England.

Dangerous ideas, indeed, especially in 1314. But, if believed by some, could these ideas have been secretly introduced into the grand tapestry of history as it was woven at Bannockburn, to perhaps one day, in more tolerant times, be trotted out as Truth?

Let's now consider how those two myths may be connected to another common root, the belief system of ancient Egypt.

In his most recent book, *Rex Deus,* Tim Wallace-Murphy reports a claim that Jesus was an initiate of the Egyptian cult of Osiris and a follower of the goddess Isis, which is largely confirmed by the well-documented Templar veneration of Isis under the Christianized guise of the Black Madonna. The belt stars of Orion are central to Graham Hancock and Robert Bauval's theories about an extraordinarily early ground plan of the pyramids on Egypt's Giza Plateau.

As I continued to study the accepted reasons given for the Scottish victory at Bannockburn, they seemed less and less credible. Moreover, the existence of an underground brotherhood of Scots and English, united in a cause that transcended national loyalty, seemed likely; and confirmation that a *secret* tale, written deep between the lines of the *official* tale, began to emerge out of the mists of time.

Some further points of interest:

In a part of Barbour's book dealing with Robert the Bruce's early days, Barbour tells of Robert being pursued by Lord John of Lorne, who used a pair of Robert's own hunting dogs. Robert the Bruce shakes the scent by wading up a stream (just as Orion and his canine companions descend nightly beneath the western ocean, only to rise again with the Sun). Barbour also pauses in his tale to deliver a strange discourse on prophecy and the conjunction of planets, perhaps to suggest that he was actually telling two tales—one tale above and one below.

A. A. M. Duncan, Barbour's most recent translator, has speculated that Barbour's fourteenth-century patron was Bishop William Sinclair of Dunkeld, younger brother to the lord of Roslin, an ancestor of the man who built the fifteenth-century Rosslyn Chapel, long considered an architectural repository of ancient knowledge and Templar lore.

THE ACTUAL BATTLE OF BANNOCKBURN

As the English army thunders northward, Robert's army waits in the Torwood, a forest south of Stirling Castle. Nowadays defined as a hill or heap, there's an interesting alternative definition of the word *tor* in the 1899 R. H. Allen book *Star Names: Their Lore and Meaning.* Referring to the ancient Druids' reverence for the constellation Taurus, Allen says some have claimed—perhaps fancifully—that the tors of England were the old sites of the Druids' Taurine cult, as our cross buns are the current representatives of early bull cakes with the same stellar association that trace a connection back through the ages to Egypt and Phoenicia. (Perhaps the claim was not so fanciful.)

Hereford's argument with Gloucester about who should lead the advance slows the English such that they must rush to Bannockburn, arriving exhausted, yet oh so conveniently in the nick of time for Robert's midday combat with de Bohun.

An English deserter named Alexander Seton (a recurring Templar surname) appears in Robert's camp on the eve of battle. He tells Robert that de Bohun's defeat has demoralized the English and that if the Scots fight on the following morning, they will surely win. As the dim light of dawn is seen, Seton utters the words "Now's the time, and now's the hour," a phrase immortalized in Scots poet Robert Burns's stirring *Ode to Bannockburn.*

In the pre-dawn darkness of June 24, the Scots quietly approach the English army and succeed in drawing a battle line closer than English prudence should have allowed. As both sides face off, the Scots suddenly kneel in prayer. King Edward thinks they are kneeling to him for mercy while, behind him, Venus has already risen, followed by Orion and the Sun. Could the widely reported event have been orchestrated to serve a double purpose—one prayer for the moment, one hidden for posterity?

Robert's greatest military innovation was his unique use of *schiltrons,* dense hedgehogs of men wielding twelve-foot spears pointed outward. Schiltrons had been successfully used before, but only as a stationary defense. Robert trained his to move, and allowed offensive use of this tactic. As Orion's three belt stars moved inexorably toward Taurus, three Scottish schiltrons advanced on the English. Among the battle flags held aloft was that of Robert's trusted lieutenant, James Douglas. It depicted *three stars on a sky blue background.*

The English army is positioned in a wedge of land between two tributaries of the river Forth, a tidal river. As the Scots advance into that wedge, these tributaries deepen—with a tide that is exceptionally high due to the Sun and the Moon being in such close proximity—giving the English little room to fight except at the front line.

Legend then has it that a fresh force of three hundred Knights Templar, led by Lord Sinclair of Roslin and followed by an exultant horde of camp followers, came screaming in from the west, throwing the enemy into an irreversible panic. Many drowned trying to flee the slaughter. Could that unusual proximity of Sun and Moon have been known long beforehand? Is that why Edward was given almost a year to assemble his mighty army? And if also known by the earls Hereford and Gloucester, who had perhaps purposely delayed the English advance, is that why their tired forces bivouacked where they did?

The 1314 Battle of Bannockburn did not end Scotland's War of Independence, but it did turn the tide. In 1322, Edward made his last foray north and found the land stripped of sustenance. "King Robert's Testament," as Robert's scorched-earth policy became known, left behind only a single meal in all the fields in southern Scotland: one lame cow.

It's highly unlikely that mainstream historians will accept as fact any of these connections but, since I have neither academic turf nor reputation to protect, I make them anyway, and welcome debate. But I would caution that further comparison of the written records with the stubbornly persistent myths will reveal other connections, too numerous to either list here or shrug off as mere coincidence. There was more going on at the battle of Bannockburn, both above and below, than history has allowed and that's just the *what* of it. The *why* is another tale . . .

The idea that myth has been persistently used as a vehicle to carry untimely, though fundamental, truths forward into a more enlightened future is difficult for many of us to process, and yet it's important we try—especially on matters of religion, and especially in these terrible times. If it's possible that all teachings are equally wrong, and grew askew from just a single and sadly forgotten spiritual source more ancient than we've been taught, then perhaps now's the time and now's the hour to consider that possibility.

11 The Pyramids of Scotland

An Orion Ground Plan Discovered in Fair Caledonia

Jeff Nisbet

Egyptian tycoon Mohamed Al Fayad, owner of Harrods and father of Dodi Fayed—Princess Diana's companion in their fatal 1997 car crash—has listed his ten favorite books on the *Manchester Guardian*'s Web site. One of them is *The Scotichronicon: A History Book for Scots,* described simply as "Scotland's debt to Egypt revealed at last."

What does al Fayed mean?

Completed in the fifteenth century by Walter Bower, abbot of Inchcolm, the *Scotichronicon* begins with "The Legend of Scota and Gaythelos." The legend claims that Scota was daughter of the pharaoh who pursued the children of Israel out of Egypt on their exodus to the Promised Land. Gaythelos, an exiled prince of Greece, was Scota's husband. Shortly after the Israelites leave, the couple are forced to lead an exodus of their own out of Egypt—going first to Spain, then Ireland, and finally to Scotland, which was named after Scota. Their bloodline flowed down the centuries through the high kings of Ireland and Scotland. But Gaythelos's pedigree was more ancient still—stretching back many more generations to the patriarch Noah of the Hebrew scriptures, eldest survivor of the biblical flood.

Although historians argue that royal families found it politically useful to invent fanciful lineages of great antiquity, could it be that the legend is more fact than fancy?

On March 27, 2000, I received the following comment from an eminent U.K. archaeologist regarding my report about an intriguing Scottish leyline configuration I'd discovered: "I do understand your quest for knowledge," she said, "but please, please beware of the whole leyline question. It is so easy to draw lines and make assumptions, from prehistory onwards, but that way madness lies."

Hmmm . . . !

For those unfamiliar with the term, a leyline is the curiously exact alignment of ancient archaeological sites, conjoined over many miles. Academics dismiss them as mere coincidence and those who discover them cannot explain the "why" of them. Crossing mountains and large bodies of water as they do, leylines never seem to follow the easily trod path—only the straight one.

So of what use were they?

I was studying the Knights Templar at the time, and my discovery was as follows:

I had noticed a geometrical connection between two preeminent Templar sites in Scotland—their earliest-known headquarters in the tiny village of Temple and that famed architectural repository of Templar and Freemasonic lore, Rosslyn Chapel. Each could be connected to a third by straight lines drawn through two small islands to the northeast in the Firth of Forth—the islands of Craigleith and Fidra. Each line connected to the Isle of May, twenty miles farther out, where one tradition tells us the Templar fleet landed after escaping from France. Historian Stuart McHardy has recently suggested that "the May," as it's locally known, is in fact the Isle of Avalon where legendary King Arthur is buried. (Glastonbury supporters, staunchly supportive of their own pet site's long-held Avalonian connections, are not impressed.)

Exactly midway between Craigleith and Fidra is a tiny island known locally as "the Lamb," which will enter the equation later.

I had then drawn three additional interconnected lines.

The first stretched exactly due south from Craigleith to the Cistercian abbey of Melrose. Founded contemporaneously by Abbot Bernard of Clairvaux, the Cistercians and the Templars are thought by many to be two arms of a single order. Interestingly, I later discovered that if the line is continued far to the south of Melrose, it arrives, unerringly, at Glastonbury.

The second line headed in a northwesterly direction from Melrose, exactly through both temple and Rosslyn, to a place called Crossford, where it intersected the third line.

That third line headed due west from Craigleith, passing through Dunfermline Abbey along the way. Robert the Bruce, quasi-hero of my "Mystery of Bannockburn" article contained in this book, was buried at Dunfermline, but his heart was removed and carried on an ill-fated journey to the Holy Land. Brought back to Scotland from Spain, which is as far as it got before the "infidel" horde put a stop to its passage, the heart was interred at Melrose, just a day's ride shy of a reunification with his body. History does not tell us why.

In effect, I had found a compass and a square connecting several Templar and Freemasonic sites in southern Scotland. And as many will know, the compass and the square are important symbols of Freemasonry. They can be seen on every Freemasonic lodge in the world—surrounding the mysterious letter *G*, which has been variously interpreted as God, Gnosis, or Geometry.

My leyline configuration buzzed with a significance that seemed to preclude coincidence. But a cautionary finger had been raised on my leyline investigation, so I put it on the back burner—but not for long.

While researching my Bannockburn piece, I often viewed a computer simulation of the eastern sky as it would have appeared on the day of the battle. Countless times, I observed the three equidistant belt stars of the constellation Orion rise invisibly in the daylight sky, and at some point I noticed they were rising over Fidra, the Lamb, and Craigleith. Throwing caution to the wind, I decided the Lamb deserved some attention—sanity be damned.

I then drew a line from the May through the Lamb and the exact midpoint between Rosslyn and Temple, just to see where it might lead. It led to a tiny spot called Tara, far away in Ireland, where the high kings of that land were crowned—kings descended from Scota and Gaythelos.

This was odd and getting odder!

On a wall of Rosslyn Chapel's underground crypt—the oldest and holiest structure in the building—is what has been called a "working Masonic drawing." It's shaped more like an obelisk than a pyramid, and yet it sang a siren song to me. The central line of the drawing passes through three pyramids—as viewed from above!

Why despoil a holy place forever with a drawing that could have been more easily scratched in dirt? Is that not odder still?

When it is visible, Orion is the most spectacular constellation in the sky—and little wonder. Of all the constellations, Orion is the least abstract—and is strikingly humanoid in shape. But of all its seven main stars, the belt stars have received the lion's share of attention over the millennia. Called simply "three in a row" by native North Americans, their relative positions have been recently correlated by the researcher Robert Bauval to the ground plan of the pyramid complex at Giza.

Fig. 11.1. The constellation of Orion rising over the horizon on the day of the Battle of Bannockburn, Scotland.

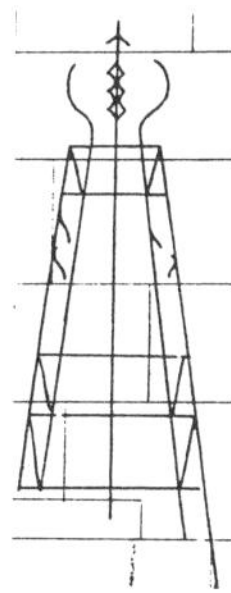

Fig. 11.2. This Masonic drawing still visible on the south wall of Rosslyn Chapel's crypt depicts the special relationship between the pyramids of Egypt and the islands in Scotland's Firth of Forth.

Fig. 11.3. A photo composite also illustrates the special relationship between the pyramids of Egypt and the islands in Scotland's Firth of Forth.

Orion and nearby Sirius, the brightest star in the sky, are inextricably linked to both the ancient Egyptian belief system and the mysterious symbolism inherent in today's bizarre Freemasonic rituals, practiced since the brotherhood's earliest days but now little understood—even by Freemasons themselves. Could the key to what has long been referred to as "The Lost Secrets of Freemasonry" have been hidden in the light of day, east–southeast of Bannockburn, on June 24, 1314?

On a wild hunch, I decided to bring Orion and Sirius down to Earth, laying the three belt stars exactly on top of the three islands in the Firth of Forth. Incredibly, Sirius lay on tiny Inchcolm Island, farther west in the Forth, where Walter Bower had written his *Scotichronicon*. In Richard Hinckley Allen's *Star Names: Their Lore and Meaning,* the author cites a Hindu astrological tradition that personifies Sirius as a hunter who shoots a three-jointed arrow that pierces Orion through the waist.

It's interesting that Walter Bower's surname derives from the craft of bowmaking. Could it be that Bower, finishing his book, let fly an arrow of forbidden knowledge toward a more enlightened future?

The other stars in the Orion/Sirius configuration, however, were not so accommodating. Bellatrix, the star that marks Orion's right shoulder, lay insignificantly in the sea, far from the May, the island my "compass" had suggested played a major role in what looked increasingly like a message from the past.

On another wild hunch I enlarged the stellar group, pivoting it on Craigleith, until Bellatrix lay on the May.

The result was riveting!

Sirius now lay on Torphichen, headquarters of the Knights Hospitaller in Scotland—the Catholic military order that absorbed the remnants of the outlawed Templers and, by the grace of Rome, acquired most of their property to boot. Recent research, however, suggests the Templars may have continued to maintain a secret autonomy within the Hospitallers.

But that's just the beginning.

A line drawn from Bellatrix through Orion's left shoulder (Betelgeuse) led directly to Dunsinane Castle, immortalized in Shakespeare's *Macbeth.*

Keith Laidler, author of *The Head of God,* relates an interesting tale about Dunsinane. He cites an 1809 newspaper article reporting that a large stone of "the meteoric or semi-metallic kind" had been discovered hidden beneath the castle. The stone was sent to London for study, but disappeared en route.

Laidler goes on to say that it was Scotland's *real* Stone of Destiny, and that the stone upon which British monarchs have since been crowned is a substitute. This real stone, he claims, is the Throne of Akhenaten, the heretic pharaoh who tried and failed to establish monotheism in Egypt shortly before the biblical Exodus. That stone began its journey to Scotland with Scota, who Laidler says was Akhenaten's daughter, while Akhenaten led the Israelite Exodus to the Promised Land under the name given to him in the Bible—Moses!

Could today's Christians and Jews be linked to a common Egyptian patriarch? The implications are staggering!

But where did Betelgeuse lie—the star between the May and Dunsinane?

My map showed a featureless landscape. But subsequent research revealed that an ancient stone circle, now "lost," had once existed to the west of the nearby hamlet of Dunino. If the lost circle proves to lie under Betelgeuse, archaeologists will have a merry time losing it again.

The stars at Orion's feet also lay in interesting locations.

Rigel, Orion's right foot, stood on the lands of Yester. Built in 1297 by the Wizard of Yester, Hugo de Gifford, Yester Castle stands over a sizable underground cavern known as the Goblin Hall. Hugo practiced his "magic" in Goblin Hall before passing it to the Hay family in the fourteenth century. Father Richard Hay later wrote a history of the Sinclairs of Roslin. Lord William Sinclair, it is said, actually moved his castle to free up the chapel's building site. Location was everything, I guess—even back then!

Saiph, Orion's left foot, stood between the towns of Musselburgh and Prestonpans, on land once owned by the Cistercian monks of Newbattle and later associated with the Templar-connected families of Seton and Kerr. Besides hosting one of Scotland's first Masonic lodges, the area hosted the first meeting of the North Berwick Witches—accused in 1590 of plotting to murder Scotland's first officially Masonic king by the "abomynable cryme of wytchcraft." The trumped-up case helped kick off over 100 years of witch persecution in Scotland, something barely covered in mainstream histories.

Here's the kicker: A line drawn from Rigel through Saiph led directly to Bannockburn, site of the great Scottish battle for independence where, on Midsummer's Day in 1314, a great message was hung invisibly in the dawn—a message meant to eventually reveal that we've been fooled for a very long time. Surprise, surprise!

Last April I drove out of Edinburgh to take photographs of the three belt-star islands, and was struck by the shape of North Berwick Law, the peak that stands just to the south of Craigleith. It looked remarkably like a pyramid, so I made some calculations.

According to Hancock and Bauval's *Message of the Sphinx,* the bottom of the square pit in the center of the Great Pyramid's subterranean chamber lies 610 feet below the pyramid's summit platform. North Berwick Law stands at 613 feet!

Care to split some very fine hairs, anyone?

From the top of North Berwick Law the islands of Craigleith, the Lamb, and Fidra lie stretched along the coast like pearls on a string. The questions cannot be avoided: How could they possibly be positioned, each to the other, like the Giza pyramids? How could they lie below the rising of Orion's belt in the Bannockburn dawn? How could North Berwick Law be

Fig. 11.4. An old map of the Firth of Forth in Scotland, with North Berwick Law prominently displayed (as "N. Law").

pyramidal? How could natural geological features be so conveniently where they are in the first place without divine intervention? And why, in that small corner of the world, do the voices of myth and history join to sing a siren song to people like me?

Perhaps I can suggest answers to some of those questions, and raise some new ones. Risking the hoots and hollers of academia, I propose that North Berwick Law and the islands of the Forth are where they are due to large-scale terraforming—that is, shaping the landscape to suit a purpose that is only now emerging from the mists of time.

On a mid-seventeenth-century map of the area, supposedly based on the original but now mysteriously lost drawings of late-sixteenth-century map-maker Timothy Pont, the three belt-star islands are shown. But there are curiosities about their presentation. The orientation of the grouping is wrong, and the Lamb is called Long Bellenden. The name is especially curious because the Lamb is not long at all. In fact, it is the shortest of the three islands.

Could it have been shortened to "sharpen" the aim over the vast distance from the May to Tara? Might not the islands have been one long island at some point—carved from the mainland by a cataclysm the ancient mythmakers would only hint at—and then cut into three? And might not North Berwick Law have been shaped from the tailings of such an enormous excavation? Just take a look at Fidra, sliced almost in two and bored clear through, and ask yourself if it was shaped by God, Nature, or the helping hand of man!

I realize I stand on shaky ground here, but not without consideration—and I welcome your arguments. Be warned, however, that this article could have been a lot longer. The simple grid shown here has blossomed into greater bloom—and I'm loaded for bear!

History tells us we're the greatest civilization ever to walk the face of the Earth. Wars have been fought since time immemorial over matters of faith—each side believing that God is on *its* side. But what if the things that make us swing our swaggersticks are wrong? Who'll forgive us for the damage we've done, fool unto fool, believing in lies?

Orion was brought down to Earth in Scotland, and then later nailed in place by tales of a legendary stone, a holy chalice, a magical sword, a battle the world would not soon forget, and a once-and-future king named Arthur.

Much care was taken, through events of much danger and tumult, to make us think. Perhaps more than ever, the time to do so is now.

12 The Enigma of the Great Lost Sailor's Map

How Did Its Makers Know What They Knew?

David H. Childress

Within a generation after Philip IV pressured Pope Clement V into disbanding the Knights Templar (October 13, 1307), maps called *portolans* began to be distributed throughout Europe. One of the earliest is called the Dulcert Portolan of 1339, which appeared just twenty-seven years after the Templars were finally suppressed.

Scholars of navigation have consistently tried to ignore the portolans because of their implications. It is accepted that they did, in fact, exist, but further conclusions about their significance have been swept aside.

Stated simply, the mystery is not so much that the portolans appeared suddenly in fourteenth-century Europe, but that they are so incredibly precise. Previously the barrier to medieval navigation was that longitude—the position east or west of any given point—could not be accurately determined. The key to finding longitude by celestial observation required measuring time with great precision. Accurate clocks simply did not exist in the medieval world, and navigators had to wait until eighteenth-century technology supplied them.

A modern expert, the late professor Charles Hapgood of Keene State Teacher's College in New Hampshire, researched the portolan maps in the 1950s and 1960s. Hapgood arranged to have his analyses checked by the Cartographic Section of the U.S. Air Force's Strategic Air Command and concluded that all the portolans seem to have been copied from one original.

All of the surviving portolans are centered on the Mediterranean world, begging the question: Did the source map from which they all derive depict a much larger area, perhaps the entire world?

If the portolans represent just the small European portion of some larger world map—or *mappamundi,* as academics would say—then the corollary must be that the rest of the world would be depicted as accurately as the small European segment.

Researcher Michael Bradley says, "I believe it is justified to assume that it is probable, with this probability verging on certainty, that Templars did possess such a map of the world. The reason for stating this so strongly is simply that modern scholars have found just this kind of mappamundi in Middle Eastern archives. Specifically, two very intriguing maps of the world have been located: The Hadji Ahmed Map was discovered in 1860 in what is now Lebanon; and then, in 1929 the Piri Re'is Map was discovered in the old Imperial Palace in Constantinople." But, supposing that a mapmaker of the fifteenth or sixteenth century possessed a very ancient but accurate map that he could copy, he would still be inclined to "improve" on it based on the best contemporary knowledge available to him.

For places that were unknown by reason of inaccessibility, such as northern Greenland, for example, or for places depicted on the mappamundi that had not yet been discovered, the mapmaker had no choice but to rely on his source map. When it came to places that the cartographer thought he knew—like the Atlantic coast of Europe and the Mediterranean area—he felt an obligation to improve things, given the best knowledge available to him. Unfortunately for the medieval or early Renaissance cartographer, and unfortunately for modern scholars, fifteenth- and sixteenth-century knowledge and mapmaking techniques were no match for the mysterious source maps, which were virtually always accurate. Consequently, the mapmaker's attempts to improve on them with then current knowledge resulted in distortions that now stick out like the sore thumb of ignorance.

THE HADJI AHMED MAP

The Hadji Ahmed Map was drawn by an Arab geographer from Damascus, who is only obscurely known to history. It is dated 1559 and shows the entire world in a somewhat fanciful projection that is more art than science, which was typical of Arab chartwork of the time. A careful look will show that Hadji Ahmed "improved" the Mediterranean according to Ptolemy, and thus distorted it. He also drew Africa according to the best Portuguese information that he could get, distorting it as well in a manner typical of the time.

But when we look at North America and South America, we see an almost modern shape that could compare well with Mercator's Map of South America drawn ten years later from contemporary explorers' information. Thankfully, Hadji Ahmed apparently had no access to contemporary maps and charts of the Americas and so was stuck with simply copying some mysterious mappamundi in his possession.

This unknown source map of Hadji Ahmed was more accurate than the best information available in 1559, and yet the map looks very modern. It shows Baja, California, which had not been mapped at that time. It shows the northwest coast of North America, including Alaska, which had not been discovered then. It shows the Hawaiian Islands in the Pacific, which were not discovered until two hundred years later. It shows a sprinkling of islands in the Pacific, a sort of vague and suggestive rendition of the Polynesian Islands, but they had not been discovered yet. It shows Antarctica clearly, and even a suggestion of the Palmer Peninsula, which had not been discovered then, either.

The Far East, insofar as it can be made out in the curious "split-apple" projection used in the map, is distorted but reasonably accurate. But the strange and unnerving thing is the region of Alaska and Asia. The curve of the Aleutian Islands is depicted accurately, but there is no Bering Strait and the whole area is land. This part of the map depicts how the world of that region actually was—but 10,000 years ago! The Bering Land Bridge between Asia and North America is shown correctly.

This fact almost defies belief. Or is it just coincidence? Perhaps a mediocre mapmaker, not knowing how Asia and North America actually terminated, decided to make things easy and simply joined them.

Hapgood and Bradley both believed that all the portolans share a peculiarity: The general accuracy is there but the sea level seems too low. On the celebrated Ibn Ben Zara Chart, most of the islands of the Aegean are shown larger than they are today, while there are some extra islands that do not currently exist, but which would exist if the sea level dropped two hundred to three hundred feet. These islands did exist 10,000 years ago, near the end of the Ice Age when the sea level was exactly two hundred to three hundred feet lower than it is today!

Since these sea-level problems are common to all the portolans and to the existing mappamundi from which the portolans seem to have been excerpted, are we to believe that the Earth was accurately mapped 10,000 years ago, and that a few copies survived to the medieval period?

THE PIRI RE'IS MAP

The Piri Re'is Map, found in 1929 at the Topkapi Museum in Istanbul, presents an even greater puzzle. It was drawn in 1519, the year that Magellan's expedition set out to circumnavigate the world. But this expedition did not return to Europe until 1521 and so the Piri Re'is Map could not have relied on the voyage. According to marginal notes presumably made by Piri Re'is himself, his map was based on "the map of Columbus" and on other maps "dating from the time of Alexander the Great."

In any event, the map caused a stir in both diplomatic and geographic circles because it showed the Americas with great accuracy. The problem was that the American continents had not yet been explored, or even coasted to any great extent, in 1519. Europeans were just then feeling their way out of the Caribbean. Cortés landed in Mexico the same year. Pizarro had not yet met the Inca of South America. What, then, could be the source of this map?

American Secretary of State Henry Stimson began a flurry of correspondence with Turkish authorities that lasted through much of the 1930s, urgently requesting the Turks to carefully search their old archives to see whether any similar maps might come to light. The Turks complied, or said they did, but nothing like the maps of Hadji Ahmed and Piri Re'is turned up.

Piri Re'is does show the New World coastline with amazing accuracy, but it may not seem that way to the average reader. It was self-evident to cartographers of the 1930s, however, who were able to see immediately that the map had been drawn according to azimuthal equidistant projection, a technique well know to modern cartographers. Experts were, and are, amazed and puzzled.

The map, Hapgood concluded, could have been made only with aerial photography!

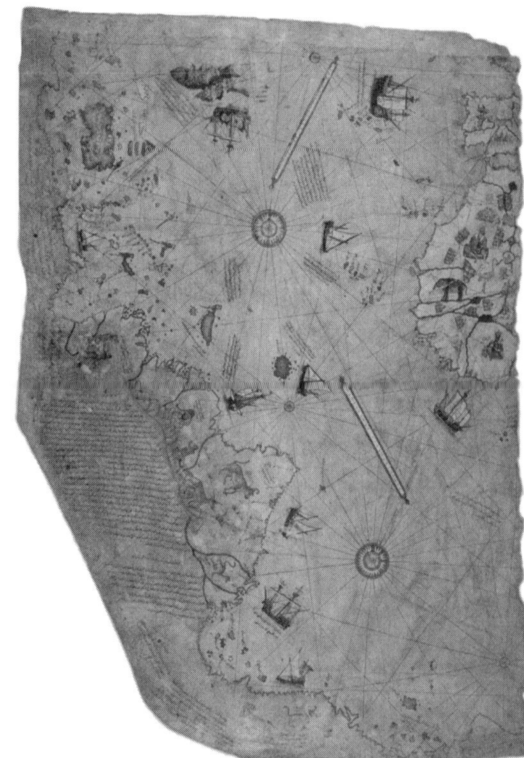

Fig. 12.1. The Piri Re'is Map reveals advanced geographic knowledge in prehistory.

THE ZENO MAP OF THE NORTH

Henry Sinclair, Grand Master of the Templars after they fled France to Scotland, apparently had a remarkable map when he set sail for Nova Scotia in 1398. This map comes down to us as the Zeno Map of the North, and was drawn by a Venetian navigator in Sinclair's service, Antonio Zeno, sometime in the late 1300s.

This map was supposedly the result of a voyage made by Antonio and his brother Nicolò from Venice in the year 1380. Their explorations reportedly took them to Iceland and Greenland, and perhaps as far as Nova Scotia. They drew a map of the North Atlantic, which was subsequently lost for two centuries before it was rediscovered by a descendant in the 1550s.

A detailed study of this map—which Hapgood conducted and recounts in detail in his book *Maps of the Ancient Sea Kings*—shows that Zeno's map was actually copied from some other highly accurate chart that was drawn on a conic projection. Antonio was not familiar with this projection, which is understandable since it was not devised until three centuries after his death, and he also "improved" things from his own knowledge when he could.

Just how ancient the original source maps may have been is indicated by the fact that Zeno's map shows Greenland free of ice. Mountains in the interior are depicted, and rivers are drawn flowing to the sea, where in many cases glaciers are found today.

As with the revelation that Antarctica at one time was free of ice and perhaps inhabited, we find similar legends of a civilized people who once lived in northern lands that are now buried under thousands of feet of ice: the legends of Thule, Numinor, and the Hyperboreans.

It is interesting to speculate that the Zeno brothers' map shows what may have been the lost land of Thule, a legendary northern land mentioned by such Greek and Roman historians as Diodorus Siculus, Strabo, and Procopius. Thule was an island in the North Atlantic, some six days' sail from the Orkneys and ten times the size of Great Britain. Even more strange, it appears that Greenland may have been free of ice at the same time!

The lost land of Thule was important in Norse mythology to the Teutonic Knights of the Middle Ages and eventually to inner occult groups in Nazi Germany.

They believed that Thule (generally identified as Greenland) had been an island to the north of Atlantis to which many Atlanteans had fled just prior to the destruction of their land. Did the Zeno brothers' map come from such a time, after the sinking of Atlantis but before the ice had completely covered

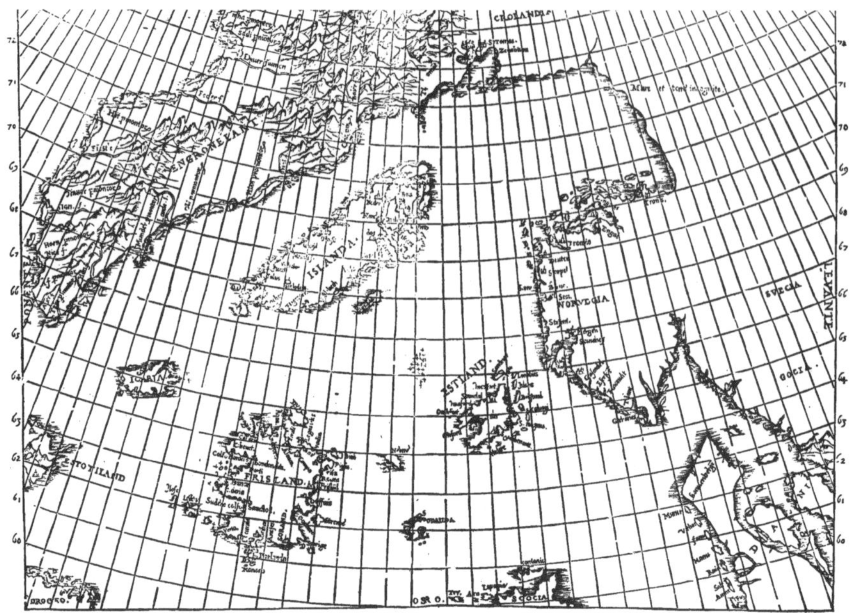

Fig. 12.2. The Zeno Map, published in 1558, comprises a set of letters and a map that resulted from the voyage of exploration taken by brothers Antonio and Nicolò Zeno throughout the North Atlantic with Henry Sinclair in the fourteenth century.

Greenland, the world's largest island? Where would these Italian navigators have run across such a thing?

As we have noted, Antonio Zeno was in the service of Henry Sinclair. Perhaps Sinclair shared with him the chart that became the brothers' blueprint. But how did a highly accurate map of the North Atlantic get to Roslin of the Sinclairs? Could it have arrived with the refugee Templars?

THE TEMPLAR CONNECTION

Two mappamundi turned up in Middle Eastern archives relatively recently: the Hadji Ahmed Map in 1860 and the Piri Re'is Map in 1929. There must have been many more such maps in those same Middle Eastern archives about 900 years ago when the Templars captured and sacked many Saracen towns and cities. It is a virtual certainty that at least some similar maps were discovered by the founder of the Templar dynasty: Godfroi de Bouillon.

The value of these ancient charts would have been appreciated at once by the Templars. Had the kingdom of Jerusalem survived, its wealth and future prosperity would obviously have depended upon trade and commerce, not upon agriculture. Palestine in the twelfth century was much as it is today. Anything that could give the de Bouillons an edge in trade would have been a treasure, and the Templars would have been given the task of guarding it.

But then the de Bouillons lost Jerusalem. They fell back on Provence, only to be massacred during the thirteenth-century Albigensian Crusade. Some few representatives of this supposed Holy Bloodline allegedly survived, but then the Templars themselves were crushed and dispersed. If there was land across the Atlantic, as both the Hadji Ahmed and Piri Re'is Maps show, then a truly secure haven from the Inquisition potentially existed. It was the Templars' job to find that haven if at all possible, and so they fled to Scotland and Portugal with their precious maps. Probes were immediately launched out into the Atlantic.

THE MYSTERIOUS CHART OF MAGELLAN

It is absolutely certain, too, that the royalty of Portugal—who were all members of the Knights of Christ, which the Templars had become—had maps that showed discoveries in advance.

Pigafetta, a navigator attached to the 1519 Magellan expedition, had this to say about a mysterious map in the possession of Magellan, copied from a map held by the king of Portugal:

> The sentiments of every person in the fleet were that [the Strait of Magellan] had no issue in the west and nothing but the confidence they had in the superior knowledge of the commander could have induced them to prosecute the research. But this great man, as skillful as he was courteous, knew that he was to seek for a passage through an obscure strait: this strait he had seen laid down on a chart of Martin de Boheme, a most excellent cosmographer, which was in the possession of the King of Portugal.

Where had this chart come from? No one knows for sure. There is no proof, but it seems at least probable that this chart came into Portugal with refugee Templars—just as it seems equally probable that Henry Sinclair's map of the north came to the Roslin refuge with dispersed Templars. The coincidences are highly suggestive, even if they do not constitute absolute proof.

Columbus had a map of some sort as well. It was possibly a copy from the same maps from which the Piri Re'is Map was formulated, or perhaps a map similar to that of Hadji Ahmed. Both of these show the New World, and neither confuses the Americas with Asia.

PART THREE

THE PIVOTAL ROLE OF THE SCOTLAND SINCLAIRS

13 The Vanished Colony of Arcadia

Did the Knights Templar Establish Outposts in North America?

Steven Sora

A curious tower stands guard over the harbor of Newport in Rhode Island. An octagon within a circle, the round stone tower has eight arches at the ground level and two raised stories with curiously placed slit windows. Since colonial times, it's been argued that it might be a grain mill, a windmill, or a remnant of the pre-colonial Norse. A recent discovery discards all such theories. The tower proclaims to all who understand its significance: Templar builders were here.

A TEMPLAR KNIGHT IN AMERICA

In 1398, Henry Sinclair, of the guardian family, rediscovered lands his Norse ancestors had sailed to centuries before. He intended to plant a colony in the New World where all were safe from persecution. This was long before Columbus, and there is evidence that Columbus was aware of Sinclair's voyage. Henry employed what would be called today a multicultural crew. His pilot was Italian; his sailors were hardy Orkney Islanders; his soldiers, remnant Templar descendants, French Normans now banded in Scottish lodges. They landed in the region now called Nova Scotia and wintered there. In spring, Sinclair split his fleet, sending his pilot Antonio Zeno home to Scotland. Sinclair told Zeno it was his intention to create a colony in this newly discovered land. With half of his fleet, Sinclair explored all of Nova Scotia and farther south into what is now New England.

Evidence of his expedition can be found in several places. In Nova Scotia, strange ruins of a shelter near the legendary Oak Island discovery site and the so-called Mystery Walls near Halifax are clues of a precolonial extended visit. In Westford, Massachusetts, an engraved granite post depicts a knight in armor whose family crest and heraldic armor were declared to be that of Sir James

Gunn, who was Sinclair's most important lieutenant in the Caithness area in Scotland. In Fall River, Massachusetts, a skeleton was found clad in armor that the poet Longfellow wrote about, even expressing belief that it was connected to the mysterious tower.

Off Rhode Island's coast, and again in Nova Scotia, were found two cannons that were among the first examples of cannon used on board ships. Antonio Zeno's brother Carlo first introduced them in a naval battle to save his home city of Venice. These early cannons had a tendency to explode rather than fire correctly; they might have been used to impress the native population, or eventually they were just tossed overboard.

This and other evidence found in various New England sites pales in importance to the tower itself and the knowledge it conveys.

WARRIORS, BUILDERS, BANKERS, AND MYSTICS

The Templars were much more than an order of warrior-monks who fought to save Jerusalem in the wars called the Crusades. They were adept in arts and sciences, banking and trade; they owned vast estates and built structures that exist today in Europe. Their most sacred architecture replicated the octagonal construction found in the Holy Sepulchre in Jerusalem. They built structures called baptisteries, or lavabos, that featured the same symbolism found in the baptismal font in any church. The circle represented the world and the eight sides to a baptismal font—or a baptistery—represented the rebirth, or resurrection, that was and is the central tenet of the Christian faith.

In such Christian symbolism, God created the world in seven days. He started on Sunday and rested on the seventh day, Saturday, the Sabbath. The eighth day was again Sunday. Further symbolism is found in the story of the death of the Son. He is crucified and killed on Friday, enters the underworld for a time, and on Sunday, the eighth day of the week, He is resurrected.

The similarity with pagan celebrations of the Sun is not much different. The Sun appears at its weakest near the time of the winter solstice. The days grow shorter and the day of the solstice itself is the shortest day of the year for those living north of the equator. While this astronomical precession has changed slightly over thousands of years, today this solstice happens on the 21st of December. The Sun is then reborn, and the Earth stays bright just a little longer each day until the summer solstice.

The summer solstice occurs on the 21st of June and, not coincidentally, the only saint in Christian theology whose birthday is celebrated, rather than the day of his death, is St. John the Baptist. He is the one who makes way for the path of the Lord.

In Celtic and pagan theology, John is the king who dies to make way for the new king. Like the symbolic death of John Barleycorn, John the Baptist is beheaded. The connection between Christian belief and pagan mythology goes beyond the Sun-Son message. Bonfires at Midsummer and candles at Christmas were remnants of pre-Christian worship, although the old traditions were never forgotten.

The Roman religion that worshipped the Invincible Sun personalized God in the form of Mithra. Mithra was also born in a cave, of a Virgin, and attended by three shepherds. His life mirrors that of Jesus in many ways and his Temple once stood where the Vatican stands today. Mithra was the god of soldiers and battle, whereas Jesus brought a message of peace.

When the Templar Knights rode out of the Dark Ages in rural France to discover many new things in the Middle East, they would find simple pleasures like candy and sugar and startling new science that Islam had both preserved and fostered in universities. In addition to the architecture in Christian sites, many in ruins, the Templars would have visited the Umayyad Mosque of Damascus.

One of the finest examples of architecture in the then modern world, it still stood in all its glory. It too employed octagonal features rare in Muslim architecture, but then this was no ordinary mosque. Built over the pagan temple of the Syro-Phoenician sun god Hadad, it never lost its original purpose. Hadad was the fertilizing Sun; his relationship to the Earth was critical, as he was needed to bring forth life. The mosque also preserved the head of John the Baptist. Muslims vowed tolerance toward all, and this particular mosque still invites those of all faiths, even Christians, to prayer. While both Christianity and Islam are guilty of concealing ancient roots, people do not forget. Even today it is not unusual for a Muslim woman to enter Umayyad to pray at the monument to St. John in the hopes of having a child.

Cynics might find a contradiction in such similarities between older and more modern religions, yet the Templars and later Freemasons viewed it differently. It was a message of tolerance: All gods are the way to the One God.

A MESSAGE IN STONE: TEMPLAR ARCHITECTURE

When the Templars returned to Europe, they brought back a broadened understanding of their faith and a much wider knowledge of science. Their new science incorporated a mixture of theology and geometry known since before Stonehenge and the pyramids were constructed, but often forgotten in Christian Europe. The Templars went on a spree of building, from Europe's most glorious cathedrals to mundane bridges. Templar soldiers and Cistercian monks left many monuments that stand today. And within these monuments are secret keys to understanding.

Zodiacs built into church floors, six-pointed stars in stained-glass windows, and depictions of the Black Virgin and Child are all evidence of an acceptance of beliefs outside Christianity. Only in the last decade or so have we had any hint that a rich blend of science and magic found its way into otherwise Christian structures.

On the tiny island of Bornholm in the Baltic Sea, the Templars built fifteen churches, eleven of which still stand. The most impressive is Osterlarskirke, meaning the East Church of St. Lawrence. The slit windows of the church were placed to admit the light of the midsummer and midwinter sunrise. The Cistercians built a similar tower in Mellifont, a remote monastery not far from Dublin. The Saint Clair chapel in southern France, the Tomar chapel in Templar headquarters in Portugal, the so-called Templar round church in Lanleff in Brittany, and the Templar Church in London are larger examples. It was not known that these round and octagonal structures had any further importance until very recently.

In many ways, the Crusades were a devastating failure. After two centuries of war against Islam, the French monarchy and the Church turned on their own. Cathars in northern Italy and southern France were targeted and massacred. Lombard bankers and then Jews were expelled from France. Soon the Templars themselves bore the blame for the military disaster of losing Jerusalem. Those who escaped arrest by going to Scotland would serve as mercenaries and play a role in that country's bid for independence. Scotland, however, was not safe. The threat of war with England was constant, and class rebellions that preceded later religious struggles also threatened.

Henry Sinclair, heir to the guardianship of the order, made the decision to create a new colony where science was not viewed as evil, where religious discussion was not settled by war, and where those placed under his guardianship might prosper. It was a utopian ideal; his colony was never heard of again. In esoteric circles the knowledge that he attempted to create Arcadia, an idyllic land where freedom and tolerance were the rule of the day, was not forgotten.

Other circles of often forbidden expression banded together as organized and secretive societies, like the Invisible College and later the Rosicrucians. Others kept their membership so secret that we still cannot attach a label. Overall, those who fostered new science and fresh thinking regarding the monarchy and the Church were said to be part of an underground stream of knowledge.

THE SEARCH FOR THE LOST ARCADIA

One member of such an esoteric society was Giovanni da Verrazano. He was born in Florence in or around 1485. Florence at that time was a hotbed of Medici-funded science and learning, as well as a target of the Inquisition. Verrazano moved to Lyons, in the south of France, where his adopted city had an equally suspect nature of welcoming alternative ideas about religion. Both cities were centers of Cathar thought, and Florence—dedicated to St. John the Baptist—was called the City of the Dove, which was a Cathar symbol. Long before Verrazano was born, the Church had carried on a devastating war against this group of Christians, massacring tens of thousands. Cathar philosophy, however, had survived.

Verrazano was a wide-ranging traveler who spent years in Egypt before returning to the sea. He would convince Francis I, the king of France, that there was good reason to send him to the New World, by bringing the king a strange treatise on alchemy and the idyllic world aptly named Arcadia. On the surface, Verrazano's mission was to find a sea route to China. But his true mission was kept secret.

When he reached the Outer Banks of North Carolina, he recorded that across that thin spit of land stretching for hundreds of miles was the Pacific Ocean. Yet he did not bother to find an entrance. He might have sailed into the wide Chesapeake Bay or the almost as wide Delaware Bay, but he didn't. Instead, he passed the future New York City, which he named Angouleme after a city whose symbol is a dragon writhing in flame, a notably Cathar device. From there he headed east, away from his stated goal.

The only place he stopped was Newport. He was greeted by Native Americans and remarkably allowed one to pilot his ship to safety in the Newport harbor. In the land he labeled Arcadia, he called on a king by the name of Magnus. He was shown the tower that stands in Newport today. While he would have known it was a Templar baptistery (as there was one in his home in Europe), his brother Girolamo labeled it a Norman villa on the map they would create.

Verrazano reported little to his sponsor, but left tantalizing clues. He described the Wampanoag people he met as peaceful and "inclining to whiteness." He described his voyage but not why he failed to explore farther west. His map was copied by other mapmakers. If a strange villa surprised anyone who viewed the map, no comments are recorded. Verrazano knew what he had found.

He labeled the future city of Newport "Refugio." It had been the refuge founded by Templar guardian Sinclair. The monument Sinclair left behind told as much of the story as was needed: The Templars had been there. Henry Sinclair had started his colony, but it did not survive.

THE LAST ARCADIA

In the heart of Paris is the Church of St. Sulpice. On the feast of the saint, the Sun rises and its light traces a path to a sundial that is strategically located. In fact, the entire church is strategically located. Inside, a brass strip called the Roseline is set into the floor, marking the Paris meridian.

St. Sulpice has been home to the Priory of Sion, the Company of the Sacred Sacrament, and other semi-secret societies that played a strong role in an underground history of France. From the early role of the Priory of Sion in the founding of the Templars to the role that St. Sulpice played in the mystery of Rennes-le-Château, little is as it appears.

In the seventeenth century, members of the Company of the Sacred Sacrament were ordered to disband. Without changing their membership list or their headquarters at St. Sulpice, they became the Society of Notre Dame of Montreal. Not all were priests; however, a most important member, Jean-Jacques Olier, would also found the Society of St. Sulpice.

The Society of Notre Dame, although Catholic, allowed commerce with French Protestants called Huguenots, and it included members who were Jansenists, a movement considered heretical, yet Catholic. While this Society of Notre Dame left few early documents (most of the membership was considered secret), we are left with a sense that it strove for the goal of tolerance, which is often lacking when faith is overwhelmed by the very institutions set up to foster it.

The Society of Notre Dame, together with French Huguenots, founded the city of Montreal in Canada. Well before the separation of church and state became a reality, the Society of St. Sulpice would actually be allowed to govern Montreal. Today, many of its old-quarter streets are named for members of the early societies that played a vital role. France would soon surrender Canada to the British, but before that took place, the Sulpicians built the last round tower.

Standing today in the city that was planned as the new Arcadia, this tower is a symbol of the last attempt to create a faith-based colony that would be tolerant of wider religious thought and accepting of individual thinking. Oddly enough, the current-day Notre Dame de Bon Secour Chapel is next to the Masonic Hall Hotel, designed by the grand master of Montreal's St. Paul Lodge.

Research into the hidden messages and secret knowledge built into such monuments from Damascus to Newport is in its infancy. Science has just arrived at the point where the existence of such deeper meaning is accepted. Isaac Newton understood that the secret of the pyramid could be found through numbers. Since his time, few have gone further. However, visitors to Newport will always find a handful of researchers standing around the Newport Tower on the days of the equinox and solstice. Someday, one may unlock its secret.

14 The Lost Treasure of the Knights Templar

Is It about to Be Found in North America?

Steven Sora

A small island off the fog-shrouded coast of Nova Scotia may conceal the world's greatest treasure, that of the order of the Knights Templar. Missing since the fourteenth century, the treasure of the Templars is reputed to contain massive amounts of gold and silver bullion, the crown jewels of royal European families, religious artifacts sacred to both Judaism and Christianity, and documents that may be as explosive now as when they were buried. The current owner of what has been dubbed "the Money Pit" estimates the value of the potential treasure to be more than one billion dollars.

The history of Oak Island's excavation begins in 1795, when three young men with time on their hands decided to search for Captain Kidd's booty. On the tiny island, they found a ship's tackle hanging from a tree branch and a

Fig. 14.1. The mysterious Oak Island in Nova Scotia, rumored to be the site of buried Templar treasure.

nearby depression in the soil. Digging two feet down, they reached a level of carefully laid flagstones, not normally found on the island. They dug farther down, and at ten feet reached an oaken platform. Successive platforms were found at twenty and thirty feet, encouraging the diggers but presenting challenges that surpassed their abilities.

Some years later, prominent citizens of the island formed a company called the Onslow Syndicate to explore further. The oak platforms continued to be unearthed until, at the ninety-foot level, an inscribed stone with a simple code revealed that treasure would be found only "forty feet below." The code may have been a false clue leading treasure seekers into a booby trap. The shaft was soon filled with seawater that not only prevented further excavation, but also remained an unbeatable obstacle for the next two centuries.

A series of flood tunnels had been dug from coves on both sides of the island. Seawater entered from clog-proof drains concealed with coconut husk and eelgrass. For nearly two hundred years, work has continued in an on-and-off fashion as one treasure hunter after another has invested one fortune after another in pumps, drills, coffer dams to stop the seawater, and even heavy construction machinery. To date, the money pit has yielded only a handful of items in exchange for the millions of dollars and the five lives it has claimed. Gold chain, an iron scissors, and a piece of undecipherable parchment are among the paltry rewards to date. There has been a wealth of theories, however, regarding the treasure's origins.

The popular but implausible theory that the treasure is that of Captain Kidd has holes in it, the largest hole being that most of Kidd's treasure was found on Gardiner's Island off the eastern end of New York's Long Island, where the Gardiner family had allowed a host of pirates access to Kidd's domain. It could be that the Oak Island treasure consists of the hidden payrolls of French and British ships, but the motive for constructing such a massive vault to house it in is thin. From Vikings to UFOs, Aztecs to Huguenots, the theory list gets longer, and the combination of means and motive is the litmus test.

One plausible theory holds that a battered Spanish treasure ship was driven off-course by a storm and diverted by currents to Nova Scotia. Mining engineers constructed the booby-trapped vault, hid their precious goods, and attempted a return to Spain to get a stronger ship. En route, another storm arose and the crew perished, together with their secret.

Until the Money Pit gives up its treasure, the debate will go unresolved.

Concurrent with two hundred years of excavation, the owners of the Money Pit and several independent researchers have attempted to determine just what treasure does lie below the surface.

Fig. 14.2. A replica of an encoded stone found in the shaft at Oak Island, Nova Scotia, alerting treasure seekers to possible buried treasure below. The original has been lost.

In 1954, the owners of the Money Pit received a letter informing them that the treasure below tiny Oak Island was not pirate gold but a treasure of far greater value. The treasure, the owners were told, would contain sacred relics and gold from the Temple of Jerusalem, together with manuscripts and documents that would add to man's knowledge of human history. From other sources came the belief that documents contained in the pit could include the Earthly genealogy of Jesus Christ. The Holy Grail, according to *Holy Blood, Holy Grail* coauthors Richard Leigh and Michael Baigent, may not actually be a chalice or dish, but rather a bloodline extending from King David through Jesus to modern times. One intriguing clue is that Sir Francis Bacon wrote of preserving important documents in mercury. Flasks with a residue of mercury have been found on Oak Island.

While the debate remains unresolved, the indisputable truth is that someone with a great deal of knowledge and engineering expertise went through a lot of trouble to conceal *something*. And it is also clear that he finished his complex project before 1795. The carbon dating process pushes the dates back to as early as 1390 and as late as the 1660s.

Who might have had the motive to construct such an elaborate complex before European colonization reached Nova Scotia? Who would have had such an important treasure to protect? And who might have had the ability and the manpower to design and construct such a sophisticated booby-trapped vault? Around the year 1118, the nine men who made up the original Knights Templar returned to France from Jerusalem. Ostensibly their mission had been to make safe the roads for Christian pilgrims visiting the Holy Land—a seemingly overwhelming task for a mere handful of men. Their real purpose might have been completely different. The early knights stationed themselves in the stables in Solomon's Temple and basically conducted a treasure hunt. When they returned to France, they received a hero's welcome and were the subject of St. Bernard's attention.

Bernard of Clairvaux preached so powerfully on behalf of the Christian warriors that he built the tiny group into an order that would rival his own Cistercians. The difference was that the Knights Templar were warrior-monks. Pledged to the Church and to their order, they answered to no other Earthly power. Young men from wealthy families of Europe flocked to join, pledging their inheritance. Nobles donated land and estates. Soon the order grew wealthy enough to lend money as Europe's first bank. Europe's first families pledged jewels and land as collateral for loans from the Templar bank.

Ironically, Templar success would contribute to the order's downfall. Nobles grew envious of the wealth and power of it, but it was not until the crusading armies lost Jerusalem and the Templars surrendered the last Christian outpost that anyone would challenge the Templar order. And then the challenge was so great that the order would fail.

The debt of King Philip of France to the Templars was great, both in terms of the money they had lent the king and because they had saved his life, protecting him from the mobs of Paris. There was, however, no mutual admiration between the borrower and the lender. When the king asked to join the order, he was refused. His hostility to the order induced him to mount false charges against the Templars and to bring in the Roman pope.

On one fateful day—Friday, October 13, 1307—the armies of France attacked Templar headquarters and arrested hundreds of knights, who were tortured until they confessed to any charges leveled by their torturers. These charges included devil worship, homosexuality, spitting on the Cross, and worshipping an idol in the form of a severed head. Many knights would die during torture; others would be burned at the stake.

Though the goal of defeating the order had succeeded, the real goal of King Philip had failed. Before that fateful October day, the Paris Temple, the headquarters of the world's only bank, had been tipped off. Its treasures was loaded onto wagon trains and carried overland to the port of La Rochelle.

There, the wealth of the order was placed aboard Templar ships. The Templar fleet then simply disappeared.

The destination of the Templar fleet has been debated ever since.

The Templars may have found refuge in Portugal, where their organization survived as the Knights of Christ. They may have found refuge in England under King Edward, who would take his time in seeking out and prosecuting them. The numerous islands off the west and north coasts of Scotland were a likely refuge, as Templars and the king of Scotland had much in common. Both suffered under the ban of excommunication, and both would soon be under attack by King Edward of England.

Robert the Bruce had earned his excommunication by stabbing his rival to death on the altar of the Greyfriars Chapel. He then gathered two important bishops and several nobles and had himself declared king on the Stone of Scone. After this, ironically, he became an outlaw and spent years living in caves, losing one family member after another to the English, only to emerge victorious at the Battle of Bannockburn. While history records many wars and battles where the English army was the better-trained and better-armed force going into battle against Scots who were reduced to throwing spears and rocks, Bannockburn was different.

The Scottish forces at first seemed to retreat, only to pull the English army in. Then a fresh force of knights emerged. The surprise to the English was devastating; they had expected an easy rout of their enemy only to find themselves fleeing for their own lives. Scotland won its most critical battle in the war for independence. And the day was June 24, sacred in Templar tradition as St. John's Feast Day.

Robert the Bruce was from a Norman family that had been part of the 1066 invasion of England. The same was true of the Sinclairs of Roslin. The Sinclairs and their French relatives, the St. Clairs, were instrumental in creating the Knights Templar. In a time when families were often as powerful as nominal kings, both the French and the Scottish St. Clairs wielded great power. The Scottish branch would soon command a navy as great as any other in fourteenth-century Europe, and their ancestral home became a headquarters for Templars in hiding.

In 1398, almost a century before Columbus, Henry Sinclair of Roslin led an expedition to lands in eastern Canada and New England that had been visited by the Norse for centuries. His pilot was Antonio Zeno, who kept detailed records and maps of the voyage. Landing in Nova Scotia on the second day of June 1398, Sinclair sent a small army to explore. He would send his Italian navigator home while he remained in Nova Scotia for at least one winter.

Fig. 14.3. Artist Tom Miller's conjectural image of Henry Sinclair's landing on Oak Island, Nova Scotia, in the summer of 1398.

From a base in Canada, Sinclair led a small army south. In Westford, Massachusetts, a skirmish with the native residents culminated in the death of a member of the party, one Sir James Gunn.

The Scottish force left a detailed carving in stone of the Clan Gunn coat of arms, which is still visible today. Another knight, unidentified, died or was killed on the route south; his skeleton and suit of armor were discovered in Fall River in colonial times. The most remarkable monument to the Templar expedition was the construction of an octagonal Templar chapel in Newport, Rhode Island. Modeled after the Church of the Holy Sepulchre in Jerusalem, Templars would erect such structures in various places throughout Europe. The only other such temple back in Scotland was in Orkney, where the Sinclair family ruled.

The Newport Tower would later become the center of great debate, although the earliest European explorer to view the Rhode Island coast was Verrazano, who recorded it on his map. Evidence of the pre-Columbian expedition would be brought home as well.

Starting in 1436, the Sinclair family planned the construction of a remarkably complex chapel in Roslin, with carvings of pagan heads and North American items—such as cornhusks and aloe—allegedly unknown in Europe until after Columbus. The Sinclairs employed construction workers—masons—from all over to build their chapel and to construct in rock a massive hiding place that could hold a treasure as well as an army. Although the masons arrived in 1436, actual work in Scotland did not begin until 1441. It would make little sense to employ workers for five years without putting them to a task.

More likely, they *were* at work. The Sinclair fleet had brought their army of masons to the soon to be discovered New World. There they would construct the booby-trapped Money Pit. Using engineering skills known to both the Templars and St. Bernard's Cistercians, the deep shaft, the long water tunnels, the false beach, and concealed drains were all put in place.

For a century the Templar treasure would rest safely in Rosslyn Chapel. The descendants of the Templar Knights would become organized as "free masons" and employed and protected by the Sinclair family. When James II became king, he decreed the Sinclair family to be the hereditary guardians of the Freemasons. This connection has not been severed in Scotland.

The affairs of state and religion, however, would soon bring the Clan Sinclair to war again. Protestant mobs inspired by Calvin swept through Scotland. Their targets were icons in Catholic churches, and the Sinclair family—ardent Catholics—gathered up the gold chalices and other goods of churches they supported. The English Crown, now in Protestant hands, rose against the families that controlled Scotland.

In 1542, the Battle of Solway saw defeat for Scotland and the loss of Oliver Sinclair, the right hand of James V's reign, to English capture. James V had predicted, at the birth of his daughter Mary, that his family dynasty would end. He placed Mary—later known as Mary Queen of Scots—in the care of the Sinclair family. Oliver, furloughed from an English prison for a short visit to his home in 1545, disappeared from Scotland and from history.

The premise of my book *The Lost Treasure of the Knights Templar* is that at this time the treasure was brought to Oak Island and sealed away. The remaining head of the Clan Sinclair, William, would share the secret with Mary of Guise, who was the most powerful woman in France and part of the extended Norman family. She proclaimed a "bond of obligation" to William. His "secret shown to us, we shall keep secret."

The existence of a vault would be known to the Guise family, but the location would be a secret passed only within the family Sinclair. Subsequent wars and religious strife took a serious toll on the family: Sinclairs died suddenly in war and in prison. At some point, the link in the chain was broken and the secret location did not pass down to the next generation.

Today the most modern assault on the Money Pit will start anew. David Tobias, the current owner, first heard of Oak Island and the treasure search when he was a pilot training in Nova Scotia during World War II. He came back to Oak Island and the search for its treasure, first as an investor, then as owner of half the island. He has not only brought millions of dollars of his own money to the table, but he has also brought the treasure search up to modern standards.

Under his direction, the search has employed and consulted with corporations and with talent from the National Museum of Modern Science at Ottawa and the prestigious Woods Hole Oceanographic Institute in Massachusetts. Tobias's group was granted a new treasure license and, as soon as some outstanding legal hurdles are overcome, Tobias and his group—known as Triton Alliance—will again challenge the capabilities of the guardians of the Templar treasure.

15 The Mysteries of Rosslyn Chapel

Were They Revealed to Mary of Guise?

Jeff Nisbet

France's Mary of Guise liked a good joke. When England's King Henry VIII proposed marriage, Mary quipped that her neck was too slender—a cutting reference to the beheading of Henry's second wife, Anne Boleyn.

Mary married Scotland's James V instead, and in 1542 gave birth to that nation's best-known monarch, Mary Queen of Scots, just a week before James died. And in 1546, during her daughter's minority reign, Mary made a curious bond with Sir William Sinclair of Roslin.

One passage of that bond has been much debated: "We bind and oblige us to the said Sir William, and shall be a loyal and true mistress to him. His counsel and secret shown to us we shall keep secret, and in all matters give to him the best and truest counsel we can, as we shall be required thereto."

In the 1999 book *Rosslyn: Guardians of the Secrets of the Holy Grail,* the authors Tim Wallace-Murphy and Marilyn Hopkins say that the "general tone of the letter is bizarre. It is more like that of a subservient person to a superior lord than that of a sovereign to her vassal."

What secret was Mary shown at Rosslyn that brought about this strange relationship?

Among the many speculations are that it was the Cup of the Last Supper, the mummified head of Christ, the Stone of Destiny, a piece of the True Cross, the Ark of the Covenant, and/or the genealogical records of a holy bloodline established by a marriage between Mary Magdalen and Jesus. And in a recent issue of *Templar History* magazine, the Grand Herald of the Scottish Knights Templar claims he "once met a chap who was convinced the chapel had been built over an ET-type spacecraft, and presented an excellent case." The mind boggles.

But while Mary may have been shown any of these things, I believe she was shown something else—something in the architectural fabric of Rosslyn Chapel that was singularly unique to a lineage she shared with William.

Let's first consider who they were.

Mary was the granddaughter of René II of Anjou and Lorraine, the grandson of René I—a mover and shaker in the heroic career of Joan of Arc. Both Renés inherited the title King of Jerusalem, a designation descended from Godfrey of Bouillon's brother, Baldwin, who first accepted the title. Godfrey had led the First Crusade to liberate the Holy Land from the "infidels." It was Baldwin who granted the first nine Templar Knights quarters on Solomon's Temple Mount, beneath which they were to busy themselves digging for a mysterious something over the next several years. Baldwin also granted the order its first insignia—the equal-end-double barred cross of Lorraine.

Fig. 15.1. Mary of Guise, the wife of James V of Scotland and the mother of Mary Queen of Scots.

Christopher Columbus acknowledged in his journals that René I granted him his first ship's command, and it's thought that Columbus voyaged westward with a cross on his sails. But did that cross have one bar or two? It is perhaps highly significant that René II commissioned the first map that shows the name America, dated 1507. That map, recently purchased for five million dollars by the U.S. Library of Congress, may ultimately prove to be little more than a spectacularly expensive piece of cartographical propaganda.

William was the grandson of Rosslyn Chapel's builder, who was himself descended from several other notable St. Clairs. One St. Clair married Hughes de Payns (who was among the original nine Templars mentioned above); one was a mover and shaker in the career of the great Scots hero Robert the Bruce; and one may have led a voyage of discovery to the New World in 1398, ninety-four years before Columbus made the first official voyage.

Mary and William clearly had a lot in common prior to her being shown the secret mentioned in her bond. Each of their respective families connects to the making of a great national hero, each connects to one or more of the original nine Templars, and each in some way connects to the discovery of America.

In my article "Further Anomalies of Rosslyn Chapel Unveiled," which follows, I talk about recent changes that have been made to the "star course" of

Rosslyn's ceiling, and suggest that the original architectural fabric of the chapel has been tampered with since the course was written—not a popular view among Rosslyn's many "book in stone" fans.

Now I'll talk about all five courses of the ceiling, and the secret I feel that William revealed to Mary when she visited the chapel in 1546, the one hundredth anniversary of Rosslyn's foundation.

Let's follow them inside.

I believe that William would have asked Mary to look up and ponder the chapel's ceiling, drawing her attention to the fact that while two of the five courses are laid out in true checkerboard fashion, with the same number of equally spaced architectural elements, the three remaining courses appear more crowded!

Bearing in mind that the architectural elements of each of these three courses would not only require more carving, but would be significantly more difficult to lay out as well, he would then have asked her why she thought that this was so.

At this point, had Mary's sixteenth-century dynastic mind not been moved into sudden revelation, William would have told her what I now tell you: Rosslyn's ceiling vault consists of five courses, each made up of its own unique architectural element of floral design, except the star course—what we will call the first course—which consists mainly of stars, laid out like the alternating squares of a checkerboard. The second course is chockablock with architectural elements, containing exactly twice the number of elements as the star course. The third has the same number of elements as the first. The fourth splits the difference between the first and the second and, although there is not as much carving as in the second course, would have been more difficult to lay out since the easy-to-replicate checkerboard template was not used. The fifth course has less carving than the fourth, but the layout difficulties would have been as great.

I believe that William directed Mary's gaze up to Rosslyn's ceiling, drawing her attention to the overcrowding of certain courses, and then told her that his grandfather, a century previously, had hidden a huge cross of Lorraine in it—with its arms tucked in!

As the graphic shows (see fig. 15.2), when we move the crowding elements away from the ceiling vault, redistributing them according to the harmony of the checkerboard pattern found in the first and third courses, the Lorraine cross is revealed with its arms extended. It is not the original equal-armed cross mentioned above, however, but instead a later incarnation that exhibits a further eccentricity that I will discuss later.

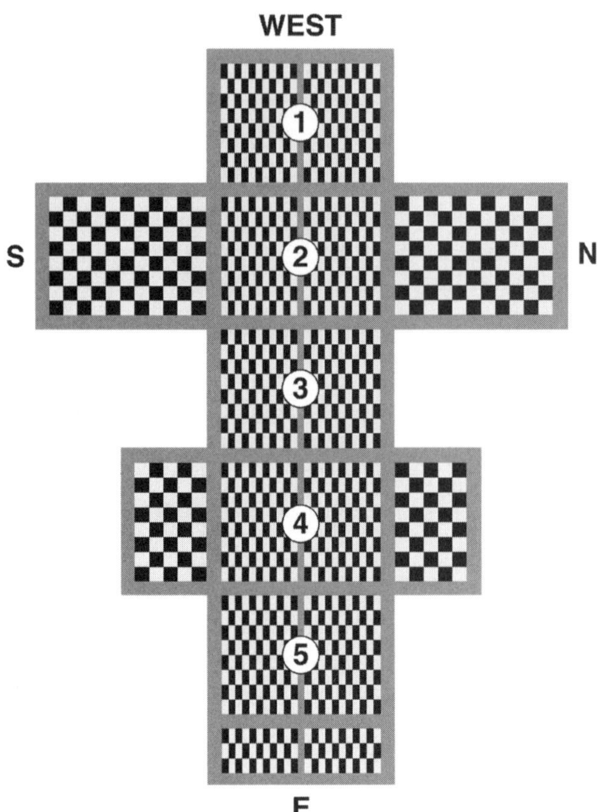

Fig. 15.2. Layout of Rosslyn's five-course vaulted ceiling with the crowding elements pulled out from the central vault, forming the reversed arms of the Lorraine cross.

The symbolism of the Lorraine cross has been explained in different ways. Writing in *Dagobert's Revenge* magazine, Boyd Rice reports that French poet and essayist Charles Peguy claimed the double-and-equal-armed cross represents "the arms of Christ, the arms of Satan, and, strangely, the blood of both."

Among other points that Rice raises in his article are these: that the cross represents "the union of opposites, the intersection of creative force and destructive force, or the union of male and female principles"; that the bar above mirrors the bar below and, as such, is symbolic of the Hermetic maxim "As above, so below"; that the House of Anjou, to which our Mary belonged, advocated "the Royal Art of Hermeticism—a tradition which according to legend was passed down to man by a race of fallen angels"; that when the ancient Hermetic text Corpus Hermeticum was first published in French, it was dedicated to Mary of Guise and that Mary "adopted the Lorraine Cross as a personal symbol."

Joan of Arc historians get irritated at the suggestion that Joan went to the stake clutching the Lorraine cross to her breast. They point to the "official" documents that record she was given one cross by an English soldier who hastily fashioned it from two pieces of wood and was given a second by an attending clergyman. But isn't it possible that the truth of a thing can be secretly hidden in the lie of it? Might not the Lorraine cross be symbolized by the two crosses that the official records say she was given? And since the French Burgundians sold Joan to the English, and the French king whom she had led to the throne ignored her plight, might we not have here a hidden reference to the expression "double-cross"?

But back to Rosslyn.

It is not the equal-armed cross that William may have shown Mary of Guise, but a later style wherein one crossbar is half the length of the other. At some point, perhaps as a way of bringing an ancient Hermetic symbol into the fold of Christian orthodoxy, the upper crossbar was shortened. This crossbar is occasionally referred to as the INRI bar, a reference to the inscribed board that Pontius Pilate ordered placed above Christ's head at the crucifixion.

But if we accept that the symbology embedded in the Rosslyn cross indicates that the star course should logically be the "above" part of the cross and that the extended lower course would be the part "below," then we can see that the crossbars of Rosslyn's cross have been reversed, with the shorter set below the longer.

Why so?

In my Rosslyn Chapel article, I write that one of the Templars arrested on October 13, 1307, and subsequently interrogated, claimed that during his initiation into the order, he was shown the single-barred Christian cross, and was told "put not thy faith in this, for it is not old enough."

In spite of the global controversy now surrounding the not-new theory promoted in Dan Brown's *The Da Vinci Code,* which speculates that Jesus Christ and Mary Magdalen were married and established a bloodline that has survived down to the present day, might not this short statement by an interrogated Templar indicate that this marriage was just another union along the course of a much older bloodline, and that the original nine Templars had found indisputable proof of it hidden within the Temple Mount?

It would, of course, have been foolish to hot-foot this heretical proof to the Vatican—especially when there were yet only nine poor Templars in the entire world. Better for the keepers of this newfound knowledge to bide their time, consider their options, and develop a viable business plan for the future—which is probably what they did.

Over the next two centuries, the Knights grew into the richest chivalric order in the world. History tells us that the order was barbarously suppressed in the early fourteenth century, but many believe its inner circle went underground in Scotland, taking its truth with it. I personally believe that the inner circle may have engineered the order's demise as part of an overall "right-sizing" operation—not a popular theory among the Templars' sizable fan base.

When William Sinclair and Mary of Guise met at Rosslyn in the chapel's centenary year, the Church of Rome was in a bit of a tizzy. Catholicism was under siege by a new and troublesome adversary—the Reformation. In one fell swoop the Christian world was cleft in twain. No longer would Rome be able to raise great armies from its subject nations to crush heresies wherever the papal finger pointed. There was no longer just one big boy on the block; another had moved in.

The mightiest church the world had ever known had been divided and conquered.

But the Reformed Church would not be allowed to remain squeaky clean. The life of Mary's grandson, the first officially Freemasonic king of both Scotland and England, would be threatened by a plot hatched by "witches" on Halloween 1590. The celebrated but trumped-up case of the North Berwick Witches kick-started over a century of Scottish witch hunts, and proved that your average Presbyterian could be just as vindictive as your average Catholic when it came to fighting Satan's minions.

While an equilibrium has been established between the two great Christian powers, neither can yet lay claim to being the saintlier, and each still has that heavy cross of guilt to bear. Another perfect double-cross, perhaps?

Interestingly, the U.S. branch of today's Sovereign Military Order of the Temple of Jerusalem (SMOTJ) uses the same reverse-barred configuration as Rosslyn's in its official insignia. Its blazer badge, "hand stitched in gold bullion," can be purchased through its web site, and part of the purchase price will be donated to a worthy charitable cause in the order's name.

In certain heraldic tomes, it is said that the double-barred cross with the shorter bar above the longer is known as the Cross Patriarchal. What if Rosslyn's builder, as his own little joke, reversed the bars in order to hang a "Cross Matriarchal" in the chapel's ceiling?

Mary of Guise would have enjoyed that joke, but would we?

Rosslyn's founder certainly used some elegant math when he plotted the chapel's ceiling, but it was not an exact fit. There are four architectural ele-

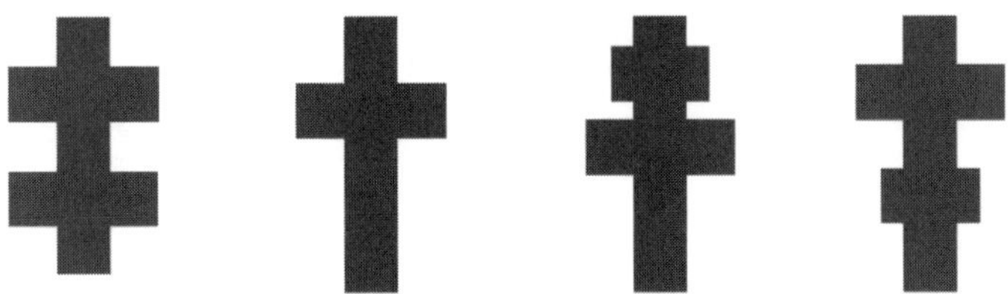

Fig. 15.3. Left to right: The Hermetic equal-armed cross of Lorraine; the Christian cross of the Crucifixion; the Christianized (INRI) cross of Lorraine; the reverse-armed Rosslyn cross, symbol of the SMOTJ.

ments remaindered in the fourth course and one in the fifth—a total of five. However, this mistake may have been perfectly planned.

I visited the Grand Lodge of Scotland's museum during my last trip to Edinburgh, and was struck by an exhibit dated to the early nineteenth century. It shows the Masonic compass, square, and level surrounded by a five-pointed star. The five points are described as "the five points of fellowship." What is truly striking, however, is that the star is upside down.

In Manly P. Hall's 1928 classic, *The Secret Teachings of All Ages,* Hall has much to say about the five-pointed star, or pentagram. He claims that the figure is "the time-honored symbol of the magical arts," and that "by means of the pentagram within his own soul, man not only may master and govern all creatures inferior to himself, but may demand consideration at the hands of those superior to himself." He further claims that the star with two points upward is called the Goat of Mendes because "the inverted star is the same shape as a goat's head." The goat, as I mention in my "Joan of Arc Revealed" article later in this book, is a recurring Masonic symbol.

Hall's most apocryphal description of the inverted pentagram is the last sentence of his chapter about it: "When the upright star turns and the upper point falls to the bottom, it signifies the fall of the Morning Star."

This is a troublesome concept, indeed.

While we watch the movements of the heavenly bodies, we do not expect to see them fall. By observing when and where they appear to us, we fix our place among them—and have done so far longer than documented history credits us with doing. But Hall's "fall of the Morning Star" eerily echoes the many far-flung world myths that talk of a cataclysmic day when the sky fell. If it again becomes an observable phenomenon, it will be we, not it, who are in motion.

I doubt we'll find it funny.

16 Further Anomalies of Rosslyn Chapel Unveiled

A Painstaking Investigation Puts the Ancient Enigma in a Dramatic New Light

Jeff Nisbet

Rosslyn Chapel sits just six miles south of Edinburgh, Scotland's ancient capital city. Built in the fifteenth century by Earl William Sinclair of Roslin, the chapel has become one of the most mysterious and controversial buildings on Earth. Recent years have seen the controversy reach fever pitch as an adversarial band of alternative-history researchers, Freemasonic "seekers of light," and treasure hunters vie to unlock the secrets they feel are hidden within the chapel walls.

THE STAKES ARE HIGH

At last tally, these intrepid questers have variously speculated that the chapel hides the long lost treasure of the Knights Templar, a piece of the True Cross, Scotland's Stone of Destiny, the mummified head of Christ, and even that Holy Grail of relics—the Holy Grail itself.

A world-class collection, no doubt—but none has yet been found. Rosslyn keeps its secrets well.

London businessman and Sinclair descendant Niven Sinclair is fond of saying that William built Rosslyn Chapel "at a time when books could be burned or banned, so he left a message for posterity chiseled out in stone." Niven's pet project, into which he has sunk a great deal of energy over the years, is to prove that William's grandfather made a voyage of discovery to America almost a century before Christopher Columbus made the voyage that history officially sanctions as the first.

Niven also believes that Christ did not die on the cross; he survived to sire children with his wife, Mary Magdalen. This marriage begat a bloodline that has flowed down the centuries through several high and mighty European families, including Niven's own. But it is still the biblical tale of Christ's ascension that wins the popular vote in the credibility department, so Niven soldiers on.

Although the expression *carved in stone* has become synonymous with "unchangeable," that is not the case with Rosslyn. Some very significant changes have been made within the chapel walls and then concealed.

LET'S TAKE A LOOK

The interior greets the eye with such a visual feast of carved stone that one barely knows where to look. Strange foliage and figures hang everywhere about the walls, arches, and ceiling, like icing on a cake. And while the overall effect was clearly meant to be Christian, closer inspection reveals that many carvings have their symbolic origins in quite different ideologies, some of them decidedly pagan.

Here and there you'll find the head of a Green Man, an ancient Celtic vegetation god, peering out from the carved foliage; and on Rosslyn's most celebrated structure, the Prentice Pillar, a daisy chain of dragons nibble away at the roots of what's been interpreted as the Nordic Tree of Life. Add to the mix carved tales from the Hebraic Hebrew scriptures and legends that resonate with Templar and Freemasonic lore, and you have an architectural recipe for perennial success. And except for a few dicey years during the Reformation, when Protestant zealots took stern issue with what they called idolatry, the chapel has been successful ever since.

But while certain details have been added to the chapel over the years, the original language of Earl William's "book in stone" is believed to be unchanged. On my last trip to Scotland, however, I found several dusty guides to Rosslyn that, here and there, tell a different tale.

Let's walk to the center of the chapel and look up.

Rosslyn's great barrel-vaulted ceiling is divided into five courses. Four courses have a floral theme, each with its exclusive tile, which repeats in cookie-cutter fashion over its entire course. But the fifth course is different from the others. Instead of flowers, it is full of stars—and *other* things!

In one corner of the course is a bearded head with an open hand raised alongside it. Niven Sinclair has described it as the head of Christ, with Christ's hand raised in blessing of Niven's ancestor's pre-Columbian voyage of discovery. But according to an 1877 article that ran in volume XII of the *Proceedings of the Society of Antiquaries in Scotland,* Mark Kerr describes this feature as simply "an open hand," and his observation is corroborated in an 1892 account written by the Reverand John Thompson, Rosslyn's chaplain.

Where was Christ's head and blessing when this book in stone was built, and why is it there now?

Fig. 16.1. The interior of Rosslyn Chapel.

Two rows up from Christ's head is the "sun in splendour," and one row up from the adjacent corner of the star vault is the emerging moon, described in both accounts as a "crescent" moon and "small star." Nowadays, the moon appears to be full, complete with surface features that should not have been observable 159 years before Galileo's telescope supposedly allowed him to look twenty times closer than anyone had ever looked before. What's been carved into Rosslyn that the founder never intended?

Toward the east end of the chapel stand two pillars that together form the basis for what has become Rosslyn's most enduring legend—the murder of an apprentice stonemason by his master. Legend has it that the master mason, who had been on a junket to Rome to study the form of a pillar he meant to duplicate in Rosslyn, returned to find that his apprentice, inspired by a dream, had finished the job before him. The master, in a fit of jealous rage, slew his apprentice with a single blow to the head.

Although both pillars are glorious, the Prentice Pillar clearly outshines the master's.

Kerr's report, while giving lip service to the Apprentice Legend, refers to the Master's Pillar as the Earl's Pillar and, in John Slezer's 1693 *Theatrum Scotiae,* the Prentice Pillar is called the Prince's Pillar. A 1774 account by Bishop Forbes of Caithness postulates that Slezer was referring to the founder's princely origins as last prince of Scotland's Orkney Islands.

Confusing, I know. To add to the confusion, back below the star vault is a carved head much studied by Freemasons. Tradition claims it is the head of the slain apprentice complete with fatal wound—a tale that resonates with the Freemasonic legend of the death of Hiram Abiff, architect of Solomon's Temple, who died in similar fashion. It has been noticed, however, that the apprentice's chin may have once sported a beard that was subsequently chiseled off. Indeed strange, considering apprentices back then did not grow beards.

Master, apprentice, earl, or prince—who's who? Is it possible that a fairly elegant shell game has been carved into Rosslyn's Book in Stone that the founder never intended, leaving us still searching for his elusive pea of truth?

In 1954, the chapel was diagnosed by Scotland's Ministry of Works as suffering from extreme damp. It was decided to coat the chapel's interior with a "cementinous slurry" meant to keep moisture out. Instead, it made matters worse. But it did more than that. Since fresh paint can cover a multitude of sins, the recent changes are no longer noticeable, and I have it on good authority that the cost of the slurry's removal, if even possible, would be prohibitively expensive. Rosslyn's fabled Truth That Conquers All, it seems, must wait for better days. Or must it?

Fig. 16.2. Some scholars believe Rosslyn Chapel to be a replica of Solomon's Temple in Jerusalem.

Increasingly thought to be the premier member of the Illuminati of his day, Earl William built into his chapel something that could never be changed—something that has waited to be noticed for a long time. And considering that the Knights Templar were ostensibly founded to protect Christian pilgrims on their way to the Holy Land, and that the earl's male progeny became hereditary grand masters of the Freemasons until the beginning of the eighteenth century, William's wild card might come as a bit of a surprise.

Rosslyn Chapel was founded upon St. Matthew's Day, September 21, 1446, and was officially dedicated to that saint on the same day in 1450. Since September 21 marks the autumnal equinox, when the sun rises exactly due east of Rosslyn, I decided to see if the earl had written something in the sky above that might have reflected the truth he'd been carving on the Earth below.

I wasn't disappointed.

It is commonly held that an inner circle of the Knights Templar escaped the order's suppression in 1307 France, going underground in Scotland while continuing to send what they believed to be Truth forward to more enlightened times by secretly hitching rides on both the astrological mythologies of a past they believed to be rooted in fact and the astronomical discoveries they knew would be found when the time was right.

Thought to have introduced both chess and tarot cards to medieval Europe, the brotherhood quietly and strategically wove long-forgotten truths into the warp and weave of the historical record—truths that would be seen only by those "with eyes to see" and heard by those "with ears to hear."

Earl William knew that even a book carved in stone could be pounded to dust, so he wrote his testament on the inviolable daytime sky and hid it in the light. In *Rosslyn: Guardian of the Secrets of the Holy Grail,* the authors claim that the site of Rosslyn had been "revered by the Druids as the oracle of Saturn, the supreme Guardian of Secrets."

According to my research, it seems they are right.

When Rosslyn was dedicated on September 21, 1450, the Sun had risen exactly due east. Throughout the day, behind the Sun and in exact alignment with the Earth, lay the planets Saturn and Neptune, a conjunction that occurs only once every thirty-six years. And they all rose invisibly in the light of day within the constellation Virgo, symbolic of various goddesses found in diverse astrological traditions.

Following the parallels I've drawn in my other articles between the belief systems of ancient Egypt and those of Scotland, however, it's interesting to note that a Greek tradition proposes that the Sphinx was originally constructed with Virgo's head on Leo's body. It's also interesting to note that the head of the Sphinx we see today looks disproportionately small—*and newer*—when compared to the much weathered body, as though carved back from a previous head. And before the weathering of the body, today's head would have looked even smaller.

Another tradition identifies Virgo with the Egyptian goddess Isis, clasping the infant Horus, last of the divine kings, in her arms. Since the advent of Christianity, however, Virgo has been identified as the Virgin Mary, with baby Jesus in her arms. But the Templars are thought to have venerated a Black Madonna, not the white one that Christian artwork has promoted for so long. Perhaps it was considered safe enough to leave the door to past belief systems open just a crack.

Far beyond our solar system, yet within the same alignment, lay the star Zaniah, known to the Chinese as Heaven's Gate. The alignment's next nearest star, Porrima, was called Antevorta and sometimes Postvorta—named for two ancient goddesses of prophecy.

Before we leave Rosslyn, let's again look at the star vault. The rows of stars alternate in chessboard fashion, except for two. Each of the two meets and mirrors the other, thereby reversing the order over the remainder of the course. Many world "myths" describe a day "the sky fell" and the heavenly order changed, an observed phenomenon much explained if the crust of the Earth had suddenly slid around its core, moving parts of the Earth out of (and parts into) polar regions, and causing the world's oceans to slosh over the land in a cataclysm now known to Christians as the biblical flood! It makes sense that it was not the great universe that moved—it was us. Two rows up from Rosslyn's full moon is a dove with an olive branch in its beak. Could it be that William meant the dove to be Noah's messenger of hope at the flood's subsidence?

When the Templars were suppressed on Friday, October 13, 1307, it is thought that the escaping Templar fleet, carrying the order's inner circle, headed toward Scotland with their treasure and their truth. Hidden below that dark night's horizon was the same rare alignment that rose at daybreak on Rosslyn's dedication day, but this time a second "undiscovered" planet, Uranus, had conjoined with it. Quite resonantly, considering the events of that Friday the 13th, the alignment lay within Libra, the Scales of Justice. It's a strong possibility, given such a grand celestial "coincidence," that the inner circle had decided that the time was right for the order's demise, and had chosen the date to coincide with the alignment. What the hell—they'd all be dead and gone when Truth finally conquered All!

On November 4, when the Templars may have reached Roslin after first gathering secreted stores of arms in Ireland, the Sun and Moon entered the alignment at dawn—a truly spectacular six-body alignment. And exactly four hundred years plus two days after Rosslyn's foundation date of September 21, 1446, Neptune was finally discovered, also during the same alignment. Quite the anniversary gift for those in the know!

Much has been speculated about what the Templars knew about Earth's early history deemed not prudent to reveal at the time, and how much of that knowledge was passed on to the Freemasons but has since been lost. Today's Scottish Templars, whose connection with the original Templars is often hotly debated, have suddenly become uncomfortably proactive in contemporary events. They have been granted special consultancy status with the United Nations, and their current pet project is to bring Jerusalem's Dome of the Rock under the control of the United Nations. They meanwhile continue to keep an aloof silence about anything they please.

Also avowed to protect Scottish history, they have shown no love for my version of it. I have been told in no uncertain terms that while I'm entitled to my opinions, they're not informed opinions. When I suggested that perhaps informed opinions are opinions one has been informed about, and so may have little to do with Truth, I got silence in reply.

One of the Templars arrested on October 13, 1307, and subsequently interrogated, claimed that during his initiation into the Order he was shown the Christian cross, and was told "Put not thy faith in this, for it is not old enough." Is it possible that all adversaries in the current conflict have been played the fool over the past few millennia in order to precipitate the much prophesized crisis of faith that will introduce a new faith the suddenly faithless will flock to?

Is it possible that in order to find the things that once made us friends, we must first discover whose bright idea it was to make us enemies—and why?

Or is it already too late?

17 A Crack in *The Da Vinci Code*

Is Dan Brown's Rosslyn Chapel Where He Says It Is?

Jeff Nisbet

Dan Brown, the author of *The Da Vinci Code,* has done what many alternative history researchers wish they'd done. He's written a blockbuster mystery that presents, to an enormous audience, theories that fly in the face of mainstream history.

I enjoyed the book immensely, and don't begrudge Brown his success. However, since a crucial section of the book deals with the Freemasonic and Knights Templar heritage of Scotland's Rosslyn Chapel, a subject I've written about extensively, I'd like to point out a major flaw in his data.

As the book's endgame unfolds, Brown writes that Rosslyn's "geographic coordinates fall precisely on the north-south meridian that runs through Glastonbury," and that this "longitudinal Rose Line is the traditional marker of King Arthur's Isle of Avalon and is considered the central pillar of Britain's sacred geometry. It is from this hallowed Rose Line that Rosslyn—originally spelled Roslin—takes its name."

Brown's positioning of Rosslyn on the same longitude as Glastonbury Abbey at a pivotal point in his narrative is one of the grander hooks upon which his story hangs—but it is wrong.

Rosslyn's north-south meridian does not run precisely through Glastonbury. In fact, it runs a whopping seventeen miles to the west.

So precisely where is that central pillar of Britain's sacred geometry?

In my "Pyramids of Scotland" article, included in this book, I talk about a strange geometry of leylines I'd discovered in Scotland's landscape. One of those lines, I report, "stretched exactly due south from Craigleith Island to the Cistercian Abbey of Melrose. Founded contemporaneously by Abbot Bernard of Clairvaux, the Cistercians and the Templars are thought by many to be two arms of a single Order." I also write that "if the line is continued far to the south of Melrose it arrives, unerringly, at Glastonbury." But while the Rosslyn meridian misses Glastonbury by seventeen miles, the chapel nevertheless lies on one of the other lines I mention in my article—and it's a highly interesting line.

Let's go back to August 5, 1999.

While visiting a friend in the village of Temple, the ancient Templar headquarters lying just five miles southeast of Rosslyn, I was shown an inscription beneath the belfry of the town's ruined kirk (Scottish for *church*). My translation of that inscription, which in part suggests that Jesus had sired children by Mary Magdalen, ran in the May 2001 issue of *Fortean Times* magazine.

I had visited Rosslyn earlier that day, and had photographed a tiny statue in the chapel's crypt—a statue of a bearded figure, thought to be Saint Peter, holding a book and a key.

When I examined the photo some weeks later, I noticed that there was a pyramidal shape carved into Peter's beard that cut across the natural flow of the hair in a way that no sculptor worth his salt would have done except by design. Immediately below the pyramid's capstone was Peter's mouth. When I noticed that his mouth was disproportionately small, I suddenly began to make a series of decidedly spooky observations.

Hidden within Saint Peter's face was a smaller face that shared his mouth, but was proportioned correctly to it. The eyes peered out from Peter's nostrils, with what appeared to be a hand raised alongside as though either saying "Hello" or waiting to whisper.

Then my spine tingled.

I noticed that the chin of that hidden face formed the head of an even smaller being, and was connected to a complete body.

There he stood—left foot resting on Peter's book and his arms making a grand thespian gesture along the shaft of Peter's key. Situated on the crypt's south wall, Peter's key pointed in the direction one would take to go from Rosslyn, through Temple, to Melrose Abbey.

It is highly ironic that Saint Peter points the way to the heretical inscription at Temple. In the 1995 book *Restless Bones: The Story of Relics,* by James Bentley, it's implied that it was the Vatican's custody of the earthly remains of that saint, as the rock upon which the Catholic Church was founded, that gave the pope's voice authority. Bentley writes that "the Pope, whatever theoretical claims were made for him, in practice owed most of his authority to the fact that he was the guardian of the body of Saint Peter."

There also seems to have been no love lost between Mary Magdalen and Peter. In the Pistis Sophia, one of the Gnostic gospels, Mary says, "I am afraid of him because he hates the female race." And in the Gospel of Thomas, Peter says, "Let Mary leave us, for women are not worthy of life." By using the statue of Saint Peter to reveal a heresy that could undermine the credibility of the Vatican by emphasizing the long suppressed importance of Mary Magdalen, Peter's sculptor would have been exacting a fair measure of revenge on Mary's behalf.

But that's perhaps not all the statue was meant to reveal. Of the charges brought against the Templars at their trial, many mention the order's secret reverence for severed heads. The first of those charges reads: "In each province they had idols, namely heads, of which some had three faces." Hmmm!

In my "Further Anomalies of Rosslyn Chapel Unveiled" article, however, I show there are elements of the chapel that are not part of its original architectural fabric. In fact, it seems they have been added relatively recently—and Saint Peter is one of those elements. Architect Andrew Kerr, referenced in my article, makes no mention of the statue in his exhaustive 1876 survey published in the *Proceedings of the Society of Antiquaries in Scotland*. So why is it there now?

One researcher has dismissed that issue to the modern Scots Templars as follows: "When any real comprehensive study, of any angle or aspect relating to Rosslyn Chapel is made, one has to accept that the subject is not static, therefore to conclude anything is not true."

I suppose that Kerr should not have believed the evidence of his own eyes, nor I his account.

I've visited Rosslyn several times since 1999, however, and must admit that I cannot see in three dimensions what I see in my photographs of Peter. Why so?

The answer may lie in the great interest shown in Rosslyn by photographic pioneer Louis Daguerre, inventor of the daguerreotype. In 1822, Daguerre invented the diorama, a technique whereby two-dimensional paintings could be illuminated in a dark room to give the illusion of three-dimensional reality. He created a diorama of Rosslyn Chapel, which received rave reviews.

Could Daguerre have guided the hand of Peter's sculptor in the opposite direction, hiding a secret in three dimensions that could only be seen in two, to create a tiny statue that would be introduced into the Rosslyn Crypt when the time was right? And is it possible that Daguerre may have even been chosen to *inherit* the knowledge that would later write his name large in the annals of photographic history? One might consider that the Shroud of Turin, recently debunked as a medieval forgery, is nevertheless a photographically "negative" image. In their 1994 book about the shroud, Picknett and Prince go so far as to suggest the relic was photographically created by none other than Leonardo da Vinci.

But on to Temple's ruined kirk.

Within the ruin is a curious grave slab, carved similarly to those described in Laurence Gardner's *Bloodline of the Holy Grail* (see the accompanying illustration for an example of a standard Templar grave slab). "In Grail imagery, just as in graphic symbolism," Gardner writes, "the Messianic succession is denoted by the female chalice accompanied by the male blade. At Rosslyn and elsewhere in Scotland, wall carvings and tombs of the Grail Knights bear this dual emblem. It is portrayed as a tall-stemmed Chalice, with the bowl face forward. In its bowl, the Rosy Cross (with its fleur-de-lys design) signifies that the vas-uterus contains the blood of Jesus."

Fig. 17.1. An example of a typical Templar grave slab depicting both a female chalice and a male blade.

The Temple grave slab, however, clearly shows a chalice, *but no blade*. Why not? Let's read the inscription. "Beatrix Lucy, wife of Henry Herbert Philip Dundas of Arniston, third baronet, born 14th May, 1876, died 6th November, 1940." It is actually the grave of a *woman* who died within living memory and, if we allow Gardner's line of reasoning, carried forward the bloodline of Jesus and Mary Magdalen! Researcher Tim Wallace-Murphy claims that it's always the *female* bloodline that's important, not the male. "Mummy's baby, Daddy's maybe," I suppose.

Temple was granted to the Templars by King David I, presumed by Gardner to be a Grail Family member. Upon the order's dissolution, it transferred to the Knights Hospitaller, and remained there until the Protestant Reformation, at which time it reverted again to the crown. During the reign of Scotland's first officially Freemasonic king, James VI, the property transferred to the Dundas family, until recently passing into the stewardship of the Midlothian Council, where it remains.

Beatrix Lucy was born Lady Beatrix Douglas-Home.

The Douglases and Homes are two families whose names have long buzzed with possible Templar and Freemasonic connections. Sir James Douglas was Robert the Bruce's trusted lieutenant mentioned in my Bannockburn article.

Fig. 17.2. Grave slab of Lady Beatrix Lucy, without the blade imagery symbolic of a male.

And Joan of Arc's battle banner is thought to have been painted by a member of the Home family. It's also rumored that a replica of Joan's ring, inscribed "Jesus Maria," was given to Home's daughter. In Glastonbury Abbey a similarly inscribed stone stands, and we might well wonder which Mary was meant to be immortalized in either case—the Virgin or the Magdalen.

Southeast of the Temple ruin stands an ancient archway, derelict in a field. It appears to lead nowhere, yet is so oriented that if you walk straight through, as I did, you are heading on the same bearing as the line that connects Rosslyn and Temple to Melrose. Alternating stones in the arch are covered in a herringbone pattern that repeats the letter *M* again and again, as though driving home a long forgotten point!

Now to Melrose, twenty-one miles away as the crow flies.

Scottish hero Robert the Bruce's heart is buried in Melrose Abbey. History tells us that a dying Robert asked that his heart be buried in the Holy Land. Carrying Robert's heart in a silver casket, James Douglas duly set off in the company of seven knights, one of whom was William Sinclair of Roslin. After dallying a tad too long in Spain, the knights were pulled into a military engagement with the Moors. Four died, including Douglas and Sinclair, and Robert's heart was returned to Scotland by the remainder of the company. If we retrace our leyline just forty-four miles to the northwest of Melrose, back through Temple and Rosslyn, we come within spitting distance of Dunfermline Abbey, where Robert's body is buried. History doesn't tell us why his body and heart weren't reunited, having come so close.

Much is made in *The Da Vinci Code* of the fact that the original spelling of Rosslyn was Roslin, tying a neat bow around the book's "Rose Line" theme and connecting Rosslyn with Glastonbury along the same meridian. But it is Melrose Abbey and Craigleith Island that lie exactly due north of Glastonbury, not Rosslyn—and Melrose also contains *rose* as a root.

Fig. 17.3. Ancient archway near Temple, Scotland, associated with the Templars of long ago.

One accepted etymology of Melrose puts the mason's hammer, or *mel,* before the "rose-colored" sandstone used to build the abbey. While the abbey sometimes exhibits a pinkish hue in certain light, the root *mel* could derive from elsewhere. The Greek roots *melas* and *mels* mean "of a darkish color, or black" and "a limb," respectively. Might I suggest that Melrose may mean a darkened branch of the rose or holy bloodline, brought to Scotland for safe-keeping by the Templars and then branded into the landscape over a long forgotten geometry that far preceded the birth of Christ?

And while etymology is on the table, let's now consider cryptology. One of the several ancient spellings of Craigleith is Craglieth—an anagram of Grail Tech!

Beatrix Douglas-Home was daughter to the twelfth earl of Home and aunt to the fourteenth, Alec Douglas-Home. Alec was secretary to Prime Minister Neville Chamberlain when Chamberlain's appeasement policy calmed world alarm over Nazi excesses until the onset of World War II became inevitable.

Alec was later appointed foreign secretary, and dubbed a Knight of the Thistle in 1962. At the height of the cold war, thanks to 1963's Profumo call girl scandal, Alec became British prime minister and later chairman of the still extant Bilderbergers, an elite association of international power brokers now thought by many to have engineered the state of the world we live in today—such as it is.

If, as the carving on Beatrix's twentieth-century grave slab may imply, the holy blood still flows—and more importantly is still known to flow by some—what agenda has this knowledge been applied to over the centuries, knowledge that we lesser mortals are not privy to? How many saints and heroes have been cobbled together to keep the common herd content with their lot, ever eager to do their bit for God and country? And how many sovereign heads have been toppled to bring us to this dark and uncertain world we find ourselves in today?

But conventional thought dictates that Jesus did not have children, and that anyone who thinks otherwise is a fool.

Nevertheless, I again claim that certain world myths have been hijacked over the millennia, and secretly woven into the warp and weft of the source documents that historians use to write our textbooks. I've found in my own area of research, for example, that John Barbour's *The Bruce* and Walter Bower's *Scotichronicon,* both roundly criticized by academia as nationalistically biased, have nevertheless been vehicles through which the underlying truths of those myths have been slipped between the lines—truths that have gained ever more purchase in recent years.

It's been my hope these truths would not be driven underground again by silence or disdain, the two reliable weapons that have so often helped shape the approved version of history we are taught in school.

But while hope springs eternal in the human breast, hope is fading fast. I fear that this particular human trait has been long recognized as a weakness, and has been used as a familiar tool over the millennia by those privileged few who pull our strings and yank our chains—those who safely push the model ships and tanks around on the great flat maps in war rooms all over the world.

Recent controversies surround Dan Brown's *Da Vinci Code* as well as Mel Gibson's *The Passion of the Christ.* While Gibson's *Passion* points the finger of blame for a divine Christ's crucifixion, Brown's *Code* challenges Christ's divinity by suggesting he had a mortal daughter who survived him. Christians and Jews are once again at odds over matters that mainstream history refuses to adequately examine and that faith continues to inadequately explain.

"A truth is not hard to kill," said Mark Twain, "and a lie well told is immortal."

18 The Real Secret Society Behind *The Da Vinci Code*

Those Surprising Rosicrucians

Mark Amaru Pinkham

As everyone knows who has read Dan Brown's *The Da Vinci Code,* the plot revolves around the clandestine activities of an ancient secret society known as the Priory of Sion. The actual existence of this society, claims Brown, is one of the few irrefutable truths woven into his fictional novel. This may have been considered true when he was writing his manuscript, but recently the authors of *Holy Blood, Holy Grail*—the nonfiction book that introduced Brown to the Priory—publicly stated that much of the information related to the organization as it appears in their book is apparently based upon a hoax.

They confessed to having been led astray by some "Prieuré documents" they discovered in Paris's Bibliothèque Nationale, an admission that for awhile deterred most researchers from further pursuing the legitimacy of the Priory. Then researchers Lynn Picknett and Clive Prince published *The Sion Revelation,* within which they examined all arguments for and against the Priory. Their surprising conclusion was that there has indeed been a secret European organization with an agenda similar to the Priory's, and that the Priory of Sion may have been invented to act as a cover for this legitimate organization.

Picknett and Prince were never able to identify conclusively this elusive order, perhaps because the secret society they apprehended is not very secretive anymore. The order they sought is commonly known as the Rosicrucian Order, although it has also been known by other related titles, including the Order of the Rose or Rosy Cross and the Brotherhood of the Rosy and Golden Cross. Although seemingly innocuous today, in the past this organization has preserved many secret rites and passed among its members many heretical secrets that are just as explosive as any information regarding the sacred bloodline of Jesus and Mary Magdalen.

The Rosicrucian Order, which we can now call the *real* Priory of Sion, first made its presence known in the seventeenth century through public documents known as the *Fama* and the *Confessio*. These manifestos claimed that the Order of the Rosy Cross was moving into a new public cycle, although it had already been in existence as a secret society for hundreds of years. Then, in 1785, one of the order's Paris representatives, Baron de Gleichen, spoke at a conference of Freemasons and Rosicrucians and claimed that the members of the Order of the Rosy Cross had been the "Superiors and Founders of Freemasonry," while additionally maintaining that its grand masters "were designated by the titles John I, II, III, and so onward," thereby ostensibly aligning them with John the Baptist, John the Apostle, or both.

These revealed characteristics of the Rosy Cross were later woven into its alter ego, the Priory of Sion, by the authors of the "Prieuré documents" and *Holy Blood, Holy Grail,* who claimed that the Priory similarly awarded its grand masters with sequential "John" titles.

Perhaps the most conclusive evidence in favor of the Priory of Sion being a cover name for the Order of the Rosy Cross is simply that the Priory is said to have called itself the L'Order de la Rose-Croix Veritas, the "The True Order of the Rose Cross." Supposedly, the Priory adopted both this epithet and that of Ormus, a name that also irrefutably ties the Priory to the Rosy Cross—Ormus is the name of the founder of an early Rosy Cross sect that existed in first-century Alexandria. Information regarding Ormus and his sect originated in the eighteenth century with the Rosicrucian historian Baron von Westerode, who claimed that Ormus, a disciple of St. Mark and a gnostic priest of the Alexandrian deity Serapis, was the founder of an early Rosy Cross sect that he named the Sages of Light.

THE ORDER OF THE HOLY GRAIL

One crucial difference exists, however, between the Order of the Rosy Cross and the Priory of Sion. The Order of the Rosy Cross never designated itself as the guardian of the bloodline of Jesus and Mary Magdalen, which was the sole raison d'être given for the Priory of Sion (this was, however, the raison d'être assigned to the Priory by the authors of *Holy Blood, Holy Grail*, not the "Prieuré documents" that first informed them of its existence). Closer inspection will, however, reveal that the two orders actually mirror each other in their fundamental mission, which for both has been the search and protection of *some form(s)* of the Holy Grail. According to *Holy Blood, Holy Grail,* the Priory of Sion has always recognized the Holy Grail to be solely the body of Mary Magdalen, while the Rosicrucians take a much broader approach. For them the Holy Grail is a subtle power that any human or object can possess. This power has been known by many names worldwide, including the Holy

Spirit, Shekinah, Baraka, and Kundalini. A seeker must simply find the right cup, sword, spear, rock, person, etc., that is endowed with this power and then absorb it into himself, thus initiating a process of alchemical transformation that leads to enlightenment and even immortality.

Those human Holy Grails who possess the greatest abundance of this power are most commonly fully enlightened masters, and objects that are ascribed the power of Holy Grails—such as the Cup of Christ and the Spear of Longinus—are normally items that have been in close contact with such masters or that held a part of them, such as their blood, and thereby absorbed their power. This sought-after Holy Grail power can also be acquired via relics of a deceased saint, such as in the case of John the Baptist, whose head was discovered in Constantinople during the Fourth Crusade and became one of the prized Holy Grails possessed by the Knights Templar.

The Knights Templar were also linked to the Order of the Rosy Cross. According to Baron von Westerode, the knights are known in Rosicrucian history as "Disciples of the Rose Cross." Their definitive eight-pointed red cross was an ancient alchemical symbol of the Rosy Cross Order. And similar to other branches of the Rosy Cross, the Templars also entitled their grand masters as John I, II, III, and so on.

BACK TO THE GARDEN

Since the Rosicrucians take an expansive view of what the Holy Grail is, their service of guarding it is also more inclusive than the reputed Priory of Sion's. While the goal of the Priory was said to be guarding Mary Magdalen and her descendants, that of the Rosicrucians has been to protect a lineage of Holy Grail masters and their alchemical teachings that can be traced all the way back to the Garden of Eden. According to the historian Arthur Edward Waite in *The Brotherhood of the Rosy Cross,* certain early European branches of the Order of the Rosy Cross maintained that their Rosy Cross wisdom was first taught by God to Adam in the fabled Garden. This secret wisdom was then passed down a lineage of enlightened "Sons of Wisdom" that included Moses and Solomon, as well as the alchemist Hermes Trismegistus.

Could the Order of the Rosy Cross have literally originated in the Garden of Eden, as Rosicrucian historians maintained? A body of surprising evidence supporting this notion can be found in the archives of the Order of the Garter, Britain's most prestigious knighted order, founded by King Edward III, who synthesized elements of the Templars, the Knights of the Round Table, and the Sufi Order of Al-Khadir to create his fourteenth-century chivalrous organization.

According to Frances Yates in *The Rosicrucian Enlightenment,* the Order of the Garter and its symbols, which include a rose and a rosy cross, were initially linked to the Rosicrucians. St. George, the Garter's patron saint, whose symbol is a rosy cross embedded in an eight-pointed star, also links the Order of the Garter to the Rosy Cross. Even more, St. George provides a link between both orders and the Garden of Eden. Today, St. George is known as Al-Khadir by Middle Eastern Sufis who maintain that his true home is Kataragama on Sri Lanka—the island paradise currently recognized by Muslims worldwide as the original site of the Garden of Eden.

St. George ties the Rosy Cross to Eden in this way, but he also provides a more direct link. According to the Hindus—who venerate St. George at Kataragama, albeit in the form of their deity Skanda-Murugan—in very ancient times St. George was physically incarnate as a great spiritual leader who first taught the knowledge of alchemy to humanity. He was suffused with the alchemical power of transformation, which he passed to his students, thereby founding lineages of adepts possessing Holy Grail power. One of these lineages was taken west by the Nasurai Mandeans, who eventually merged with the Jewish Essenes to produce the sect of the Nasoreans or Nazarenes, the sect that John the Baptist and Jesus were born into.

John received this Holy Grail power and wisdom from his Nasorean teachers before passing it to Jesus and other masters who founded gnostic sects, including the founders of the Alexandrian sect that produced Ormus. Jesus eventually passed the power and wisdom to his successors, John the Apostle and Mary Magdalen, who in turn transmitted it down a line of Holy Grail masters that culminated with the Knights Templar. Thus, in the end, the power and secret teachings of the Holy Grail came into the possession of many branches of the Order of the Rosy Cross, the *real* Priory of Sion.

PART FOUR

THE POWER AND REACH OF HIGH-RANKING FREEMASONS

19 "The Star-Spangled Banner" and America's Origins

Were the Founders of the United States Guided by an Ancient Mandate?

Jeff Nisbet

My article "The Mystery of the Battle of Bannockburn," which is included in this book, proposed that the great 1314 battle for Scottish independence had been stage-managed by a clandestine brotherhood that stood on both sides of the battle line, and had been forever fixed in time as an event of great symbolic significance by uncannily mirroring a simultaneous encounter in the heavens above.

Bannockburn, I proposed, was an epic contract between enemies of convenience, written in the invisible ink of the stars at daytime and sealed with the blood of battle. It follows that many of the rank-and-file who fought that day thought they were fighting for Freedom only, but in fact were also fighting so that certain forbidden truths could be sent quietly forward to a more enlightened time. The brotherhood knew that books could be burned and messages carved in stone could be crushed into dust, but the arrangement of the heavens would forever be safe from tampering. And so it was there, supported by some pointed hints in the official record, that they hid their secrets!

Five hundred years after the Battle of Bannockburn, that brotherhood would meet again to fix yet another date in time and to reaffirm their ancient contract. Once again they would pretend to be enemies, and once again they would hide their secrets in the sky.

Let's go back.

Very early on the morning of September 14, 1814, a young American lawyer named Francis Scott Key stood on the deck of a British truce ship, waiting for the dawn. In a letter to a friend, Key would later describe the dawn's arrival as a "bright streak of gold mingled with crimson shot athwart the eastern sky, followed by another and still another, as the morning sun rose in the fullness of his glory, lifting 'the mists of the deep,' crowning a 'Heaven-blest land' with a new victory and grandeur."

Fig. 19.1. Francis Scott Key observes the aftermath of the British attack on Fort McHenry, Maryland, on the morning of September 14, 1812.

He had just witnessed the end of the twenty-five-hour naval bombardment of Maryland's Fort McHenry, the fort that guarded the entrance to Baltimore Harbor.

The sight of an immense American flag, flying "o'er the ramparts" of the fort, would inspire him to scribble down the lyrics to "The Star-Spangled Banner." That anthem would be Key's single claim to fame, and would commemorate the most memorable event in America's otherwise most forgotten war.

Often referred to as America's second war of independence, there were several reasons for the War of 1812, but the immediate reason was the British navy's nasty habit of boarding American ships and "pressing" certain of the crew into its own ranks on the grounds that they were British deserters. The action rankled, and America went to war for the first time as a sovereign nation.

Fig. 19.2 An American flag similar to this star-spangled banner was hoisted over Fort McHenry, Maryland, after its assault by the British, inspiring Francis Scott Key to write his famous anthem.

Much has been speculated about the early foundations of America. It has been proposed that the country was begun as a grand experiment of the brotherhood of Freemasons, a fraternity thought by many to have grown out of the Knights Templar, the mysterious order of warrior-monks barbarously suppressed in France on grounds of heresy, among other charges, in 1307.

It has also been proposed, however, that many Templars escaped to Scotland, and delivered the decisive blow against the English at Bannockburn. Going underground, the order then cobbled together yet another brotherhood within the civil sector that would survive the Protestant Reformation—the great church schism that gave the Vatican a new force to reckon with. Although the Templar connection is still hotly debated, that new brotherhood is thought to be the Freemasons.

Almost three hundred years after Bannockburn, in 1603, the Crowns of England and Scotland would finally unite under the first officially Masonic king, Scotland's James VI. Shortly thereafter, the great migration to the New World would begin in earnest.

In Michael Baigent and Richard Leigh's *Temple and the Lodge,* the authors claim that many of America's founding fathers were Freemasons, and that the precipitating acts of the American Revolution were planned by that brotherhood. Many Freemasons, they claim, were key participants in the famous Boston Tea Party. One of them was Paul Revere—famous for his midnight ride to Lexington, where "the shot heard round the world" was fired.

It is interesting to note that from George Washington on down, a disproportionate number of Freemasons were among the American high command, including a general Arthur Sinclair, a descendant of Sir William Sinclair who built Scotland's Rosslyn Chapel, the world's most revered repository of Freemasonic lore. William, in turn, was a descendant of the man thought to have led the Templar charge at Bannockburn, who was himself descended from Henry Sinclair, who arguably may have organized a voyage of discovery to the New World in 1398, long before Columbus was a twinkle in his father's eye.

Baigent and Leigh also imply, however, that the top British commanders were Freemasons as well, and showed little zeal to win the war. It was perhaps thought more prudent to let the new land govern itself, while each country's movers and shakers remained bound by brotherly bonds. A mutually beneficial dialogue could then be quietly maintained, while highly motivated hordes of European immigrants proceeded to kick America's indigenous people about, from place to place, in the great march west.

But they needed a flag to march behind.

It is well known that the first American flag was commissioned by George Washington and was sewn by Betsy Ross. But it is less well known that Betsy's husband was a Freemason, and that Washington described the flag's circle of stars as "a new constellation."

While we are taught that the circle symbolizes the thirteen original states, could Washington have had something else in mind? Might he have been secretly invoking the hermetic dictum "As above, so below," a phrase much bandied about whenever Templars, Freemasons, and "underground streams of knowledge" are discussed in the same breath? Could that stellar circle also symbolize the letter O, for Orion, the constellation that played such a pivotal role at Bannockburn?

America's Declaration of Independence, signed by Washington and many other Freemasons, is thought to have been inspired by Scotland's Declaration of Arbroath, which was signed shortly after Bannockburn by many individuals associated with the survival of Templar and Freemasonic ideals. That stirring document can still be interpreted as a testament to the equality of men and as strong advice to any temporal ruler unwise enough to hold the will of the people in contempt.

During the years following the American Revolution, however, the young nation somehow failed to develop a unity of spirit that the world's major powers would respect. The War of 1812 would change all that, and the bombardment of Fort McHenry would force the world to see the Stars and Stripes with new eyes, and would give the American people a song to sing.

The British assault on Baltimore was, like the English assault at Bannockburn, a two-pronged affair. British General Robert Ross, who had shown remarkable restraint by burning only government buildings during his earlier sack of the nation's capital, led his men toward Baltimore by land. The assault

Fig. 19.3. British naval forces assail Fort McHenry, Baltimore.

failed when Ross became one of the first casualties and, with an effect eerily reminiscent of a similar event at Bannockburn, his men lost morale.

Meanwhile, the British fleet had anchored broadside to Fort McHenry.

At 7:00 A.M. on September 13, and continuing for twenty-five hours with just one break of several hours, British warships bombarded the fort. Key's lyrics, however, tell us that the bombs were "bursting in air" before reaching their targets. The fuses had been inexplicably set too short to go the distance. But the light of the bombs and "the rockets' red glare" did manage to give "proof through the night that our flag was still there!"

It was quite a show, and a relatively cheap one. Only four Americans are known to have died during the attack.

But there was a much bigger show going on above—one that would outlive the tale we are told today.

At 3:41 A.M., the morning star, Venus, rose above the eastern horizon midway between the forelegs of Leo, just minutes before the rising of Regulus, a significant star in Masonic tradition. If the night had been dark, clear, and eventless, they would have made a pretty pair. But it was raining, the air was full of smoke, and all eyes were trained on the light show below.

Mercury rose at 5:16 A.M., as Leo appeared on the horizon in a stance well reminiscent of the flag carried at Bannockburn—the flag Scots still fly today—followed quickly by the war planet Mars. Even if the bombardment had not been the main focus of attention, these events would already have faded in the light of the approaching dawn.

Just twenty minutes later, giant Jupiter would rise behind the Sun, followed shortly by the Moon.

Toward the east, if we include the Sun and Moon, six denizens of our solar system lay within just thirty degrees of sky—all but one of those lying within seven degrees—a surprisingly rare alignment.

The planet Pluto surprised me even more.

Pluto is the outermost planet in our solar system—so far out that it takes approximately 249 Earth years to orbit the Sun. Not discovered until 1930, many years after the siege of Fort McHenry, Pluto takes a very long time to get from one side of the solar system to the other—and yet there it was, due west of the battle but part of the same alignment.

But the biggest surprise was the planet Neptune, not discovered until 1846, with an orbit time of 165 years. When a line was drawn between Neptune and Pluto, and another line drawn between Neptune and the midpoint of Pluto's easternmost orbit, a compass was formed. When another line connected the two endpoints, a pyramid was formed. And when a line was drawn between

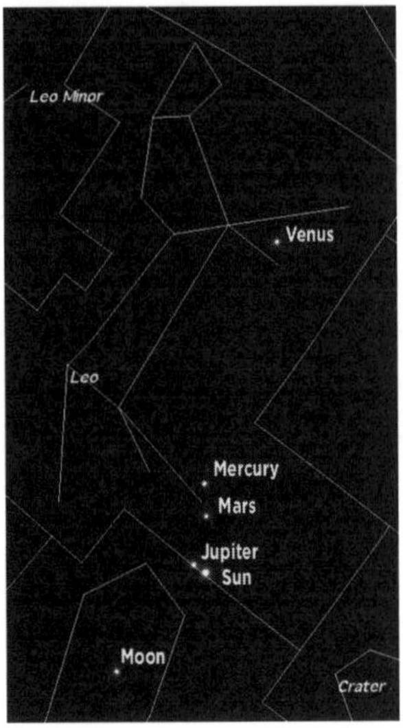

Fig. 19.4. The position of the stars and planets shortly after dawn on September 14, 1812.

Neptune and the Sun, everything weirdly doubled. Astrologers call this particular configuration a "T-square," and I am told it usually portends events of a sinister nature. (But more about astrology later.)

As reported, the assault had ceased at dusk on September 13 and had resumed at 1:00 A.M., when the first belt star of Orion broke the horizon. Some 3,000 miles to the east, dawn was breaking in the sky above Bannockburn, and Leo stood defiantly on the Scottish horizon as the bombs again began "bursting in air" above Fort McHenry.

It was a long and noisy night, but the Brits eventually set sail at dawn, leaving the grand finale to the Americans. Meanwhile, in the skies east of Bannockburn, Hercules slew Serpens Aquaticus, the many-headed water serpent. How's that for synchronicity?

The Battle of Baltimore was fought on many fronts, indeed!

It is a common misconception, not corrected in most history books, that the immense thirty-by forty-two-foot Fort McHenry flag, currently undergoing restoration in Washington, D.C.'s Smithsonian Institution, was the flag that was flown throughout the bombardment. It was not.

Fort McHenry commander Major George Armistead had ordered two flags to be made, and had required that one of them be large enough so that "the British would have no trouble seeing it from a distance." It was the smaller flag that was flown during the bombardment. It was the larger flag, hoisted at dawn, that inspired Key's song.

What else about the flag, and the continuing mystery of the bombardment itself, might warrant a closer look? Here's the short list:

- Stitched prominently in red on the third white bar from the bottom is what has variously been described as a patch, the letter *A* for Armistead, or an inverted *V*. We might ask ourselves the following: Why would someone patch a white bar with a red patch, leave off the crossbar of a letter *A*, or turn a *V* upside down? Might I suggest that this element symbolizes the ever-enigmatic Masonic compass? It is also highly provocative that the letter *B* is almost invisibly embroidered near the top of that compass, perhaps to commemorate Bannockburn.
- Architecturally, Fort McHenry was star-shaped, and had been named after Freemason James McHenry, U.S. Secretary of War during Washington's presidency.
- There is a legend that, as the British fleet retreated, a rooster crowed defiance from the top of the flagpole. That "herald of dawn" is prominently displayed on the seal of the Sinclair clan, with the motto "Commit thy work to God."
- The Francis Scott Key Bridge spans the Potomac River from Washington, D.C., to Rosslyn, Virginia, perhaps another quiet symbol of the secret transatlantic arrangement made so many years ago.
- The very name Scott Key resonates with the suggestion that one key to unlocking this great mystery will be found in Scotland.

While I have described the astronomical arrangement of the skies above Fort McHenry and Bannockburn, and have tipped my hat to the ancient mythological connections, I have paid only brief lip service to astrological considerations because astrology is not a field I have studied enough to feel comfortable with. Astronomy and astrology were once virtually inseparable disciplines—but not today. Though astronomy has acquired a gloss of scientific respectability, astrology has not fared so well.

I have nevertheless asked Rab Wilkie and Ed Kohout, both knowledgeable in the understudied field of Masonic astrology, to weigh in with their thoughts on my theories in "100 words or less." Stingy, I know! They have so far weighed in with thousands, and deserve a forum—larger than this article can provide—to properly present their views and do them justice. I thank them both for helping me adjust the accompanying heliocentric graphic into something the average reader can visually comprehend. They have also enthusiastically convinced me that what each of us has seen so far is "just the tip of a rather large iceberg."

These are interesting times, indeed!

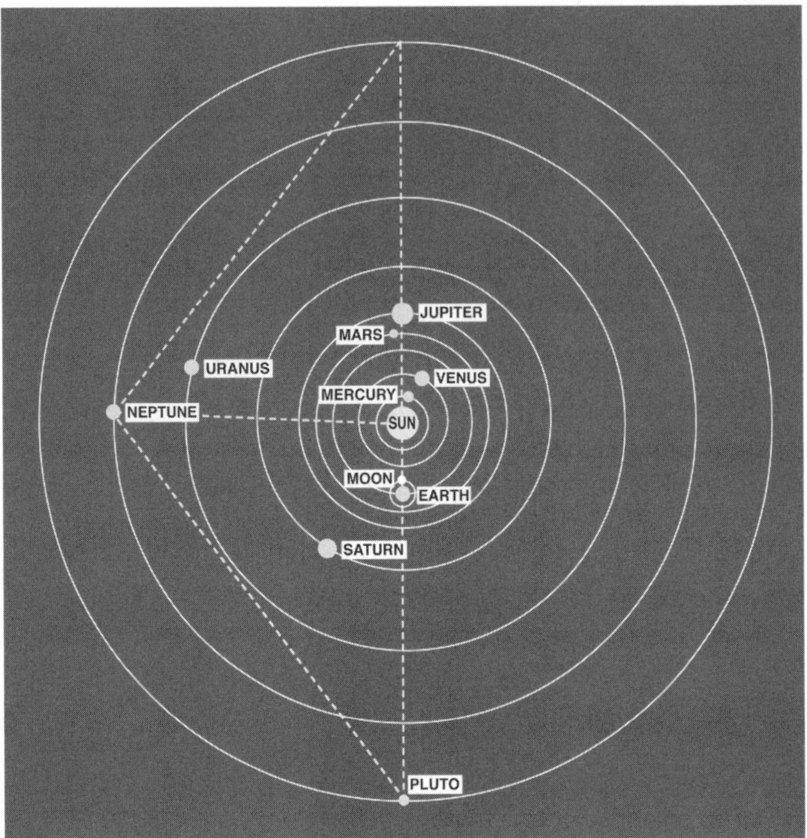

Fig. 19.5. Compressed heliocentric view of the solar system at dawn, September 14, 1814.

Some final thoughts about the subject at hand:

Consider that the most famous song inspired by the Battle of Bannockburn was "Scots Wha Hae," written by Scots bard and Freemason Robert Burns. Consider that Freemason Francis Scott Key wrote "The Star-Spangled Banner" during the War of 1812. Consider that Freemason John Philip Sousa's last performance was to conduct his "Stars and Stripes Forever" in 1932. And finally, consider the possibility that a small yet influential clandestine brotherhood was marching in secret to its own drum since 1314, if not earlier.

Considering all those things, one might well wonder what the Freemason George M. Cohan had in mind when he penned the last few lines of "You're a Grand Old Flag" using a phrase from the Robert Burns megahit "Auld Lang Syne." Could Cohan have written those lines for brothers "with ears to hear"?

Every heart beats true 'neath the Red, White and Blue,
Where there's never a boast or brag.
But should auld acquaintance *be forgot,*
Keep your eye on that grand old flag!

Like religion, flags have always had the uncanny ability to keep large groups of people united, ready to fight for a common cause at the drop of a hat. Unfortunately, flags and religion have also been found useful in keeping even larger groups of people apart and, for the most part, that's why the great chess game called War has never lacked for pawns.

But who plays the game, and who are the pieces?

20 America's Ancient Architect

Were America's Founders Pursuing a Hidden Agenda?

Steven Sora

The history of the United States was forged by the power of secret—often elite—societies. George Washington, John Hancock, and Benjamin Franklin were all members of Masonic lodges. Connections made through Freemasonry allowed them to provide the spark that incited America on the road to liberty, and supplied her with goods, ammunition, and allies to fight the battle and, through years of defeat, arise to strike the decisive victory.

Hancock was a smuggler. As a shipowner and an heir to his uncle's merchant empire, he resorted to smuggling because Britain had made illegal almost any import that did not come from England. A full one-third of Boston's families depended on Hancock for their livelihood. The city depended on him for foodstuffs and commodities. He in turn needed to depend upon people whom he could trust.

While he belonged to an elite lodge where fellow merchants and sea captains made up the privileged few, he also belonged to the rank-and-file lodge of St. Andrews, where he could meet and be acquainted with the men he would hire. What greater place could he find to recruit those whom he needed to sail, build, outfit, and load and unload his ships? Sworn to secret oaths, acknowledged by secret handshakes, and pledged to assist fellow Masons, being a lodge brother meant that one could be counted on to be a trusted employee. When considering a potential employee, the key consideration was often whether or not the man was "on the level" or "on the square." This ensured trust.

In 1767, a ship owned by Hancock, propitiously dubbed the *Liberty*, was boarded by customs agents. It carried Madeira wine, a commodity that was not allowed to be imported on colonial ships. While some of Hancock's men locked the customs agents in a room, others unloaded the ship. The king's men were not amused and seized the ship anyway. This began a series of measures and reactions that culminated in the Boston Tea Party.

That night, thirty men dressed as Mohawks threw 10,000 pounds of the

Fig. 20.1. The Masonic symbol of the compass and the square.

king's tea into Boston's murky harbor. Twelve men were from the St. Andrews Lodge, which met at the Green Dragon Tavern. The rest were from two revolutionary cells, the Sons of Liberty and the Loyall Nine (sic). Their actions closed the port and enlisted the other states to the cause.

Washington was a farmer, a surveyor, and a military man. To further his business, his brother clued him in to the importance of joining a lodge. It meant connections, assistance, and—as in the case of Hancock—being able to trust those you brought into your business or up in rank. The future president took the same lesson to war. Washington operated through the "field lodge," a new development in Freemasonry that began in the French and Indian War, when Washington's career began as well.

As the army moved, a stationary lodge was of no help. The field lodge was a tent where the Masons met. It was a refuge where privates could speak freely with officers and where Washington could assemble with his generals, as many of whom were Masons also.

Washington embraced the Masonic ideals of liberty and fraternity, and risked his property and his life for his principles. A more religious man than Hancock, Washington belonged to a church, but always left the service before the communion. It is said that his brand of religion was Deism. He believed in one God, a God that created the universe. He avoided the dogma that had brought suffering and war to Europe for centuries. Washington's belief was one that was shared with several of the other Founding Fathers.

To Masons, the creator God was the Great Architect. His powers were represented in the sciences, the most important of which was geometry. This is the basis for other sciences, significantly building. The surveyers' tools were symbolic of their belief, and practical in Washington's early career.

Franklin was a self-made millionaire. He recognized the value of Freemasonry as soon as he moved to Philadelphia. As a printer, lodge brothers referred business to other brothers. Having made his fortune by age forty, Franklin went on to establish fire companies, libraries, and the post office of which he became postmaster. Being a postmaster at this point in time meant being a spymaster, as this position controlled the movement of information.

Franklin's European counterparts, many in sympathy with the American cause, freely shared information, and spread dis-information when it served to further the cause.

As a Mason and a man of science, Franklin could move freely within European society. In England, he was invited to stay at the Medmenham Estate, where the Hellfire Club held weekend-long parties that would shake modern sensibilities. The central figure of the hedonistic group was Sir Francis Dashwood, who had been initiated into Masonry in Italy and whose personal proclivities leaned toward the occult. Dashwood may have had a quality that redeemed him to Franklin in that Dashwood was England's postmaster. Together Franklin and Dashwood were able to control and disseminate intelligence more effectively than the military.

Dashwood's circle would unite many in England who were prominent royal subjects and yet actively promoted the cause of the colonists. One was John Wilkes, who called those who challenged the English king the "Sons of Liberty." The title caught on and soon resistance groups in several colonial cities were happy to operate as Sons of Liberty. England soon became too dangerous for Franklin, as many suggested he be arrested, so he moved to France.

One very elite lodge, the Lodge of the Nine Sisters, was pleased to welcome Franklin as a brother. That lodge included many who would be active in the struggle for liberty. Some were prominent merchants whose importance in getting supplies and ammunition to the colonies was critical. Others were prominent thinkers who would influence public opinion. (Franklin was present at Voltaire's initiation into Freemasonry.) And one was England's top spy in France, Dr. Edward Bancroft. Franklin moved in circles where if not for his participation in Freemasonry, he would have spent a lifetime earning a welcome.

The importance of the role played behind the scenes by Franklin and a handful of other Americans has been marginalized by history. It was, however, at least as important as the military role. Not only were connections with the Freemasonry organization established in France, but even those at odds with Freemasonry were enlisted in the cause.

The Knights of Malta—ardent Catholics loyal to the pope—were not on friendly terms with Masonry. Catholics regarded Masonry as an institution that, by this time, was anti-Church. From a practical point of view, however, both the Knights of Malta and the Masons considered England to be an enemy in need of comeuppance. Twenty knights joined the war effort and thousands of foot soldiers came along, including the original French Foreign Legion. The French navy was under the command of Admiral de Grasse, a Knight of Malta, who delivered badly needed supplies to Yorktown.

Looking at the war that became the American Revolution from a military stance, it is hard to accept that Washington's army was victorious. Defeated in all but a handful of battles, undermanned, poorly equipped and unprepared, the Continental army was chased from one state to another. Bordering on starvation, lacking uniforms and even shoes, the army managed to strike a blow every so often that wore down England's appetite for the lengthy conflict. Washington himself survived assassination plans by the English and the plot of a cabal of Americans that wanted to replace him as commander. At a time when commanding officers were sought-after targets, Washington survived one battle after another, even though he rode into the field on a large white horse.

Whereas the battles of Saratoga, Monmouth, and Yorktown are known to students of American history, the story of the "secret war" has remained a mystery. Of all the plots that took place off the battlefield, perhaps the greatest is the story of Admiral George Rodney. Appointed to command the English navy, Rodney had a serious problem. His gambling debts forced him to flee England for France. In France, he incurred even more debt and was unable to leave.

Commanding a fleet in war was a lucrative opportunity, as a commander was entitled to take a one-third share in the spoils of battle. Rodney saw a way out of debt, but not out of France. To his rescue came the maréchal duc de Biron, the military commander of France's French Guard. Although the two countries were days away from a formal declaration of war, the highest-ranking French officer lent a huge sum of money to the soon-to-be highest-ranking English naval officer.

The circumstances beg two questions. Why would Biron lend this fortune to an enemy? The answer may lie in the fact that his nephew, the duc de Lauzon, was leading the French Foreign Legion in battle. Biron felt the American revolutionary effort was, at best, a romantic adventure. The Americans, outmanned and outnumbered by the superior forces of the British, were surely headed for defeat and he was afraid for his young nephew.

The feeling was shared by the uncle of the Marquis de Lafayette. Lafayette and his brother-in-law the Viscount Noailles, as well as the count of Ségur, were barely out of their teens when Silas Deane, an American, recruited them to the cause. Lafayette's uncle laughed and called them the Three Musketeers, until to his horror, he found they were serious. Not since the Crusades had young nobles so gladly rushed off to war.

The second question is: What did the duc de Biron expect in return from Rodney? The answer becomes evident. Rodney needed to supply the British forces under Cornwallis before de Grasse supplied the American and French forces in Virginia. The showdown was a certainty. The race was on between the two navies. Rodney understood the importance of beating de Grasse at sea, or in the race to Virginia, and indicated this in letters to his commanders and even to his wife. He then inexplicably failed to engage the French navy three times, split his fleet, and sailed home to England, complaining his prostate was acting up. The French admiral de Grasse supplied fresh troops and ammunition to the siege at Yorktown and the world was turned upside down. Cornwallis surrendered.

The admiral's commanders were astounded and complained to Lord Montagu that Rodney was singularly responsible for the failure to supply the troops. The crafty admiral outmaneuvered them and returned to the Caribbean to defeat the French navy in the Battle of the Saints in 1782. He lost the war and only won the late battle and, despite criticism in the English newspapers, returned a hero.

The defeat of Cornwallis was soon followed by the treaty that recognized America's freedom. Those who won the war would win the peace. The inauguration of Washington as the first American president was a Masonic celebration. The marshal of the day's events was Freemason and General Jacob Morton. The inauguration oath was administered by New York State's grand master, Robert Livingston. Washington's escort was Freemason and general Morgan Lewis. The Bible used was the Bible of St. John's Lodge in New York.

Another celebration followed shortly when the new capital, Washington, laid out by Mason Pierre Charles L'Enfant, was dedicated. This ceremony also was complete with baptism by corn, oil, and wine more common to ancient mystery religions than to either Christianity or Americana. The new symbols of the country were the all-seeing eye, truncated pyramids, and obelisks. While having no significance to most Americans, the significance was fully understood among Freemasons. As it still says on the one-dollar bill, over and under the pyramid: *Annuit Coeptis and Novus Ordo Seclorum*. The first phrase is a prayer to the god Jupiter, the second phrase means: "A New Order of the Ages."

Washington may have understood that, despite funding a nation based on fraternity and equality, there was a danger in allowing a secretive force, even

Masonry, to become too powerful. The adage "Power corrupts and absolute power corrupts absolutely" seemed to indicate that the European concept of kings and inherited nobility was not to be trusted or allowed.

After the Revolution, a society of officers that fought together was created. The Society of the Cincinnati consisted of American officers and nearly all of the French Knights of Malta. When Washington found that they planned to limit future membership to their descendants, he declared it elitism and threatened to quit the group. The order changed its policy. Washington was also offered a lifelong presidency of the order, which he refused.

The American Revolution was followed by more than a century of revolutions in France, in the Italian states, in Latin America, and finally in Russia. Secret societies and conspiracies would topple entrenched ruling classes and governments that had existed for centuries. The French and Russian Revolutions would turn into bloodbaths that saw opportunists and repressive dictators take the reins of power. Only in America was democracy forged.

Before the new order of the ages would be one hundred years old, secret societies would show a darker side. Within Masonry, a murder and cover-up by Masons in New York saw the movement self-destruct as public clamor halved membership and shuttered lodges. Nationally, power and self-interest asserted the ability to corrupt the new democracy. Plots were made to return to England, to split the new country, and to assassinate Presidents Harrison, Taylor, and Lincoln. When victory could not be attained through Congress, darker means were employed.

As the country enters its third century, secret and elite societies are alive and well—and prospering. They have the ability to control the government, to topple it, to enrich themselves, or to safeguard the principles on which the nation was founded. The survival of ideals such as liberty and equality may rest in the balance between the mob and the elite, the powerful and the masses. It may depend on the vigilance of those with overriding principles or the intentions of Washington's Great Architect.

21 National Secrets

The Truth Might Be Stranger Than Any Fiction

Steven Sora

The reviews are in for *National Treasure,* Hollywood's take on the esoteric origins of America, starring Nicolas Cage. The critics hated it, but the good news is that the public loved it.

The story centers on Ben Gates (Cage), a descendant of one of the signers of the Declaration of Independence. The signers, it seems, may have left more than a blueprint for democracy on the Declaration. America's founders, led by Freemasons, had—the movie suggests—hidden an actual treasure, indeed, the legendary treasure of the mysterious Knights Templar.

To this day Freemasons consider themselves to be the heirs of the Templars. The treasure, though, according to historical accounts, had its origin even before the Templars are said to have carried it home to France from Jerusalem after the Crusades. It is said that only a handful of men (the film purports that these included the Founding Fathers) once knew of the treasure, and only by correctly interpreting many mysterious signs and symbols could its location be uncovered. In the movie, the most important clue is a map on the back of America's most sacred and protected document, the original Declaration of Independence.

The fact that the reaction of film critics goes against popular opinion should come as no surprise, but it is interesting to examine just why they chose to pan such an overwhelmingly popular film.

One critic argued that no serious historian has ever believed that there was a Templar treasure. We beg to differ.

The Templar treasure is no myth. During the persecution of the Templars in the fourteenth century, strong evidence of the treasure's existence was part of actual court testimony in at least one Templar trial. In contrast to their French counterparts, British proceedings against the Templars never took on a hysterical tone. The English trials, in fact, were quite orderly and free from the fantastic accounts of devil worship and spitting on the Cross that had become familiar features of continental trials. Even the use of torture was minimal and then only as a result of pressure from the Church and the French king.

In England, the record reveals that knowledgeable and influential figures testified that, just before the Friday 13th, 1307, raid that destroyed their organization, the Templars had been warned of the king's warrants. It is no secret that, before the raid, the Templars had served as virtual world bankers—receiving deposits of treasure from the rich in many locales and issuing payments on demand drawn on those deposits in other locations. While scholars may question the existence of the Templar treasure, it is clear that the raiders of their strongholds failed to find it.

This begs the question: What actually happened to the vast deposits that the Templars certainly held? According to the testimony, upon receiving warning of the pending raids, the knights feverishly loaded all the valuables in their care onto a hastily assembled wagon train and quickly and quietly transported the immense hoard—the holdings of what was then the only bank of the world—to the French port city of La Rochelle. There the treasure was loaded onto ships of the Templar fleet—the largest in the world.

From La Rochelle, many believe, the fleet sailed to the one place a fugitive order could find protection—the free nation of Scotland, where the upstart king Robert the Bruce had been excommunicated for declaring his country's independence.

The outlaw order seeking protection and the outlawed nation in sore need of ships and knights established a mutually rewarding relationship. Very soon, at the greatest battle in Scottish history, Bannockburn, the fugitive Templars proved their value. Just as English forces appeared to be sweeping the field, a fresh cadre of knights charged from the forest and routed the enemy. It was the feast day of St. John, patron saint of the Templars, destined to remain the date of their last great victory in the field. They soon went underground, concealing their true identity behind the Masonic mask.

When James VI of Scotland was crowned King James II of England, the Scottish family at the heart of the Templars, the Sinclairs, was rewarded with the title and responsibility of hereditary guardians of Freemasonry. The honor would be confirmed again in 1601. The Sinclairs had protected the treasure since it was brought to their estate at Roslin, and would protect the order as well.

In the fourteenth century, as anti-Catholic sentiment led to attacks on churches and the destruction of long-preserved relics, it is believed that the Sinclairs grew concerned about possible threats to the immense but secret treasure in their possession. Once again—almost a century before Columbus crossed the Atlantic—the vast cache was moved, this time, apparently, to Nova Scotia.

In most of America, the story of the first Sinclair voyage to the New World in 1398 is taken lightly. Not so in Nova Scotia, where in Guysborough, a statue of Henry Sinclair remains a testament to belief in the voyage. Further corroboration comes from maps and charts from this early Atlantic crossing, which were used by Gerardus Mercator in preparing his own maps and by Martin Behaim in producing his globe.

The second criticism of the movie *National Treasure* was that there is no evidence of any treasure ever being pinpointed by secret symbols placed strategically for others to follow. Wrong again.

Once the Templar treasure was safely stashed away in a massive vault complex deep underground on a small island in Mahone Bay, Nova Scotia, the Sinclairs built Rosslyn Chapel. Carved in stone on Masonic pillars in the church are depictions of American maize, corn, and aloe. A hidden vault beneath the chapel long concealed the resting place of Sinclairs who had fought as Templars. Skull and bones, the markings on tombs, signified that only bones were needed for resurrection. Crossed legs meant that the deceased had been a Templar.

Across the ocean in Nova Scotia were still more clues. Oaks were planted on what would be called Oak Island to distinguish it from other small islands in the bay. Today the island has become a focus of sensational worldwide media speculation over the purpose of a gigantic and as of yet unexplained shaft, the full contents of which remain a mystery.

THE "MONEY PIT"

For fifty years Oak Island has been owned by two men who do not see eye-to-eye. Fred Nolan, a surveyor, discovered numerous symbols including a ten-foot equilateral triangle with a cross in the middle. Before anyone could decipher its meaning, Nolan realized it was part of an even larger triangle. Within the area, he found drilled rocks with metal ring bolts, and a heart-shaped rock within another smaller triangle. Another formation was made up of ten-ton granite boulders, again forming a cross, its intersection being a skull shaped rock showing evidence of artificial construction.

The other side of the island—the location of the notorious Money Pit—is owned by David Tobias. Excavation of the shaft began before 1800 with the discovery of flagstones at a three-foot level and then, every ten feet, a layer of oak planking. Ninety feet below the surface, an elaborate booby trap has persistently flooded the shaft and, for more than a century, has thwarted the dreams of treasure hunters to dig farther down. Even after it was determined just how the shaft was flooded, the advanced hydraulics of the ancient builders have continued to defy modern excavators.

Is there a treasure-laden vault under the small island? Both men still believe there is, and despite their advanced age, they continue to work to get it to the surface. Tobias is considering a new proposal for a massive shaft that will miss nothing in expanding the original Money Pit shaft. The price tag would be fifteen million dollars, adding considerably to the five million dollars he is said to have spent already. Nolan has brought in his son-in-law and recently purchased a nearby island and its treasure rights.

Oak Island's Money Pit, though, is not the only potential repository of wealth and secrets in the Americas.

VIRGINIA'S BRUTON VAULT

In Colonial Williamsburg, Virginia, lies the Bruton Vault. It too is connected to a secretive group with connections to the Templar-Masonic heritage. The vault itself is in one of the most visited American family destinations.

Here the original settlement has been restored and developed into a major park. For many, it is a great alternative to the hustle of nearby Six Flags, and an opportunity for Americans young and old to gain a sense of their history. Few know that it conceals an unusual secret, one that no visitor will ever see.

The secret is that more than one of the most significant items reputed to be part of the Templar treasure may have been hidden under the original Jamestown Church. These items are believed to include works by Sir Francis Bacon, as well as the Ark of the Covenant, said to have been brought to France by the early Templars from Jerusalem. What could these celebrated artifacts be doing under the Jamestown Church?

The fact is that the history of England's colonial origins in America has been altered, largely to fit into an acceptable orthodox framework. The true history borders on the bizarre.

Perhaps the greatest secret influence behind the persuasion of Queen Elizabeth to join the French and Spanish in racing to the New World was a mysterious man by the name of Dr. John Dee. The mysterious Dr. Dee was a magician and an astrologer as well as a scientist on a level with the great Copernicus. His tricks of levitation, experiments with alchemy, and his magic mirror brought suspicion upon him. He was booted out of school for actually levitating items on stage during a school play. For awhile he was even forced out of England. But he did come to have the queen of England as his protector.

When Elizabeth took the throne, she relied on Dee's ability to read the stars and to see the future, calling on him to choose the date and time of her coronation. His influence on the queen and the history of England is both incalculable and rarely mentioned. He coined the term Britannia, planned the Royal Navy, and convinced Elizabeth that sacred England owned the seas.

He also convinced her that she was a lineal descendant of Arthur, who went westward when he suffered his possibly mortal wounds. As a result of King Arthur's voyage to the West, Dee argued, England and the queen had the right to America. She granted him a patent to all the lands north of 50 degrees latitude.

If it had just been England's "mad monk" influencing Elizabeth, the country might not have taken the course in did in the history of the New World, but Dee had Sir Francis Bacon in his corner. Bacon wrote *The New Atlantis* and urged Elizabeth along.

The new colony was to be founded by the Virginia Company. Named ostensibly for England's Virgin Queen, it had less to do with her than with a virgin goddess older than Christianity. The flag of the state of Virginia shows the goddess Athena (known as Minerva to the Romans) holding a sword and spear and standing with one foot on the chest of her vanquished enemy. Athena, the goddess of Wisdom, was nicknamed the Spear-Shaker, a war goddess like Poseidon the Earth-Shaker.

Even operating under the permission of the queen, Bacon and others envisioned a world where monarchy and religion had no power. While other adventurers and merchants joined the bandwagon, colonization for Dee and Bacon was a divine mission. Bacon's writings on the subject of such an Arcadian paradise were a long held theme in war-torn Europe. To keep the queen as his patron, he wrote under the name of a butcher's apprentice, William Shakespeare.

While this might come as news to many, the Bacon-as-Shakespeare controversy is centuries old. The mystery of how an illiterate butcher's apprentice could have written on so many subjects—from law to science, medicine, and history—without the advantage of ever having owned a book has led many to suspect that he served as a "beard" for someone else.

Within the confines of a brief article, it is impossible to cover this subject fairly, but suffice it to say that four hundred books have been written on the topic; authors have included Benjamin Disraeli and Walt Whitman.

The original Shakespearean manuscripts, it is said, as well as some Bacon texts, were brought to America. Francis Bacon didn't survive long enough to enjoy the lands granted to him, but his family was well represented. However, in 1676, the Bacon family found itself at odds with Virginia's government. Virginia was, after all, a royal colony and Bacon represented an anti-government philosophy.

In the year of Bacon's Rebellion, as the history books recall, the contents under the Jamestown Church were moved and placed in a ten- by ten-foot vault twenty feet below the tower of the Bruton Parish Church in Williamsburg. Nevertheless, despite the efforts—legal and borderline illegal—of modern researchers and other groups, the secrets of the vault remain secure. At least for now.

THE KNIGHTS OF THE GOLDEN CIRCLE

It is over a century since an impoverished parish priest in Rennes-le-Château, France, tracked clues to an astonishing amount of money (a case made famous by the the books *Holy Blood, Holy Grail* and *The Da Vinci Code*) but much more recently, American treasure hunters have followed signs and symbols to caches of money hidden across the South and even in the West. National treasure? Not exactly, as the stashes were part of a plan to keep the Confederacy alive during, and even after, Lee surrendered at Appomattox.

Researchers Warren Getler and Bob Brewer describe a series of esoteric graffiti that include reference to biblical passages, dates, and coded letters, all serving to signal the way to secret stashes. The small hoards were buried by groups of Masons and by the Knights of the Golden Circle, a group whose members were often recruited through Masonic lodges.

HIDDEN IN PLAIN SIGHT

Although *National Treasure* was confined to two hours, the film did manage to make references to some deeper secrets. On the desk of one of its characters, Abigail Chase, is David Ovason's book, *The Secret Architecture of Our Nation's Capital.* While it is known that the city of Washington was laid out according to Masonic geometry, Ovason points out that there are numerous zodiacs built into both the plan of the city and many of its buildings.

One of the most intriguing clues in *National Treasure* is found on the back of the one-hundred-dollar bill. The clock tower points to a certain time of day, indicating its shadow will give the next direction. Here the movie makes a mistake. The treasure hunters had first thought they missed the critical moment, and then figured daylight savings time meant they were just coming up on the moment. Daylight savings time, however, had been proposed by Franklin, but was not yet in effect when Independence Hall was built.

The meaning of that critical time remains a secret.

22 Bacon, Shakespeare, and the Spear of Athena

Occult Origins of England's Role in the New World

Steven Sora

William Shakespeare, we are told, was born of illiterate parents, educated only through grade school, and apprenticed as a butcher's boy. Five years after he got married, saddled with three children, he decided to leave his family and hometown for London. Once in the great city, he began writing plays, and joined an established acting company that would perform them. His plays displayed knowledge of English, French, Greek, and Roman history, legal and medical principles, military and naval terms, falconry, horsemanship, and terms used only on the campus at Cambridge. In short, the plays exhibited everything outside of his realm of experience.

After a long career, he headed home, where he put the sixth and last signature of his life on his will. His will left household items, including a bed, but no books, and—notably—no folio of work. His death received no notice either in Stratford or in London until years later.

Writers are generally voracious readers, book lovers, diary keepers, and keepers of correspondence; the actual individual known as William Shakespeare, however, was the opposite. He most likely couldn't read or write, never owned a book, and never kept a diary, and it wasn't until long after his death that anyone got the idea to celebrate "the playwright." It was also years after his death that a "folio" of his work was put together. This was not an original folio, as none of those is known to exist.

Certainly the original plays were written, and copied, yet none has ever surfaced. With such a large body of work, this is suspicious, to say the least.

Trying to put William Shakespeare in the role of the writer of his plays was and is impossible, and soon the effort attracted detractors—Walt Whitman, Mark Twain, John Greenleaf Whittier, Benjamin Disraeli, and Ralph Waldo Emerson among them—who believed Shakespeare himself could *not* have been the author.

The man believed to be the bard was born in 1564. Queen Elizabeth I had been on the throne since January 15, 1559, and ruled with a capricious but iron hand. On a whim she could arrest or execute anyone, from her court to her countryside. Her court included Sir Francis Bacon, born in 1561; Christopher Marlowe, born in 1564; Edward de Vere, the earl of Oxford, born in 1550; and Henry Wriothesley, the earl of Southampton, born in 1573. It was a full-time job keeping Elizabeth happy. Sir Walter Raleigh was sent to the Tower for impregnating one of her ladies-in-waiting. The earl of Essex was punished for getting married a second time, and for his role in putting on the play *Richard II* was beheaded. Her physician, Ruy Lopez, was suspected of plotting against her and was drawn and quartered.

Speaking freely had its price.

None of William Shakespeare's plays included his name until 1598 and beyond. If producing *Richard II* was treason, then why was the writer allowed to go unpunished? It may have been that Essex was actually considered the author. Edward de Vere, earl of Oxford, was also a candidate. He wrote plays, owned a theater, and had been to Italy. Oxford, some believe, faked his death on June 24, 1604. It was the feast day of St. John the Baptist, a sort of patron saint of esoteric knowledge. James I had eight Shakespearean plays performed as a tribute to Oxford.

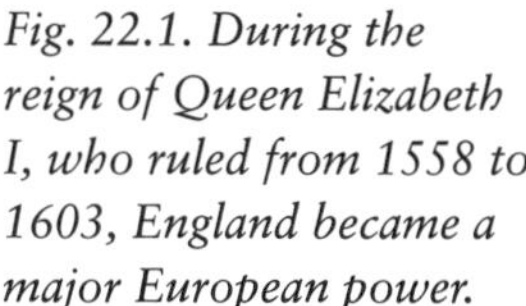

Fig. 22.1. During the reign of Queen Elizabeth I, who ruled from 1558 to 1603, England became a major European power.

While both Essex and Oxford are suitable candidates to have been the writer of the plays attributed to Shakespeare, with education and worldly knowledge, the most common candidate for the Bard's works is Sir Francis Bacon.

Although the prolific Bacon could not have written *Richard II* without fear of the chopping block, he did have the requisite knowledge attributed to the young butcher's apprentice. Bacon had studied at Cambridge, studied law at

Fig. 22.2. The Globe Theatre in London, where many of Shakespeare's works were performed.

Grey's Inn, and was fluent in languages. He loved cryptology and had invented his own sophisticated code. He was also, many believe, a quiet homosexual who surrounded himself with handsome young men. One of these was Henry Wriothesley.

In 1592, the first recorded Shakespearean play was dedicated to Henry. The sonnets, in which the poet speaks of his love for the youth, were also dedicated to Wriothesley. Coincidentally, it was in 1592 that Henry Wriothesley became a patron of William Shakespeare. More likely this is the year that Shakespeare and Bacon made a deal. In 1592, Shakespeare received a large sum of money and bought the second largest house in Stratford. He bought other property as well, traded commodities, was party to lawsuits, and collected taxes.

A deal, if made by Shakespeare and Bacon, served them both well. Sir Francis Bacon avoided the executioner's ax and William Shakespeare became a landowner. The two men could not have been more different. Bacon was educated, worldly, sensitive, and genuinely interested in changing his world. Shakespeare could barely sign his name, was brash and greedy, and had few qualms about leaving his wife and children. A typical Stratford man might have a working vocabulary of 400 words, while a Cambridge graduate might have one of 4,000 words. The author of the works attributed to Shakespeare had a vocabulary of 20,000 words.

A POET BY ANY OTHER NAME

Why did Bacon pick Shakespeare to "front" his work?

When Bacon studied at Grey's Inn, he was the driving force behind an invisible knighthood called the Order of the Helmet. The members dedicated themselves to an ancient goddess, the Pallas Athena, who was depicted with helmet and spear. Her epithet was the Shaker-of-the-Spear. Meeting a country bumpkin by the name of Shake-spear might have seemed almost divine intervention. Bacon's motto was *Occulta Veritas Tempore Patet,* meaning "Hidden truth comes to light in time." In the last five years of his life, notably after the death of Queen Elizabeth, he could be more open in his writings.

Notably, he penned his *New Atlantis,* searching for a peaceful world where royalty ruled as a result of wisdom. Under King James, he also translated what would be called the King James Version of the Bible. In Psalm 46, the forty-sixth word down from the first verse is "Shake"; the forty-sixth word from the end is "Spear." He also authored the *Sylva Sylvarum,* discussing numerous scientific experiments, including one to preserve documents in mercury and another on creating artificial springs.

Fig. 22.3. Monument to Sir Francis Bacon above his tomb at St. Michael's, St. Albans, England.

FINDING AVALON

England was a latecomer in the rush to colonize the Americas. It was Elizabeth's astrologer, Dr. John Dee, who convinced her she had rights in the New World. While the illustrious John Dee would serve well as a model for a character in *The Hobbit,* he did convince Elizabeth of the need for a strong navy, as well as of the "fact" that Arthur's Avalon was indeed America. Intellectually, she lived vicariously through her wizard. Dee, a magician and alchemist, wrote about Rosicrucianism and navigation. His estate held 4,000 books and a "magic mirror" to tell the future.

The queen's adventurous side was lived through the likes of Sir Francis Drake and Sir Walter Raleigh. She sent them to conquer lands, steal treasures, and explore the seven seas.

When Elizabeth's life and reign expired, Bacon's status was elevated. He was able to convince King James to become more serious in efforts across the ocean. Bacon made sure that he and his circle were granted lands in the New World. They shared grants in Newfoundland and Nova Scotia, gaining additional powers as part of the Virginia Company. With Bacon as lord chancellor, the Jamestown settlement was establsihed in Virginia. Named for the "Virgin" queen Elizabeth, the seal of Virginia that has survived to modern times depicts Athena. She is the ruler, complete with helmet and spear, of the land where her wisdom will prevail.

BACON'S NEW ATLANTIS?

There was a great deal of secrecy in the settling of the colonies, which would also serve as the repository of knowledge for those secret societies that grew around Bacon. In an era when Copernicus was afraid to publish his theory that the Sun was the center of the universe, Bacon and his circle kept much in secret. The original texts of the plays attributed to Shakespeare might have been just a small part of a secret Masonic/Rosicrucian library.

In 1911, Dr. Orville W. Owen, who had spent many years decoding Bacon's ciphers, mounted an expedition to England. Under the Wye River he expected to find a secret Masonic/Rosicrucian library. A secret vault was found. Unfortunately, it was empty. Obviously, someone had stopped the river's flow long enough to build the vault, and conceivably fill it and empty it again. Employing such hydraulic abilities was nothing new. The body of King Lear had similarly been placed in a vault under the river Soar. The body of Attila was safe under the Busento River in Italy.

Nine years later, Burrell Ruth, who had followed Dr. Owen's work, believed the original folio of Bacon's Shakespearean works had been moved to Nova Scotia in the New World. In Mahone Bay, underwater booby traps had been placed by builders adept in the science of hydraulics. Mercury flasks had been found on Oak Island, where the longest treasure search in history was under way.

A search has now been in progress for two hundred years.

More recently, the owners of half of Oak Island have broadened their search to other islands in the bay. Tunnels are believed to connect two or more islands, and a spiral staircase leading underground is said to be on an island near Oak Island.

NATIONAL TREASURE

The Virginia Company, established in 1606, was made up of Bacon and his inner circle. Interestingly enough, it included both Virginia and a new colony called Bermuda. The first mention of Bermuda is in *The Tempest,* a Shakespearean play about a shipwreck on a small island.

The Virginia Company would also engineer a place to house its own secrets. Among the first jobs completed at Jamestown was the construction of an underground repository and, over this vault, the first Jamestown church. The vault was used to house documents brought over in 1635.

In 1676, the documents were moved to a new vault located in Bruton parish. The area was known as the Middletown Plantation and later would become Williamsburg. A brick church was built, and twenty feet underneath the vault was placed. This church did not survive, and a newer church, which exists today, is on the Duke of Gloucester Street; it's both a tourist attraction and an Episcopal church. Somewhere under the churchyard lies a spiral staircase leading to the vault.

In the 1920s, the Rockefeller Foundation bought much of Williamsburg to create a tourist destination. Oddly enough, it also bought Stratford-on-Avon, which had already become such a destination. The actual site of the Bruton vault was owned by the Anglican Church and could not be bought; instead it was given to the U.S. government.

In recent years, a group called Sir Francis Bacon's Sages of the Seventh Seal has sought permission to excavate the site, particularly under a pyramid-shaped structure known as the Bray monument. Fletcher Richman, a Baconian scholar, believes that beneath the monument, accessed by the underground spiral stairway, is a vault containing the writings of Bacon and others, writings that may have significant implications for the future. Permission so far has not been granted. Richman says this is just one of many hidden libraries.

For now, they remain hidden.

23 Unlocking the Shakespeare Riddle

New Light on a Perennial Mystery—Was the Bard Really the Drunken Actor from Stratford-on-Avon or Someone Else?

Virginia Fellows

In February of 1999, just in time to pick up a handful of Oscars, a surprising film appeared on wide screens everywhere. Miramax's *Shakespeare in Love* did what the literary world had not been able to do for some time—it brought the cult of Shakespeare back into the limelight. Although certainly never obliterated, the popularity of the world's greatest dramatist had been on a downward spiral since the early twentieth century.

The young of today have, to a degree, relegated the wonderful plays to a category of "don't-bother-to-read" classics. They knew little and cared less about the genius who wrote them until handsome young Joseph Fiennes appeared in the ever-powerful medium as a composite character of the youthful playwright and his most favored creation, Hamlet. Screenwriters Tom Stoppard and Marc Norman had done the unimaginable—they had brought Shakespeare into focus again. In the process, they won the award for Best Original Screenplay from the Writers Guild of America. All of a sudden "the bard is back" became the topic of the day!

What would the author of the plays have thought about all this? Those who consider Shakespeare a man of mystery due to the scarcity of facts about his life can only guess at an answer. Those who feel better acquainted with the true identity of the author can say with conviction: "He would have been delighted!" Obviously the plays were written to entertain audiences, and, with the release of the movie, that was now happening on a broader scale. But it was also the intent of the playwright to instill strong visual representations of the whole range of human psychological errors into sluggish minds.

The hope in doing so was that recognizing wrong attitudes would help to raise consciousness a notch. "Shakespeare is able to examine the depths of our souls and bring to the surface issues which, on some level, we must deal with," says one discerning modern commentator. A third but little recognized purpose of the author was to "conceal at the same time as reveal" one of the most poignant and tragic stories ever told, the story of his own personal life.

That the works of Shakespeare were intended as a cover text for a cipher under which the secret history of the author could be hidden has long been known by a few researchers. Now, in this millennial time of unexpected exposures, the real story can be told without ridicule.

Would this mysterious author have approved of the choice of Joseph Fiennes as the lead? The screenplay uses the clever device of allowing the movie character to quote himself as Shakespeare/Hamlet. When the true story of the playwright is accepted, one is able to imagine a young Fiennes as a very recognizable Hamlet, the prototype of the youthful author himself—handsome, sensitive, slightly fantastic, aristocratic, and troubled. It is in this way that the secret history reveals him—a true prince of England, not of Denmark.

It is not presumptuous to assert the intents and motives of the famous author when one learns actual details of his personal life—details that are certainly not known about the uneducated peasant from an obscure and drab country village: Stratford-on-Avon. Mainstream scholars strive to come up with a believable biography for the country lad, son of an illiterate family by the name of Shaksper (or Shakstpur, or Shagster—there is a variety of spellings of such a name). But they are attempting the impossible.

There is no indication that their candidate ever received more than a year or two's education in a one-room, one-master country school. Nor can it be shown that he ever had an acquaintance with French, Latin, or Italian literature not yet translated into English, or an understanding of recently discovered Latin and Greek classics, or even a speaking acquaintance with the law, medicine, poetry, the aristocracy, the affairs of the British and French courts, or any of the other myriad topics that are displayed in the dramas.

Recognizing the dichotomy between the works and the supposed author, certain researchers have been convinced that the immortal blank verse could not have been written by country-bred Will Shaksper. Ralph Waldo Emerson wrote, "Shakespeare is a voice merely; who and what he was that sang, we know not." Henry James said, "I am haunted by the conviction that Shakespeare is the biggest fraud ever practiced on a patient world." Samuel Coleridge asked, "Does God choose idiots to reveal divine truths?" And more recently, the Yale Research Society has agreed unanimously that the plays could not have been written by the Stratford man.

So where does one find an alternative? One hundred and fifty years after the

Fig. 23.1. Martin Droeshout's engraving of William Shakespeare, which adorned the first folio edition of his works (1623).

1623 publication of the first folio, a clergyman from a village neighboring Stratford, James Wilmot, spent many hours in and around Stratford in what turned out to be a fruitless search for information about the great playwright. Reluctantly he had to admit that not one single item could be found to indicate that a poetic genius of any kind had ever lived in the village. Few villagers could even write their own name (both Shaksper's wife and his two daughters among them); there were no books that could have been used by the author; and not one inhabitant remembered even a small detail or anecdote about the life of so famous a name. The rector concluded that the only man in England of the time who was qualified to write such works was the brilliant, superbly educated philosopher, psychologist, and lawyer Sir Francis Bacon. Wilmot confessed his secret only to the Ipswich Literary Society, demanding that they keep it mum. So faithfully did they keep the secret that it wasn't discovered until the early part of the twentieth century in their private files.

Since then, numerous contenders have been named for the honor of authorship—Christopher Marlowe, Herbert Spenser, various British lords such as Derby, Essex, Pembroke, Rutland, and Oxford—even Queen Elizabeth herself. Francis Bacon has long been the undisputed favorite, strongly promoted by the Baconian Society, a London group founded in 1876. The society has published over 150 periodical journals containing hundreds of articles filled with their careful research.

Currently, however, it is Edward De Vere, the seventeenth Lord Oxford, who has been receiving much attention as a likely candidate. Such recent and worthy researchers as Charleton Ogburn and Charles Vere Lord Burford, an Oxford descendant, are pushing the earl to the top of the list.

Lord Oxford is not an unlikely choice; he was a highly educated aristocrat, an insider in Elizabethan court affairs, and a multilingual and classical scholar conversant with works that had not yet been translated into English. He was also a sportsman well acquainted with falconry, horsemanship, and other activities never engaged in by the peasantry but talked about in the plays. Oxford was a European traveler, a military expert, and a participant in every cultural upper-class privilege of the British aristocracy. He was even a protégé of Elizabeth's illustrious secretary Lord Burghley, generally recognized as the prototype for the pedant Polonius in *Hamlet.*

Francis Bacon, however, as well as Lord Oxford, qualifies under all of these terms with even more impressive credentials, as it turns out. His supposed mother, Lady Ann Bacon, was even the sister-in-law of Burghley.

There are a few stumbling blocks for Oxfordians—the earl died in 1604, twenty years before the bulk of the Shakespearean dramas were published or could even have been written. Their only defense is that he must have begun some of the plays and left them to be finished by someone else. Of necessity, they deny that the great play *The Tempest* was part of the canon since it could not have been written at that early date. Another major problem is that the poetry known to have been written by Oxford is dull and uninspired, in no way to be compared with the brilliant verse of the dramas.

Then there is the consideration that the young lord's character—demonstrably wild, wayward, quarrelsome, and irresponsible—is not in compliance with the philosophy and moral stature that is so obviously portrayed in the plays. Of Bacon, contemporaries said kinder things. "All who were great and good loved him," said his chaplain Rawley. "I loved him this side of idolatry," said Ben Jonson. "He was the ornament of his age," said others.

Such complications are readily overlooked by Oxfordians and it is important to realize that Oxford was one of the poetically minded young dandies who joined with the much younger Bacon in the exclusive and prestigious literary group known as the Areopagus Society. The lives of the two men were frequently intertwined. There is, however, one major circumstance that gives Bacon an undeniable lead over Oxford, the one concrete proof of authorship that cannot be disputed. This is the discovery of a secret story hidden in the very body of the plays—a so-called code or cipher system that the original playwright had painstakingly concealed in the actual writing of the plays—to reveal truths that he dared not speak aloud.

As fantastic as it sounds, an entire secret biography of the true author, Francis Bacon, had been inserted at the time of the original writing of the plays. There is no possibility that this could have been done by anyone except the original author himself.

At the end of the nineteenth century, a doctor from Detroit by the name of Orville Owen made a startling find. A great fan of Shakespeare, he had memorized every word of his plays. After becoming thoroughly familiar with the dramas, he found some very strange discrepancies that he could not explain.

Years of close study and experimentation revealed an amazing thing—all the plays of Shakespeare contained an inner play, an actual play-within-a-play, a device that the author had also been fond of using in the outer works. Certain phrases from the originals were marked by special keywords to be lifted and arranged in a different context that told an entirely different story.

After tedious scrutiny and study, Owen learned that the inner play, or the cipher story, was actually a personal and totally unexpected biography of the true author of the plays, Sir Francis Bacon. The puzzle was, why had Bacon used this method to leave his incredible life story to posterity? The answer was that his life depended on secrecy. The truth of his birth was a great secret of state. His true name was not Francis Bacon but rather Francis Tudor—the true child of Elizabeth the Queen of England and her lover, the dashing Robert Dudley, Lord Leicester!

The two had carried on a lively romance, which has been well documented historically. Not so well known was that a bigamous marriage had been performed by a monk while they were both prisoners in the Tower of London. (Leicester was already married but his wife was conveniently and shortly thereafter killed by a mysterious fall from her balcony.) Elizabeth subsequently refused all suitors for her hand although she delighted in portraying herself as the chaste Virgin Queen wedded only to her beloved country.

Careful scrutiny of historical records of the time reveal many hints as to the possibility of this situation, although it would have been considered treasonous and punishable by death to divulge them. The first child of this union was given to the queen's matron of honor—the pious Lady Ann Bacon and her honorable husband Sir Nicholas Bacon—to raise. A pact was made between Lady Ann and the queen promising that the truth would never be revealed. Elizabeth herself dramatically broke that pact at the time Francis was sixteen years old, as is revealed in the secret account.

A second son born to this odd couple was given to the Devereux family to raise. This was the fascinating young Lord Essex whom history sees as having been Elizabeth's strange young lover. Much history is clarified when it is realized that the odd relationship was that of a mother with her adored but rebellious child rather than that of an aging queen and a glamorous youthful courtier.

There were many tragic events concerned with Elizabeth's story and her cat-and-mouse treatment of her two sons, initially promising to acknowledge them, then threatening their very lives. Essex cracked under the strain, tried to take over the throne for himself, and was beheaded in the Tower. Francis relieved the nearly unbearable strain by determining to leave a true account to the world. He knew, however, that to reveal the truth would have meant a death sentence. Inspired by a vision in a dream, he conceived of the device of the cipher to tell his story.

As Owen went on decoding the Word Cipher, as Bacon had named it, he hired two women to assist him in the tedious work. One of the assistants, Elizabeth Wells Gallup, a Detroit school superintendent, found as she proceeded that a second cipher was also included. The second cipher was based on the so-called bi-literal system, which Bacon had carefully explained and demonstrated in his own acknowledged work *The Advancement of Learning.* It is an alphabet based on various arrangements of five letters or units, much as the Morse code is. Gallup pored over these works until she was almost blinded, but what she discovered was amazing. She was reading, in prose, the exact same story that Owen had discovered written in the Shakespearian blank verse of the Word Cipher. They corroborated each other exactly.

Dr. Owen, following instructions given in the cipher itself, constructed what he called his Cipher Wheel. It is an awkward and huge contraption consisting of two large wooden wheels with over a hundred feet of linen stretched between them in such a a way that they could be rolled back and forth on the principle of a modern reel-to-reel tape player or an ancient parchment scroll.

Onto this linen are glued pages cut from books of plays—the scroll can be rolled back and forth for easier viewing. According to certain clues and keywords, Owen would mark the relevant passages and read them off to his assistants, who would then type them onto slips of paper. Owen would then place them in correct order, thus revealing the secret history.

Both Owen and Gallup published their cipher findings in book form and both, needless to say, were unmercifully ridiculed. Although now out of print, all these books are still available in various public and university libraries and used-book stores.

Through a set of remarkable coincidences, perhaps what Jung would call "synchronicity," this strange machine came into my possession from the hands of its most recent owner, Elizabeth Hovhannes, a well-known American musician. It is now stored in a safe place and is being examined by alert young students who are enthusiastically attempting to duplicate the cipher findings through the use of a computer.

Not surprisingly, the cipher story has not received universal acceptance; mainstream scholars think that it just couldn't be true—ergo, it isn't true. They see the books and conclude that they were concocted by Owen and Gallup themselves.

Before his death, Dr. Owen advertised an offer to demonstrate his method of deciphering to any and all who would listen. Few came, but in the early 1900s Detroit's leading newspaper, *The Tribune,* sent a reporter to one of Owen's lectures. The paper then published a scathing review ridiculing the process. Owen immediately got a judgment for ten thousand dollars and an injunction against the paper, which prohibited publication of further issues. He offered to demonstrate his findings to whomever the paper chose to examine them. A Miss Sherman, *The Tribune*'s best arts critic, was sent and Owen went to work. He showed her his method of deciphering, gave her the relevant materials, and left her alone in his office to experiment. When he returned, she had followed his instructions and had come up with the identical passages that he had found.

An apology appeared on the newspaper's front page and the injunction was lifted. Others were able to duplicate Dr. Owen's findings, but still others refused to accept them, their only argument being that it must have been faked. However, if Owen and Gallup had been so creative as to insert the cipher into the plays, both would have had minds more brilliant than the author himself—two new rivals for the genius of Shakespeare!

It is time now for some of the anomalies of earlier centuries to be put right. One of these anomalies must be a resolution of the Shakespeare mystery, revealing the true story of the brilliant Francis Bacon and granting him full credit for the service he performed.

As a charter member of the Virginia Company and a colonizer of America, as an active promoter of Freemasonry and Rosicrucianism, as an advocate of experimental science, and as an author working under the pseudonym of William Shakespeare, he was of prime importance in preparing for the incoming age of enlightenment. But, as he often wrote of himself: "Mihi silentio"—"Of myself I am silent." "To dare; to do; to be silent." But there is no longer the need for silence. It is time for truth to be known.

Incredibly, denied acknowledgment by a jealous and selfish mother, Bacon was forced to carry on his brilliant work undercover. He left his amazing life story to the offhand chance that some alert student would one day discover the secret and reveal the truth of a man whose credit is long overdue. As he frequently said in cipher: "Truth is not dead; it merely sleepeth."

24 Francis Bacon and the Sign of the Double A

Did the Great Scholar and Statesman Leave Cryptic Clues for Future Generations to Uncover?

William Henry

The greatest bard of all, William Shakespeare, is closely connected to an esoteric mystery that is as obscure as its solution is profoundly illuminating: the cryptic AA symbolism.

Facsimiles published during Shakespeare's time of the *Sonnets, Hamlet,* and *Richard III* all bear the light A and the dark **A** on their title pages. Why? What does it mean? As seekers of the mysteries, what's in it for us if we divert the river of our precious consciousness to pore over this symbolism? The answer will probably surprise you. It also will connect the dots between some of the greatest literary works in history.

For instance, the A**A** also appears in the King James Bible (1611). Some symbolists note that the A is closely associated with God, the Trinity. The AA in this view are the Greek letters alpha (A) and omega (Ω), signifying the first and the last.

One reason both the works of Shakespeare and the King James Bible bear the A**A** symbolism is that, it is claimed with persistent controversy, Sir Francis Bacon (1561–1626) covertly guided these works to fruition. Some believe the titled, gentleman/genius Bacon, who is the shaper of modern Free-

Fig. 24.1. The "Bacon Double A": two A's, one light and one dark.

masonry and the author of *New Atlantis,* among other works, is the author of the works attributed to Shakespeare.

Fig. 24.2. A period portrait of Sir Francis Bacon (1561–1626).

William Henry Smith, whose *Bacon and Shakespeare* was published in 1856, launched the Bacon-is-Shakespeare theory. Whether or not Bacon authored the Shakespearean works, he is considered an illumined mind gifted with prophetic vision. He seemed to be able to see through time, describing inventions of great imagination such as a pillar of light at the center of the New Atlantis. A true initiate, he hid his secrets in cryptograms buried in works his shop produced—many bearing the **AA** headpiece—including books written by other authors under his direction. Five rival publishers independently produced the works of Shakespeare bearing this headpiece, lending credence to the idea that this headpiece is, indeed, the signature of a hidden author: Francis Bacon.

Bacon had his own wood blocks bearing devices or emblems—some of which were his own design—and every book produced under his direction, whether or not written by him, was marked with one or more of these logos. Authors he published include Edmund Spenser, Christopher Marlowe, Shakespeare, and Walter Raleigh.

As he was a master of ciphers and symbols, Baconians say he used the works he printed to send messages or to pass on teachings. Many would read through these works, Bacon hoped, and knowledge would be increased, fulfilling the End Time prophecy of Daniel.

BACON AND ENGLISH

Above all, Bacon's greatest code of all may be the English language. When Bacon was born, English as a literary language did not exist. But during his life, he succeeded in making the English language the greatest piece of software possessed by mankind. It is the human brain's most wonderful tool.

As a boy, Bacon witnessed the progress of French—through the efforts of a group of poets dubbed "La Pleiade" (the Seven) in Paris—transformed from a barbarous tongue, blossoming into a literary language. Bacon was thus inspired to create a language capable of expressing his highest thoughts.

The English language, it is widely acknowledged, owes a profound debt to the English translation of the King James Bible (which, some believe, God enabled and Bacon guided) and upon the plays of Shakespeare. There are about 22,000 different English words in the plays, of which 7,000 are *new words,* introduced—as Murray's Oxford Dictionary tells us—into the language for the first time.

In fact, it may be stated, "God speaks *English!* (not French, German, Italian, Greek, Hebrew)," one of Bacon's triumphant messages of the KJV and the flood of English literature that roared from the Elizabethan Renaissance.

As I discussed in my book *The Language of the Birds,* according to the French alchemist "Fulcanelli," interpreting ancient names and place-names in the English language reveals original, hidden meanings. This code equates words that sound alike in different languages, connecting word concepts by sound *in English.* These language connections reveal astonishing literary and historical synchronicities, or meaningful coincidences, that point to the interconnectedness of all creation, which Bacon's works are meant to show us.

A good example of how Bacon used this literary technique to convey information is his pen name: Shake-Speare.

THE SPEAR-SHAKER

The name Shake-Spear is a reference to the Greek goddess of war and wisdom, Pallas Athena, the Spear Shaker. The mother of the Athenians, she was worshipped as the Holy Virgin in the Parthenon, where she stood with her phallic Pallas spear or rod with a serpent coiled at her feet. The Athenians called themselves "serpent born."

According to Bacon authority Peter Dawkins, A-thena and A-pollo (the god of the Sun) stand for the Double A sign, or the Double A.

With this understanding, we are deep into the code of Bacon. If we persist, says Harold Bayley, an early-twentieth-century symbolist and author of *The Tragedy of Sir Francis Bacon,* we'll uncover an El Dorado of information awaiting disentombment from Elizabethan Renaissance literature . . . and perhaps elsewhere.

For the AA's usage and possible meaning, I have found, is traced well beyond Greek myth to ancient Sumeria and Egypt, where it was used as a cabalistic signature. Athena is a remake of the Egyptian Isis and the Sumero-Babylonian Is-Tara, the goddess of love, both of whom shook spears or rods upon which a serpent was coiled and raised—à la Moses lifting the healing serpent. As in the story of Moses, the serpent symbolizes wisdom, the conduit to the Light, and the Messiah.

BACON AND THE CATHARS

Another node in the web of the AA symbolism is found closer to Bacon's home and era. While living in Europe, Bacon was initiated into the mysteries of the Order of the Knights Templar and the true secret of Masonic origin. His connection with them may be traced through his father, Sir Nicholas Bacon, a descendant, according to S. Baring Gould, of Jacques de Molay—"the last Templar"—who was martyred for his faith by Philip of France in 1314.

The following is from Mather Walker on the subject.

> While Francis (= *Free,* from pri, *pure*) was in France during the period from 1576 through 1579, a number of works were published exhibiting his AA handiwork. The AA also appeared in Alciato's *Emblems,* "the little book" of riddles by the Italian genius Andrae Alciato (1492–1520) first published in 1531. Classified as a collection of religious love emblems or symbols, Alciato's emblems tell the story of the religion of love. This was the religion of AMOR (French for "love") of the Cathars of Southern France, who were associates of the Templars and the victims of the first European genocide.

The Cathars called themselves the Pure Ones. Interestingly, the English word *free* is from the Sanskrit root *pri,* meaning "to love," and so the root meaning of free = love. The Cathar church of love claimed possession of Jesus's secrets for making over an ordinary human (whom the Cathars regarded as prisoners of Rex Mundi and Roma) into a Pure One or a Free Man. Free, that is, from the grip of the Church of Roma.

Harold Bayley also investigated these marks. He bequeathed to the future his enormously intriguing study *The Lost Language of Symbolism,* one of the finest collections of religious papermarks ever assembled.

Bayley connected the Cathar's secret teaching of Jesus to a symbol system traced to the pre-Christian era. The Cathars believed that "Jesus Christ"—called Alpha and Omega by Christians—had no human existence, but rather was the personification of the abstract qualities of Truth, which were hidden from the masses. Their emblems encoded the sacred teachings—the abstract science—of the hidden Christ, AA.

A jealous Catholic Church attempted to exterminate the innocent Cathars, eradicate their revolutionary secret teaching during the horrific Albigensian Crusade of 1200–1244, and buttress its competing brand of Christology.

After the attempted genocide of these "heretics," surviving Cathars turned to papermaking. Fearing further persecution—they were only a few murders away from extinction—the Cathars made use of coded symbols as a means to convey their secret religious teachings. They embedded these symbols of "pure Christianity" as watermarks in the paper they manufactured.

Turning to Bayley, we find the AA of Bacon's works are answers to the Cathar emblems of the holy pillar (or *sacred cross*) at the holy mountain. We notice that the Cathar symbolists put two A's together to form the twin-peaked holy mountain or the holy M. The cross or Ladder to God emerges from between the two A's. In this way the mysteries of the letters *A* and the *M* are joined to the mysteries of the crucifixion.

I have traced the source of this double A = M symbolism to the Babylonian sun god Shem or Shamash (meaning "heavenly"), who was portrayed on cylinder seals rising through an M-shaped gate from the underworld with his rod in hand. The sun god Shamash enters Earth through a gateway composed of two A-shaped cones with a branch, wand, or ray of light in his hand. Note that two cherubim guard the gate, as in the gate of Eden story.

In my view, the Cathar emblem and the ancient seal tell the same story: The Son of God rises through the AA or M-shaped gate.

The first Christians, in particular the Gnostics of Alexandria, Egypt, were highly influenced by the mythology of Shem. *The Paraphrase of Shem* is part of the lost Nag Hammadi Library hidden by the Gnostics when they were ruthlessly persecuted by Rome. It tells of Shem's ascent into the heavenly realms and is based upon the Sumerian story of the savior, also called Shem, who arose and crossed into the heavens through the AA or M-shaped gate.

From this, it is easy to see that Bacon's use of the AA indicated a continuous chain of usage from Cathar, Gnostic Christian, Egyptian, and Sumerian symbol systems.

As we shall investigate now, the AA symbolism is meant to connect the works bearing this mark to the ancient myths of the gate of the gods and the means to safely pass through the underworld of the gods.

BACON AND HIS SECRET SOCIETY

Vital data concerning Bacon's connection to the gateway to the gods, vis-à-vis the AA headpiece symbolism, is found in Mrs. Henry Pott's *Francis Bacon and His Secret Society* (1911). She comments that Bacon and his society, the Rosicrucians (Rose ✠), expanded and diversified the Cathar papermarks.

Three papermarks that Mrs. Pott found were especially associated with

Francis Bacon and his brother Anthony. They are to be seen embedded throughout the printed books ascribed to Francis. These marks are the double candlesticks; the bunch or cluster of grapes; and the pot or jug.

Mrs. Pott notes that few of Bacon's letters, and none of his acknowledged books, are without one of these marks. They are included because, like the AA headpiece, they point to him as their author or acknowledge the touch of his hand as a reviser or editor of the book.

I believe the double candlesticks may well be the AAs, the twin peaks (towers or pillars) through which the Son or Sun rises.

The cluster of grapes, says Mrs. Pott, signified to Bacon and his society the "fruit of true knowledge"—or Gnosis—which gathered in clusters. Bacon, says Mrs. Pott, worked the wine press, collecting his clusters (like Joshua, Numbers 13:23) and storing up the grapes' precious juice so that in due season, it might be poured upon other men's vessels.

The pot or vase contained the "heavenly juice" or "liquor of knowledge." In Cathar papermarks, pots and jugs are shown spewing bunches of grapes—the fruits of knowledge—and pearls—the dew of heaven—or *manna,* the pure food of the gods.

The manna, say the Hebrew scriptures, was collected at Sun's rise and stored in the Ark of the Covenant along with the golden pot and Aaron's rod that budded.

Now, the Egyptians, says Sir Laurence Gardner, called manna *mfkt.* It was a mysterious substance with phenomenal qualities that came from a hyperdimensional realm.

At Abydos—Egypt's oldest oracle—we find a depiction of a rod tended by two angels whose bodies form an M. A "head"—Gerald Massey says the Egyptians called it mfkt—"floats" on the rod. It belongs to the cow-headed goddess Hathor, who, we can more easily note here, peaks and speaks from between an M, the twin peaks, or the AA. Putting Massey's definition together with Gardner's reveals that the mfkt headpiece may be part of a utensil through which the goddess peaks or speaks: that is, utters oracles.

To the Egyptians, says Gardner, Hathor was representative of the Babylonian goddess Is-Tara. Her hair or headpiece symbol was shaped like the omega Ω. Hathor wears the same headpiece. Hathor, Athena, and Is-Tara are all the same goddess.

The reason these goddesses are so closely connected to the Omega is that they are one half of the Alpha and Omega. The Abydos rod, which is topped by a serpent, is an earlier variation of the rod of Moses and Is-Tara and the spear shaken by Athena.

It is the secret behind the AA headpiece: the Emblem of Abydos with the mfkt headpiece.

According to the Egyptian *Book of the Dead,* Abydos is the entrance to the Tuat, or underworld. One wonders if this is another term for the hyperdimensional realm from whence mfkt emerges.

Mythologist Barbara Walker notes that Apollo, the other half of the AA, is the Greek name for the Egyptian Apep, the serpent of darkness that guards the Tuat underworld and, in fact, is the personification of the underworld itself. In medieval alchemy, says Walker, the serpent Apep was confused with the serpent Ouroboros. Ouroboros could reveal the secret of the Philosopher's Stone, which Gardner notes is another term for mfkt. This is the stone of light, guarded by the dragon that grants entrance to the gate of the gods.

I'm not convinced the alchemists were mistaken. Strangely—or perhaps not—in English (the Bard's tongue) the AA is a pun on Two A or Tu A, the root of Tuat or Am-Tuat, the Egyptian word for the underworld.

The meaning of the AA symbolism on the headpiece of Bacon's works is now clear. It represents a rodlike utensil that opens the gate to the underworld. This is likely the pillar of light at the center of Bacon's *New Atlantis*. From these connections, it is reasonable to propose that Bacon (Shakespeare) was the oracle of the Elizabethan age. He was the holder of the magic rod that opened the underworld, or Spear Shaker.

PART FIVE

VISIONARIES AND ALCHEMISTS

25 The Nostradamus Perspective

Did a French Mystic from the Fifteenth Century Have Something to Tell the People of Today?

J. Douglas Kenyon

In the middle of the last millennium, the bubonic plague still ravaged Europe. Before it was done, the Black Death would kill fully one-quarter of the continent's inhabitants. But even in that darkest of times, not all hope was lost.

In France, an enlightened physician fought back, saving many lives with what author John Hogue calls "a mixture of cleanliness and vitamin C (rose pills)." Ironically, though, posterity would show little interest in the heroic healing contributions made by Michel de Nostradamus at that time. He is remembered, instead, mostly for his many obscure and complex prophecies of times to come. In *The Centuries,* begun in 1554, Nostradamus offered what was to be a ten-volume series, each consisting of one hundred four-line verses called quatrains, which purported to offer details of ages yet unborn.

Contrary to popular belief, Nostradamus was not a prophet of doom (at least not for our time). Although many of his prophecies were dire, he saw no end to the world before the eighty-sixth century. The quatrains have attracted millions, especially as great events have sprung seemingly, straight from his pages. Some argue that he predicted the French Revolution, Hitler's birth and rise to power, and the assassination of John F. Kennedy. The most recent Nostradamus revival comes on the heels of the September 11, 2001, attacks on the World Trade Center in New York City. The wide circulation of highly questionable "quatrains" attributed to Nostradamus and apparently describing the disaster has created something of a sensation.

According to a *USA Today* article written ninety days after the attack, "All things Nostradamus are suddenly 'in.'" Books and videos are flying off the shelves. Web search engines claim more searches for "Nostradamus" than for any other word in the last two years. Reuters even reported that "sex" had been knocked out of the number one position.

The phenomenon, says the *London Sunday Times,* is simple enough—

Tibet's sixteenth-century Leh Palace was an important stopover on trade routes along the Indus Valley between Tibet to the east and Kashmir to the west, and ultimately between India and China. In 1887, the Russian traveler Dr. Nicolas Notovitch claimed to have uncovered, in a monastery in Himas, ancient texts about the life of Jesus that suggest that Jesus discovered his divinity after undergoing spiritual training from Eastern sages.

Morning sunrise over the Dome of the Rock in Jerusalem. Jerusalem was invaded during the Crusades, and when it was finally captured in 1099, the Dome of the Rock was converted from an Islamic shrine to a Christian one and renamed Templum Domini (Temple of the Lord).

As with Mel Gibson's depiction of Jesus in the film *The Passion of the Christ,* the painting *The Entombment of Christ* (by Raphael) reinforces orthodox Church doctrine.

This chalice is based on a creation by Benvenuto Cellini (1500–1571), the noted Italian goldsmith. Some scholars argue that the famous cup of the Last Supper (the Grail Chalice) may have been carried by the Templar fleet that sailed secretly from La Rochelle, France, in 1307, to escape persecution by the French king and the Church.

Many similarities between Jesus and the ancient Egyptian god Osiris—shown here with Isis in this image from *The Egyptian Book of the Dead*—lead some to believe that much of Christian tradition is borrowed from ancient Egyptian sources.

In the distance lies the fortress of Masada on the banks of the Dead Sea, where, in A.D. 70, Jewish Zealots committed mass suicide rather than surrender to attacking Romans. Ancient copies of Dead Sea Scrolls found at Masada link this community with the Maccabean Revolt of the first century A.D., contradicting the long-held notion of a pacifist Essene community at Qumran.

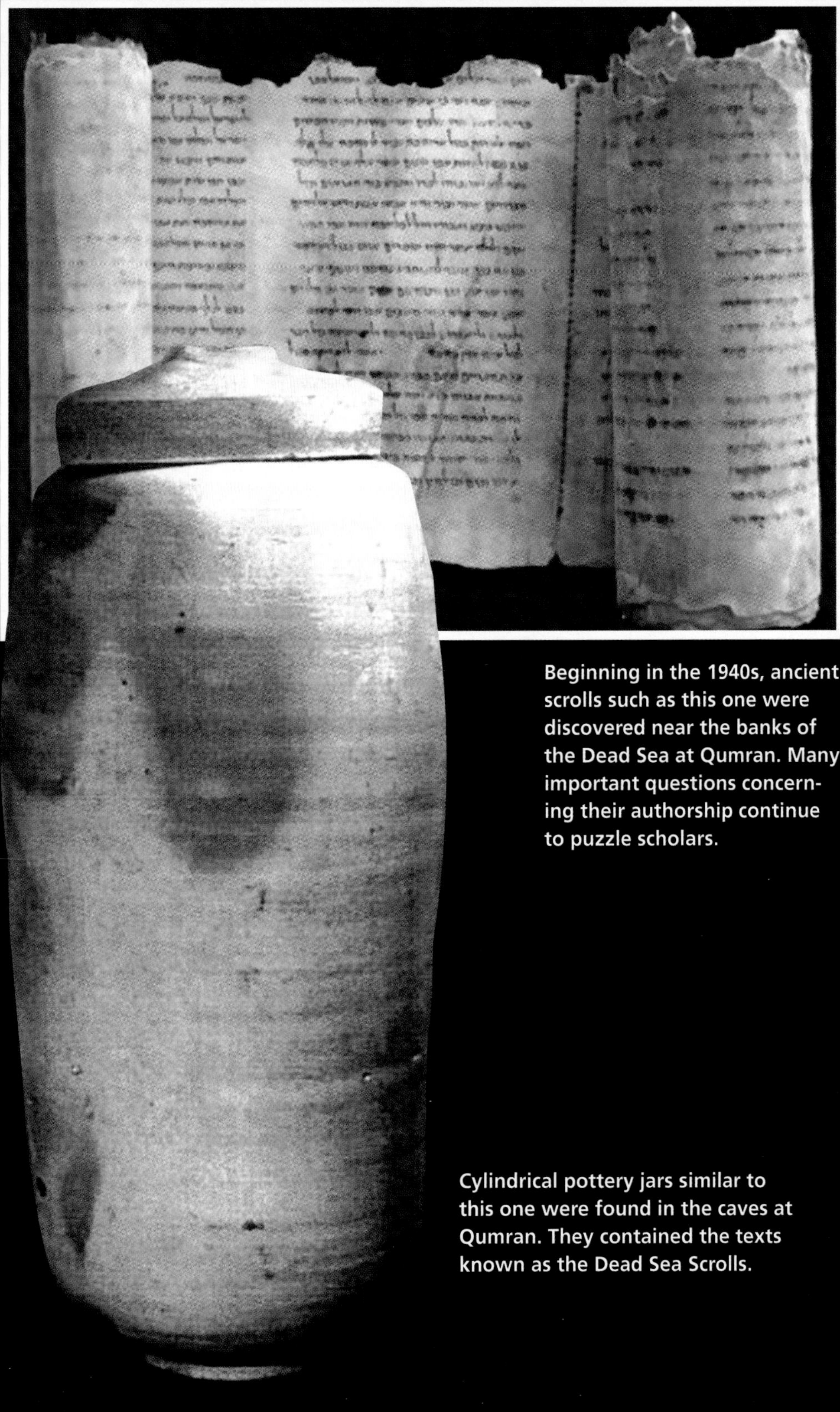

Beginning in the 1940s, ancient scrolls such as this one were discovered near the banks of the Dead Sea at Qumran. Many important questions concerning their authorship continue to puzzle scholars.

Cylindrical pottery jars similar to this one were found in the caves at Qumran. They contained the texts known as the Dead Sea Scrolls.

An antique rendering of the famous Battle of Bannockburn, between the Scots and the English in 1314. It has long been suspected that the Scottish troops were supported by sympathetic Templar knights who had fled the continent, and to whom Robert the Bruce, leader of the Scots, had given safe harbor.

Robert the Bruce (1274–1329) led Scotland to independence. His courage and determination have made his name synonymous with Scottish nationalism.

Jacques De Molay, the twenty-third and last grand master of the Knights Templar, was tortured for years before being burned at the stake on March 18, 1314. With his dying breath, De Molay cursed his persecutors Pope Clement V and King Philip IV: Both men were dead within the year.

An image of a Templar knight on crusade in the Holy Land.

Rosslyn's ceiling vault consists of five sections comprising floral or star motifs. This ceiling may conceal a Lorraine cross in its encoded design. The Lorraine cross was carried during the Crusades by the original Knights Templar, its use granted to them by the patriarch of Jerusalem.

The ghost of a Templar knight pursues an ancient dream through the ruins of Edinburgh Castle. (Painting by Tom Miller)

A painting of the door to Rosslyn Chapel.

Rosslyn Chapel is a fifteenth-century medieval chapel rich in unusual carvings and Masonic symbolism. It was founded in 1446 by Sir William St. Clair, third and last St. Clair prince of Orkney.

A stone in Westford, Massachusetts, commemorates Henry Sinclair's journey to North America in 1398. Evidence of his travels is found in many strange and inexplicable artifacts up and down the New England coastline.

A bust of Henry Sinclair, the Scottish Templar knight whose journeys to North America a century before Columbus may have included Nova Scotia and Newport, Rhode Island.

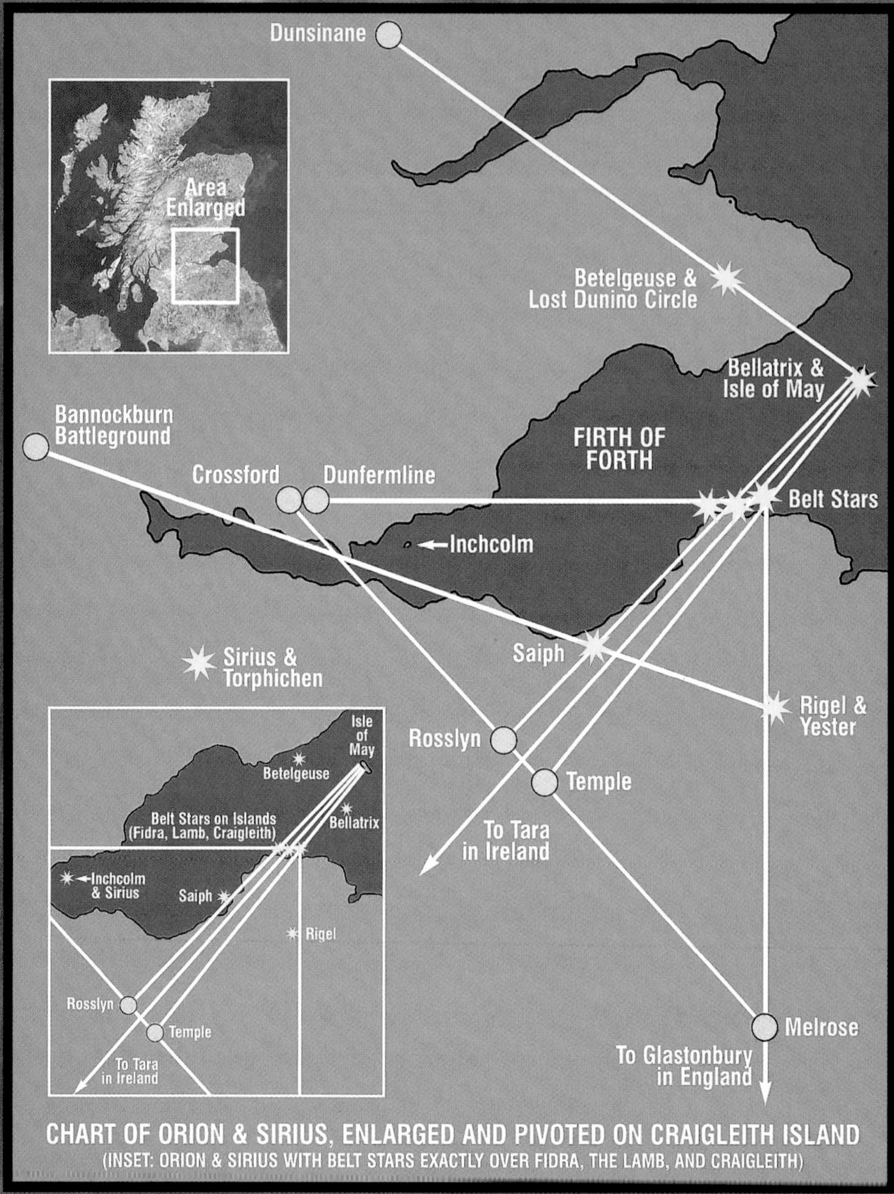

A chart of Orion and Sirius, enlarged and pivoted on Craigleith Island. The inset is of Orion and Sirius with Orion's belt stars exactly over the islands of Fidra, the Lamb, and Craigleith in the Firth of Forth, Scotland.

Sir Francis Bacon (1561–1626) was the great essayist, lawyer, statesman, and philosopher who many suspect was the real author of the plays attributed to William Shakespeare.

Some historians believe that ships such as this were sailed by Templars doubling as pirates, in a vendetta against the Roman Catholic Church. It has been argued that the "Jolly Roger" flag was actually a Templar flag in disguise.

Benjamin Franklin

John Hancock

The Great Seal of the United States, a well-known Masonic symbol featuring the pyramid and the all-seeing eye of the deity, was placed on the one-dollar bill by Franklin Roosevelt.

American ideals of liberty, due process, and democracy were influenced by Masonic thinking. Founders like George Washington (shown here), John Hancock, and Benjamin Franklin were all Freemasons.

An early portrait of Joan of Arc (1412–1431). Joan led the French army against the English during the Hundred Years' War. Many of Joan's comrades were members of the Scots Guard—a group thought to have strong ties to the Knights Templar.

The great mathematician and scientist Sir Isaac Newton (1642–1727) was a student of alchemy and the occult mysteries for most of his life.

"like a religion: you either believe or you don't"—and according to Curtis Hsia, a psychologist at Boston University's Center for Anxiety and Related Disorders, it's not surprising. "People are looking for an explanation," he told *USA Today,* "and are trying to get a sense of what is out there and how we can predict what's going to happen next."

It is also not surprising that the intellectual establishment—representing, as it does, a materialist secular paradigm—would write off the phenomenon as superficial, if not superstitious. Such thinkers are not likely to take encouragement from public insistence on deeper and more profound explanations for current events than those provided by today's custodians of ultimate truth.

The remarkable and immediate changes in society following the events of September 11, 2001, seem abundant and largely positive. Not only has a new spirit of unity replaced the petty and quarrelsome politics to which we had become accustomed, but also vigilance has been transformed from "paranoia" to "common sense," and patriotism has become politically correct. Many have also noted, simultaneously, a subtler shift—which may ultimately prove the most significant change of all. The search for deeper answers to life's mysteries has intensified—witness the mushrooming interest in Nostradamus.

However, where there is a great appetite, there will always be some prepared to fill it—legitimately or otherwise. As that pertains to the widely circulated "Nostradamus Quatrains," the latter, unfortunately, is the case. One verse making the rounds is:

In the City of God there will be a great thunder,
Two brothers torn apart by Chaos,
while the fortress endures,
the great leader will succumb,
The third big war will begin when the big city is burning.

The lines, it turns out, were not written by Nostradamus, but rather were taken from a web page produced by Nostradamus debunker Neil Marshall in an attempt to show how vague imagery could create an important-sounding stanza.

The problem has been compounded by the addition of even more phony quatrains:

In the year of the new century and nine months,
From the sky will come a great King of Terror.
The sky will burn at forty-five degrees.
Fire approaches the great new city.

In the city of York there will be a great collapse,
Two twin brothers torn apart by chaos
while the fortress falls; the great leader will succumb;
third big war will begin when the big city is burning.

Here again it appears that the counterfeiters have been at work. The second quatrain is a complete concoction. In the first quatrain, lines are taken from two different prophecies and put together for effect. The first line here is actually tied to a reference to July of 1999 (or possibly 2000) and previously associated with many other events. (One is reminded of the common practice of quoting the Bible out of context, as in, "And Judas went out and hanged himself . . . Go thou and do likewise.")

Author John Hogue has written extensively on the French seer. He says you can always smell a rat when Nostradamus is quoted without a reference. "Even in his own day, [he] had to counter the publication of false books of prophecy attributed to his name. He protected himself and us by indexing every prediction for verification."

Should Nostradamus be discarded as a prophet for our times? Hogue believes we do so at our peril. "[Nostradamus] spoke of a new type of world war to come," comments Hogue, "one using surprise and ambush. A rogue leader from the Mideast will trigger it. He is a terrorist, code named in the prophecies as 'Mabus' or the 'Third Antichrist' (Napoleon and Hitler are considered to have been the first two). This man will be one of the first to fall in his war. He could become a symbolic martyr for terrorists who will soak the world with blood for twenty-seven years. Nostradamus spoke of the great new city made of high 'hollow mountains' near the garden of the world.

"The state of New Jersey, from whose shore one can view the great hollow mountains of New York City, is known as 'the Garden State.' In two of Nostradamus's prophecies, a thing his sixteenth-century mind can only call 'it' cuts a path to these hollow mountains. They are then seized and boiled in a cauldron. Over four centuries ago, Nostradamus may have seen those great hollow mountains hit by a huge, 'scattered flame.' He implied that the flame could not be put out and the smoke and debris would rise and ferment in boiling clouds, as if they were 'plunged in a vat.'"

Century 6 Quatrain 97 reads:

At forty-five degrees, the sky will burn,
Fire approaches the great new city,

Immediately a huge, scattered flame leaps up,
When they want to have verification from the Normans.

As Hogue explains it, "New York City is near latitude 45 degrees. It is relatively young as cities go, and there are no cities exactly on this latitude that one could call 'new' and significant enough to alert Nostradamus's attention. Lines

Fig. 25.1. Did Nostradamus foresee the destruction of the twin towers in Manhattan in 2001?

two and three could describe the flaming engines of two jet airliners approaching the great new city. They crash into the World Trade Center towers. Huge fireballs of 'scattered flame' erupt while intelligence sources in the U.S. seek verification from their French opposites about rumors of an imminent attack on America."

"Another possibility (other than 'latitude')," notes Patricia Spadaro, coauthor of *Saint Germain's Prophecy for the New Millennium,* which analyzes Nostradamus and other key prophets, "is that Nostradamus is 'seeing' the incident from ground zero, where he is looking up at a 45-degree angle as the airliners dive into the towers."

A novel alternative interpretation of the word "Normans" is offered by Elizabeth Clare Prophet. "Normans literally means 'men of the north,'" she writes. "If you were to write in code, you might describe the heaven-world as 'north' and its inhabitants as 'men of the north'—that is, the angels, masters, and saints who reach out to us spiritually from the heaven-world. Perhaps we will be turning to these enlightened ones at the time of the fulfillment of this prophecy to understand the spiritual significance of what is taking place."

Century 10 Quatrain 49 reads:

Garden of the world near the new city,
In the path of the hollow mountains:
It will be seized and plunged into a boiling cauldron,
Drinking by force the waters poisoned by sulfur.

Hogue points out, "If you were to stand on the western shore of the Hudson River, in New Jersey ('the Garden State'), and look across to Manhattan Island, you would see the man-made 'mountains' of New York. Even New Yorkers describe their boulevards as 'canyons' among the mountainous skyscrapers.

"'In the path' of those 'hollow mountains' raced terrorists in hijacked jet liners ready to unleash their mortal blows. The hollow mountains are 'seized and plunged' into the boiling 'vat' or *cuue,* as Nostradamus describes it in Renaissance French . . ." Hogue believes the use of *cuue* is a poetic attempt to capture the vision of vast, mountainous buildings being pushed down by gravity: "It describes the hollow mountains as crumbling and melting away in the ferment of boiling clouds made of their own pulverized debris. The last line may attempt to describe the toxicity of the debris cloud that blanketed New York City with the stench of asbestos-laced dust."

Hogue also believes the final line of this quatrain could augur a future and far more catastrophic attack on New York. On "Mabus, the Third Antichrist" and his twenty-seven-year war of terrorism, Hogue refers to Century 2 Quatrain 62:

Mabus will soon die, then will come,
A horrible undoing of people and animals,
At once one will see vengeance,
One-hundred powers [Nations], thirst, famine, when the comet will pass.

Century 8 Quatrain 77 continues the theme:

The Third Antichrist very soon annihilated,
Twenty-seven years his bloody war will last.
The heretics are dead, captives exiled,
Blood-soaked human bodies, and a reddened, icy hail covering the Earth.

Hogue has long interpreted the appearance of the comet Hale-Bopp in 1997 as the clue to Mabus surfacing in our near future. Nostradamus points to Mabus (at least in part), says Hogue, in a related Quatrain 72 of Century 10 as the "king of terror, descending from the skies" either in "1999 and seven months" (July 1999) or "1999 plus seven months" (July 2000).

Although few can ignore the apt comparison of civilian jets crashing into the Pentagon and the World Trade Center towers as a "terror descending from the skies," Hogue believes the advent of Mabus has arrived, if slightly later than expected by Nostradamus. "I for one," he says, "do not fault a man predicting events 450 years in the future who misses his written date by two years and four months or fourteen months, depending on which July Nostradamus intended."

Generally, unraveling of the true meaning of Nostradamus seems to be much like interpreting the Bible, especially the Book of Revelation. A great deal remains in the eye of the beholder, but this is no reason to discard the process. In fact, it could be the point.

Joseph Jochmans, another authority on Nostradamus, said in a recent article in *Atlantis Rising:* "The more one studies what [Nostradamus] actually wrote in his original Old French verses, the more one realizes there are several potential meanings to his prophecies, which can lead to several possible directions that the prophecies can take. In essence, what Nostradamus did in his prophetic messages was to set a mirror before us, showing us the different pathways we can take that already exist within us. Which of his prophecies we choose to fulfill remains up to us." According to Spadaro, the prophets tell us that prophecy is not set in stone. It's a warning, she says, and the changes we make in our own lives will influence its outcome.

Even in the ancient warfare of good and evil, all *change,* both internal and external, unfolds according to rules—the "laws" of dramatic episode. In classic theatrical form, borrowed from ancient temple ritual—as understood by scholars from Aristotle to Goethe—the audience experiences catharsis: purging, release, or change—after being conducted vicariously through a number of defined steps (inciting moment, denouement, climax, and so on). In the tragedies of Shakespeare, the conflict present in Act One is ultimately resolved after the protagonist and antagonist have worked their way through the dramatic formula or recipe to the preordained climax. It's called metamorphosis and can be described as the path by which a caterpillar becomes a butterfly or a bud becomes a rose. For the alchemists, such change, which was to be sought, was the great work of transmuting the base metal of the primitive soul into the refined gold of the higher self—sometimes called the changing of water into wine.

For this school of thought, the outer world is but a reflection of a preexisting world within—"As above, so below." Could the much dreaded "end of the world," as presented in apocalyptic literature, in actuality represent a great episode of change that must occur within us, if not without? External catastrophe without (in the physical world) ensues when the needed changes have not occurred within. As we pass inwardly through the episodes prescribed, we are freed of spiritual tyrants such as materialism and idolatry that bind us to lesser states of awareness.

In his 1998 book *Hidden Millennium, the Doomsday Fallacy* author Steven Koke deals with these issues. Koke believes the Book of Revelation, the apocalypse, and the Last Judgment are concerned entirely with psychological subjects. "The Biblical apocalypse," writes Koke, "is not a statement about the physical world, but indicates great changes in human consciousness and attitudes. The world of the psyche or soul is the subject of the apocalypse."

As psychological research scholar Joseph Ray explained, "The hidden language of the Bible is allegory and metaphor. What one understands depends upon the degree of spiritual awareness one has cultivated and allowed to develop in oneself." He goes on, "The metaphor of the lost continent, Atlantis, rising could mean the return of lost knowledge to a person." And, as Koke adds, "What millennium (or doomsday) prophecies may reveal is a renaissance, not a catastrophe."

"We are in a time of unique challenge and unique opportunity," says Spadaro. Prophets—from Nostradamus to John the Revelator, from Edgar Cayce to Saint Germain—have foreseen a coming rite of passage for America, with the same challenges that brought down Atlantis.

"The prophets and sages of East and West," says Spadaro, "tell us that war is a reflection of the inner warring within the citizens of Earth. And they say we can influence outer conditions when we engage in a process of inner transformation. What's important is not so much matching incidents to prophecies, but learning and growing from events that take place—and changing the outcome of prophecy by changing our consciousness."

That is not to say we will enjoy the transformation. "The mind does not normally want to be transformed," says Koke, "because change looks like an entrance into chaos and strangeness." Psychoanalyst Carl Jung, in his own efforts to comprehend human behavior, identified fear of the strange—*misoneism,* he called it—as a powerful determiner of behavior.

Certainly the spectacle of giant aircraft piloted by mad assassins crashing into the enormous towers of New York and killing thousands before a worldwide television audience constitutes an event of truly biblical proportions—one that might be expected to provoke thoughts of death and doomsday. As such, it could form the catalyst for a kind of accelerated thinking, which could not appear in more tranquil times. But whether this is a product of a preordained great change or the cause is not the issue. The inescapable fact—as many have said—is that we will never be the same again.

So let us make the most of it.

26 Giordano Bruno

Why Was He Burned at the Stake?

John Chambers

Until recently, most people knew Giordano Bruno only as the brilliant Dominican priest who was burned publicly at the stake in Rome on February 17, 1600, for proclaiming not only that the Earth goes round the Sun, but that the universe is infinite and contains an infinite number of worlds. Over the past half-century, an even vaster Bruno has been emerging. It's now apparent that the reach of his thought and its predictive quality were truly astonishing, extending to almost every human activity.

At least one modern commentator, Ramon Mendoza, doesn't hesitate to call Bruno the founder of modern cosmology. It's long been known that the Italian priest's accurate descriptions of our physical universe anticipated by centuries the discoveries of modern astronomy. Bruno even wrote in the late 1500s that "[i]n space there are countless constellations, suns, and planets; we see only the suns because they give light; the planets remain invisible, for they are small and dark."

Bruno's prescience was strikingly greater than that. Mendoza and other commentators make clear that this thinker, trained by austere Catholic seminarians, was even a non-dualist—someone who believed that mind and matter are not separate but rather aspects of a single, underlying reality—a belief that has found receptive ears only in our century.

Mendoza writes in *The Acentric Labyrinth* (1997) that "[t]he cornerstone of Bruno's ontology is [t]his insight: matter is intelligent and intelligence is material." It is of the essence of matter to be self-propelling, to evolve, and to bring forth from within itself all the forms it is capable of adopting. Matter is self-organizing and self-metamorphosing.

With such notions, Bruno seems to have anticipated chaos theory, whose proponents argue that matter tends to organize itself spontaneously into more-complex arrangements. He seems to place himself on the side of those who believe in a "zero-state" universe, one in which an implicit, energetic order of reality is seen as underlying all of space and time. Indeed, with his notion (derived from the ancient world) of the *anima mundi,* a universal soul

Fig. 26.1. Giordano Bruno, a seventeenth-century visionary executed for his beliefs.

or "God-consciousness"—one aspect of that total reality of which matter is another aspect—Bruno is not far from the position of the new prophets of quantum holography, who maintain that every portion of the universe is contained in every other portion.

Bruno's genius was not only cosmological. Julia Jones, a Los Angeles–based writer currently researching the heretic-philosopher, comments that Bruno was a tireless promoter of the cause of ecumenicalism, who in a time of bloody sectarian battles advocated, predicted, and actively sought the reconciliation of all religious systems, Catholics with Protestants, Christians with pagans.

"'Unity' was his watchword," says Jones, who believes Bruno would have been delighted and unsurprised to learn that in mid-June of 1998, the Vatican agreed to end a 500-year-old rift with the Lutherans by co-signing a declaration that both parties "share a basic understanding of how human beings receive God's forgiveness and salvation." Jones points out that the *New York Times* ran this story on its front page, side-by-side with a report about a newly discovered planet orbiting a red dwarf star only fifteen light-years from our Sun. Bruno would have been equally unsurprised by this report, she says, and would have seen both stories—and even their pairing!—as affirmations of his belief in the fundamental unity of all things.

There is yet another area, which researchers are only just now beginning to explore, where Bruno may have been not only 400 years in advance of his time, but even in advance of our time as well. That is regarding the concept—eagerly seized upon by modern-day New Agers—that the human mind has endless power to mold, create, penetrate, and understand reality. "Our thoughts create reality" has become a catchphrase.

Bruno went well beyond this understanding by advocating—in an age that discouraged even the slightest form of free-thinking—that we all could, and should, aspire to become like God, so that we could enter into his understanding and therefore have personal power over our world. "Make yourself grow to a greatness beyond measure," he wrote, "by a bound free yourself from the body; raise yourself above all time, become Eternity; then you will understand God. Believe that nothing is impossible for you, think yourself immortal and capable of understanding all, all arts, all sciences, the nature of every living being."

Contemporary New Agers are criticized for the arbitrary nature of their belief in this power of the mind to create reality; they're accused of indulging in undisciplined and irresponsible "just plain wishing." What's not always known about Bruno—because it is deemphasized by researchers who are increasingly focused on his achievements as a theoretician of science—is that all his life, this Italian-born philosopher/priest, who also lived in France, England, and Germany, strove to discover a set of tools that would enable him to harness, in a disciplined fashion, the powers of his mind.

He found those tools—and elaborated upon them personally with strikingly original additions—in the quasi-science of astral magic, which had, a century before, gripped the imaginations of the greatest minds of the Italian Renaissance.

In our time, thinkers and writers such as Schwaller de Lubicz and—more recently—Robert Bauval have argued that ancient Egyptian civilization reached back in time much farther than we thought, and that in the mists of a vanished antiquity, there was a possessor of arcane knowledge who bestowed great spiritual and practical power on that people. Many modern-day New Agers often think they have picked up on that knowledge—usually in the area of mind-control—either through channeling or by reading ancient sources.

We seem somehow to have forgotten that, in fifteenth- and sixteenth-century Europe, thinkers such as Marsilio Ficino and Pico della Mirandola held exactly the same beliefs. So did Giordano Bruno, who, in fact, flaunted himself to the Church as an "Egyptian" philosopher who had picked up the torch of those vanished beliefs and was presenting them, throughout Europe, as being vastly superior to the beliefs of Roman Catholicism. It was his readiness to carry this torch that would, most of all, eventually deliver Bruno up to the flames of the Inquisition.

Bruno would come to believe that we could communicate directly (to use his word, "copulate") with the anima mundi, the soul of the universe, by addressing it in its own language—the symbols of magic as animated by the human imagination. It was the wisdom of the ancient Egyptians that would provide him with the tools for doing what the ancient Egyptians themselves had done. This ostensibly ancient body of knowledge was all the more compelling in its contemporary newness; it had entered Europe from the Middle East only in the mid-fifteenth century.

Bruno scholar Francis Yates writes that "[t]he Egyptian God, Thoth, the scribe of the gods and the divinity of wisdom, was identified by the Greeks with their Hermes and sometimes given the epithet of 'Thrice Great.' The Latins took over this identification of Hermes or Mercurius with Thoth." About 1460, a monk brought from Macedonia to the court of Cosimo de Médici in Florence a Greek manuscript containing a copy of the Corpus Hermeticum. This work was thought to have been written in remotest antiquity, possibly before the time of Noah, by an all-wise Egyptian priest—possibly Thoth himself, which gave it its name, Hermeticum.

De Médici ordered the great scholar/thinker Marsilio Ficino to translate the document immediately; Ficino did so, becoming enamored of its wealth of knowledge particularly relating to astral magic. The translation caused a sensation; along with other ostensibly ancient Egyptian works then entering Europe—and in addition to first-time translations of the Cabala coming up through Spain—Ficino's work wrought a minor intellectual revolution that, a century later, was still powerful enough to capture the imagination of Bruno.

Astral magic taught that it was possible to draw down from the stars and planets powers that would be beneficial to the practitioner—to "draw upon the life of the heaven," as Ficino put it. This could be done through the manipulation of a complex set of precise images, some drawn from the signs of the Zodiac. And yet, as Yates stresses, astral magic escaped from astrological determinism by gaining power over the stars—in part from the signs of the decans, the thirty-six parts into which the ancient Egyptians had divided the heavens.

It was essential to have these images in front of one, or to contemplate them at all times in the mind. It was equally important to back them up with the presence of corresponding objects, such as colors, or precious stones, or vegetables. These Italian Renaissance magi would have argued that if the pyramids of ancient Egypt were arranged to correspond to the shape of a constellation, this was intended to draw down the power of those stars and not the result of a primordial visit from otherworldly beings. They would have maintained that the model of the heavens said to be on the ceiling of the tomb-chamber of the first Chinese emperor, Qin Shi Huangdi, was there to draw down upon the body of the emperor the power of those celestial bodies.

Ficino and his fellow thinkers believed the Egyptians had been able to manipulate these cosmic energies in such a way as to cause spirits to enter into statues and animate them. They took at face value the statement in the Picatrix—the first book of the Corpus Hermeticum—that "Hermes was the first who constructed images by means of which he knew how to regulate the Nile against the motion." Since the Church frowned severely on the pagan

Egyptian elements of astral magic, thinkers like Ficino and della Mirandola practiced it only mildly, though enthusiastically.

Bruno was quite different. He was, as Yates puts it, "to take the bolder course of maintaining that the magical Egyptian religion of the world was not only the most ancient but also the true religion, which both Judaism and Christianity had obscured and corrupted."

For Renaissance thinkers, the precise if complex images of stars, planets, and decans essential to astral magic were far more than just images: They represented an interface between the physical realities of the Earth and the divine world of the anima mundi. Bruno, however, took things one step further. He believed there was nothing in the universe but matter—or, to be more precise, two kinds of matter, corporeal matter and incorporeal matter. However, while matter might be fundamental, incorporeal matter was animated by the anima mundi—the soul of the world. Moreover, all matter was immortal and divine by virtue of the presence of the anima mundi.

Bruno believed the soul of the world had a principal faculty, which he called the "universal intellect" *(intelletto universale),* and which "directly governs and transforms matter in its endless vicissitudes." He has a wonderful sentence about this matter that he considered to be the ground of all being, writing in *De l'infinito* that "tired of the old appearance [*specie*], [it] lies in wait, yearning for the new one, for it desires to become everything and, according to its own forces, to be similar to every being."

In operating upon matter, the intelletto universale had to take into consideration this tendency; it could not work its way upon matter completely arbitrarily. Bruno explains, "According to the diversity of dispositions of matter and according to the capability of the active and passive material principles, [it] manages to produce diverse configurations and to bring about diverse capabilities, showing sometimes living beings without sensation, some other times living and sentient beings without intelligence . . ."

For Bruno, then, matter and spirit were essentially one, but matter was primary. This made all the more potent his assertion that, by manipulating his images of astral magic, he could communicate with the anima mundi in such a way as to change physical reality (including, or so he intimated, the stars in the sky and the planets in their orbits!); he created his images on the assumption that the anima mundi and physical reality were one and the same. Is this what frightened the Venetian inquisitors so much? Did they know more than we know—namely, that Bruno had discovered a way to stir up the very physical universe itself? Is that why they condemned him to a terrible death at the stake while suppressing most of the records of his trial and execution?

Only one eyewitness account of the burning of Giordano Bruno has come down to us; until the early nineteenth century, the Roman Catholic Church steadfastly denied that it had ever carried out such a dire act against its outspoken Dominican priest.

A commemoration service was held for Bruno in 1889, at the very place in Rome where he met his death. On account of this event, says Julia Jones, some 30,000 people rioted throughout Europe, some furious at the service, others joyful over it. The pope went into seclusion and fasted, hoping to ward off any evil effects stemming from the event.

A little more than a century later, on February 17, 2000, a commemorative service attended by thousands was held at the Campo di Fiori in Rome—the place of his execution—to honor the four hundredth anniversary of Giordano Bruno's death. Despite the Catholic Church, which ignored the celebrations, Bruno's rehabilitation is proceeding slowly and seemingly with a degree of sureness. There can be little doubt that his brave and brilliant presence is badly needed in the world today.

27 Joan of Arc Revealed

What Has History Left Out of Her Strange Saga?

Jeff Nisbet

On May 30, 1431, a young girl was burned alive for heresy and witchcraft in Rouen, France.

According to one account of the day, when she had succumbed to the flames, the fire "was raked back, and her naked body shown to all the people, and all the secrets that could or should belong to a woman, to take away any doubts from people's minds. When they had stared long enough at her dead body bound to the stake, the executioner got a big fire going again round her poor carcass, which was soon burned, both flesh and bone reduced to ashes."

Although history tells us the victim was Joan of Arc, a simple shepherdess known then as Joan the Maid, the account of her execution shows even her gender was in doubt at the time—a doubt put to rest perhaps just a tad too neatly in the historical record.

Joan deserves a closer look.

Born on January 6, 1412, Joan is one of history's best-documented figures—hardly surprising considering that the records of her several trials still survive.

At the age of thirteen, a voice told Joan she had been chosen by the "King of Heaven" to bring "reparation to the kingdom of France, and help and protection to King Charles."

With much of France under English domination, French sovereignty was in dire straits. The forces of England's Henry V had invaded in 1415, dealing the French a crushing defeat at Agincourt. When Henry died in 1422, the English controlled all of France north of the Loire River, and in 1428 laid siege to France's last stronghold in the region—Orléans.

Making matters worse, the French throne was itself in dispute.

King Henry had married the daughter of Charles VI of France, and under the terms of the 1420 Treaty of Troyes, Henry's son was named heir to the throne over the Dauphin Charles, son of the French king. Adding insult to injury, the tale was spread that Charles was illegitimate—a tale his own widowed mother, Isabeau, endorsed. Isabeau was enjoying the protection of the French Burgundians, allied to England, so what's a mother to do? While the Burgundians held Paris, the Dauphin held a pitifully ineffectual court at Chinon.

Then, on March 4, 1429, Joan showed up.

She was granted an audience with the Dauphin on March 6 and, with divine help, recognized him even though he was in disguise. She impressed him by privately relating a secret only he should know. She was then vetted by a court, which recommended that Charles set Joan at the head of his armies. The rest is a history that is known well enough to be covered only briefly here. Joan raised the siege at Orléans and drove out the English.

She then led the Dauphin to his coronation as King Charles VII and, after a brief yet glorious military career, was captured by the Burgundians, sold to the English, tried, and then burned at the stake, while France's new king looked the other way.

Twenty-four years later, Joan was tried again—posthumously—and in 1456 the original verdict was nullified. More than five hundred years after her birth, Joan of Arc was canonized Saint Joan in 1920—cold comfort to Joan the Maid.

But the "sworn testimony" that paints the picture of Joan that we are now expected to accept is a weird mix of the believable and the unbelievable, the commonplace and the miraculous. Although many swore to the testimony given, only a few privileged hands recorded it—so why must we believe what they have written? Perhaps instead of accepting what they wrote, we should look elsewhere.

In previous articles, I have proposed the existence of a secret brotherhood with both the knowledge and the clout to orchestrate certain historically pivotal events on Earth that simultaneously mirror the arrangement of the heavens above. The articles suggest that these events are staged not only because out of the resulting smoke and thunder are born heroes and symbols guaranteed to weather the winds of time, but also because they are scripted to shape a nation's sense of identity for centuries to come.

Scotland has Robert the Bruce.

America has the star-spangled banner.

France has Joan of Arc.

One need only look at Joan's entourage during her glory days to see a troupe now recognized as players in the underground stream of knowledge game. Under the terms of the Auld Alliance between Scotland and France, many of Joan's comrades were members of the Scots Guard. This was a group thought to have held strong ties to the Knights Templar, whose inner circle may have

Fig. 27.1. Joan of Arc Kisses the Sword of Liberation, *a famous nineteenth-century painting by Dante Gabriel Rosetti.*

escaped from France to Scotland upon the order's 1307 suppression for heresy, at which time they chose to quickly disappear. While today's sizable Templar fan club subscribes to that theory, my opinion is that the Knights' inner circle had taken the forward-thinking view that it was time to "right-size" the corporation, and it had done just that.

And then there is René d'Anjou, one of Joan's companions on her trip to meet the Dauphin. One of René's many titles was King of Jerusalem. Purely titular, the designation had nevertheless descended from Godfroi de Bouillon, who, as Michael Baigent and Richard Leigh assert in their book *Holy Blood, Holy Grail,* had founded the shadowy Priory of Sion, which, in turn, had founded the Knights Templar. René is known to have been a close friend of the young Leonardo da Vinci, who, later in life, is thought to have been grand master of the Priory. "Many have made a trade of delusions and false miracles, deceiving the stupid multitude," Leonardo wrote. He also held the highly heretical belief that Jesus was a twin! But more about twins later.

One of the suspiciously precise details we know about Joan is her exact time of birth—one hour after sunset on January 6, a day variously known as the Feast of the Epiphany, the Day of the Three Kings, and the Twelfth Day of Christmas. Surprisingly, neither Joan's mother nor any other witnesses at the nullification trial mentions that Joan's birthday was an official holy day. Considering the trial was meant to show that Joan's mission had indeed been divinely inspired, I found that silence curious. And so I decided to consult a record I had discovered during my previous research—that of the arrangement of the heavens on the day in question.

Shortly before dawn on that day of January 6, 1412, the planet Mercury, messenger of the gods, rose above the bow of the constellation Sagittarius, the Archer, while Venus, the morning star and symbol of the goddess in many pre-Christian traditions, sat on the bicep of the arm that drew the bow. Then came the Sun, hiding the heavens in the light of day.

In Shakespeare's *Henry VI,* written 179 years later, the Dauphin challenges Joan to a mock swordfight. Soundly trounced, Charles calls Joan the "bright star of Venus, fall'n down on the Earth."

Let's now consider the name Arc, which in French means "bow" and has also come to mean the leap electricity makes between unconnected points. It's intriguing that on Joan's birthday, Venus drew the bow, perhaps to indicate that a woman had been chosen to let fly an arrow of hidden truth into the future, while Mercury, also known as Hermes, would speed it on its way. And though the Shakespearean Dauphin's reference to Joan as Venus fits this scenario neatly, a prophecy that had caught the imagination of the day fairly shivers with resonance. Attributed to Merlin, the prophecy foretold that a virgin riding Sagittarius would save France!

Uranus followed the Sun on Joan's birthday. Oldest of the gods, Uranus sat on the head of Capricorn, the goat—a figure some speculate is of enormous Templar significance. One common depiction shows a winged creature with the head of a male goat on a human torso, with female breasts and a mid-forehead star. It is presenting a bright moon above and a dark moon below, a very telling Hermetic image. Considered by some to be Baphomet, the entity the Templars were accused of worshipping, it waits eighteen years to appear again in the life of Joan.

When Joan is received by the Dauphin on March 6, Venus is riding the back of Capricorn, and in *Henry VI* a messenger brings news of Joan as "a holy prophetess new *risen up.*" In an initiatory rite of the Freemasons, a fraternity thought to have continued the legacy of the Templars, initiates are raised into the order from a symbolic death, and one of the persistent tales told about the rite is that initiates must also ride the back of a goat.

But back to Joan's nativity.

As the Sun set in the west, the Orion constellation rose in the east. Since I have discussed Orion's significance in previous articles, I will not do so here—except to add that tiny and distant Pluto sat above Orion's head like an invisible crown.

To Orion's left, the planet Neptune, god of the oceans, separated the Gemini twins, and the Twelfth Day of Christmas became Twelfth Night—the night that Joan was born. One hour after sunset, weather permitting, Orion and Gemini would be shining brightly in the eastern sky.

Scholars have long argued the significance of Shakespeare's title *Twelfth Night, or What You Will,* since the play offers no explanation. It is the story of twins, male and female, who are separated by a storm at sea, each thinking the other has drowned. The woman masquerades as a man and, until the end of the play, there is much gender confusion, with a little cross-dressing thrown in for good measure.

Since the historical record conveniently tells us that Joan was born on Twelfth Night, it's interesting that Neptune, named after the god of the oceans, separated the Gemini twins on the night of her birth, just as Shakespeare's twins were separated by a storm at sea.

Methinks perchance the Bard's mighty quill writ two tales—one hidden in the other!

Apart from the King James Bible, commissioned by Britain's first officially Freemasonic king, no books have enjoyed greater sales figures than those containing the plays of William Shakespeare. And yet their authorship remains hotly debated. A top contender as the author/editor of both works is Francis Bacon, the English philosopher who lived contemporaneously with Shakespeare. Thought to have played a key role in the birth of the Rosicrucians—an esoteric brotherhood with Templar and Freemasonic ties—Bacon may have secretly worked to put a system in place whereby lost knowledge might eventually be rediscovered. He also shares resonant connections with the Twins.

Bacon's coat of arms shows two soldiers—likely Castor and Pollux, the Gemini twins. His motto, "*Mediocria firma,*" has been interpreted as "the middle ground is safest." In an age when heresy could get you burned at the stake, perhaps Bacon was merely protecting himself by not taking credit for saying too much too soon—preferring to let his rather milquetoast motto speak sterner stuff in times to come.

In the 572 years since Joan's death, historians have been plagued by two pesky groups of revisionists—the "bastardizers" and the "survivalists." The bastardizers claim that Joan was not a simple shepherdess, but was in fact the illegitimate daughter of Queen Isabeau and her brother-in-law, Louis of Orléans, which would make Joan the half sister of the Dauphin and also, consequently, the aunt of Henry VI of England through the marriage of the Dauphin's sister to Henry V. The survivalists claim that Joan escaped execution thanks to the secret efforts of her principal judge, Pierre Cauchon, and others in the English camp.

Within twenty-five years of Joan's execution, several brave souls claimed to be Joan of Arc. It is interesting that one of these "impostors" was pardoned in 1457 by no less a personage than René d'Anjou, Joan's companion at arms and titular King of Jerusalem.

It is highly unlikely that Joan was born on the day that history records—a day when the heavens were oh-so-conveniently arranged. It is more probable that she was born earlier and then delivered to foster parents on that astronomically auspicious day—for the record. It is also more probable that Joan of Arc's miraculous career was orchestrated by the will of a *cognoscenti* that followed a mutually agreed-upon secret agenda from opposite sides of the battlefield—a brotherhood that counted the many thousands of ensuing war casualties as acceptable collateral damage and which would continue to quietly promote a spirit of nationalistic and adversarial competition that would become very useful when the time came to divvy up and populate the New World soon to be "discovered" to the west.

The first cartographic appearance of the name America appears on Martin Waldseemüller's 1507 map produced under the patronage of Duke René d'Anjou II, who had inherited the title King of Jerusalem from his grandfather. The map has recently been purchased by the U.S. Library of Congress for five million dollars and will be the crown jewel of its map collection. *Caveat emptor!*

Finally, whereas the positions of the six ancient planets on Joan's official birthday could have been easily predicted at the time, the positions of the three "modern planets" should have been problematic. Uranus, conveniently on the head of the goat, would not be discovered until 1781; Neptune, between the Twins, in 1850; and Pluto, above Orion's head, in 1933. Hmm!

Perhaps they were simply allowed to be prudently rediscovered when the time was right!

Francis Bacon wrote: "I begin to be weary of the Sun. I have shaken hands with delight, and know all is vanity, and I think no man can live well once but he that could live twice. For my part I would not live over my hours past, or begin again the minutes of my days; not because I have not lived well, but for fear that I should live them worse. I envy no man that knows more than myself, but pity them that know less. Now, in the midst of all my endeavours there is but one thought that dejects me, that my acquired parts must perish with myself, nor can be legacied amongst my dearly beloved and honoured friends."

Although the girl whose body climbed the sky in a plume of smoke over Rouen on May 30, 1431, may never be known for who she truly was, she might someday be known for who she was not. Francis Bacon, in his way, made sure of it.

"All the world's a stage, and all the men and women merely players." Indeed!

28 The Alchemist's Resurrection

Did the Ancient Arts of Transmutation Die with the Middle Ages, or Do They Still Survive in Different Disguises?

Mark Stavish

Mention alchemy to someone and what does he usually think of? The Middle Ages with old men in some forgotten attic, laboring over bubbling flasks filled with some unknown fluid, or in front of an oven, trying to turn molten lead into gold. These are the images of the alchemist that time, mythology, and prejudicial history have handed down to us.

It is true that many of the early alchemists were the forerunners of the modern scientists. Physics and chemistry are indebted to these early "puffers," as they are disparagingly called. From their hours of sweat and travail, a host of modern advances came—porcelain, alcohol distillation, acids, salts, and a variety of metallic compounds; all are the results of early alchemical experiments. But if alchemy wasn't just a foolish waste of time in the search for a means to turn base metals into gold, what was it?

THE EGYPTIAN CONNECTION

The word *alchemy,* or *al-kemi,* is said to be derived from Arabic or Egyptian, meaning either "divine chemistry" or possibly "black earth," referring to the silt deposits from the annual flooding of the Nile River. However, regardless of where the word *alchemy* began, it has come to mean a very special form of spiritual development.

From Plato's Greece to the European Renaissance, ancient Egypt was held to be the land, if not the origin, of all things mystical. The Egyptian god Thoth, called Hermes by the Greeks, was said to be the father of all magical arts and sciences, with numerous books on the laws governing creation being attributed to him. These books became the basis of most Western occult teachings, and are known as The Hermetic Corpus or the Body of Hermes, which refers to the total collection of works attributed to the "scribe of the gods."

Fig. 28.1. An alchemist in search of the Philosopher's Stone discovers phosphorus.

Fig. 28.2. L'alchimiste, *by David Teniers the Younger.*

The teachings and practice contained in these writings are called Hermeticism and, in the Renaissance, came to include aspects of Jewish mysticism (kabbalah), alchemy, the use of ritual, and communication with super-celestial beings, or angels. It is important to remember that in the ancient world and until the end of the Renaissance (the sixteenth century), magic was seen not as superstition, but as a logical and coherent means of understanding the universe and controlling one's destiny. Magic, imagination, and magnetism are all related, both through their root *mag* and how they are seen through the mind of the magician or alchemist.

For the magician, or even the alchemist, the universe is perceived as a reflection of the imagination of the Godhead. Its laws are consistent and logical, and if we are created in the image of the Creator, then we can also create as the Creator has—through the power of imagination. Intense imagination creates a stress on the fabric of the universe, drawing to it magnetic power, thus bringing our images to fruition.

The fundamental ideas of Renaissance magic and alchemy are also found in Eastern Yoga, and are the basis for the New Age movement, as well as hypnotherapy, guided visualizations for mental health or cancer treatment, affirmations, and an assortment of other psycho-spiritual practices.

Until the last half of the twentieth century, though, most of these spiritual practices were kept secret or hidden, mostly out of fear of political or religious persecution. Hence, they became known as occult, or hidden. Since many of them used the same signs, symbols, and literature as contemporary religions—such as Christianity, Judaism, and Islam—the hidden, occult, or Hermetic arts and sciences became known as esoteric, or the secret meaning behind *exoteric* or everyday religious practices and dogma.

This fear of persecution, of imprisonment or death, limited instruction in esoteric practices to a trusted few, and was carried out only through a process of slow, careful symbolic rituals and cryptic teachings known as initiations. Each of these initiations symbolized a step, or grade, in a student's inner journey toward illumination.

During the seventeenth, eighteenth, and nineteenth centuries, dozens of initiatic orders and societies were established across Europe for the dissemination of spiritual teachings, the most prominent of them being the Rosicrucians, Freemasons, and Knights Templar. Some of them taught their members through moral instruction, such as the Freemasons. Others, such as the Rosicrucians, taught practical mysticism, the use of ritual, the structure of the universe through Kabbalah, and laboratory alchemy. Many of these organizations exist in Europe or the United States in some form today.

In alchemy, however, each of its steps or phases represents not only an interior awakening (initiation), but also a physical, practical technique performed in the laboratory. The physical, laboratory work becomes a means of verifying spiritual and psychic expansions in consciousness.

Alchemy, it is said, is an initiatic system in which one has no delusions. It is the only initiatic path where there is an objective control in the laboratory: If an experiment shows that one has gone beyond the ordinary material laws of the universe, it shows that one is an alchemist who has had an interior awakening. This awakening corresponds to the rule that says, "You will transmute nothing if you have not transmuted yourself first," says Jean Dubuis, founder and first president of the French alchemical organization the Philosophers of Nature.

Dubuis has actively practiced alchemy and related esoteric arts for nearly sixty-five years. Because of his extensive professional career in electrical engineering for a major international electronics firm in France, and his work in the field of nuclear physics with Nobel Prize winner Joliot-Curie, he has been described by fellow alchemists as one of the few people easily at home with both a periodic table of the elements and a kabbalistic diagram.

His spiritual path, he says, began when he had a spiritual awakening at the age of twelve in the island cathedral of Mont Saint-Michel, off the coast of Normandy. This awakening led Dubuis to a lifetime of activities and intimate involvement in European esoteric circles. He has held positions in the French-speaking branch of the Rosicrucian Order, AMORC—presiding over its Illuminati section of higher-degree students—as well as in a number of esoteric orders and societies.

After tiring of the various levels of secrecy and often the self-aggrandizing use of the power such vows bring, he renounced his memberships and established the Philosophers of Nature (PON) to open the paths of alchemy and kabbalah to everyone of good heart and mind. This is expressed in his view of the basic philosophy behind alchemy: "Alchemy is the Science of Life, of Consciousness. The alchemist knows that there is a very solid link between matter, life, and consciousness. Alchemy is the art of manipulating life and consciousness in matter to help it evolve, or solve the problems of inner disharmony. Matter exists only because it is created by the human seed. The human seed, the original man, created matter in order to involute and evolve. You see, if we go beyond what I said, the absolute being is an auto-created being, and we must become in its image auto-created beings," Dubuis said during a recent interview at the annual conference of the Philosophers of Nature.

A similar statement was made by fellow Frenchman and alchemist François Trojani during an interview with Joseph Rowe in the summer 1996 issue of *Gnosis:* "It [alchemy] is the dimension of interiority and of meaning in the deep sense: the meaning of life, the meaning of my life, questions about the relationship of spirit to matter, of the purpose and value of my own actions—the questions 'where did I come from?,' 'why am I here?,' 'who am I?' I'm not saying that alchemy provides precise answers to these questions, but that it operates in the dimension where these questions arise."

MODERN PSYCHOLOGY

Just as esoteric initiation seeks to repair the psychic damages in humanity, so does its stepchild, modern psychology. As a result, most folks today are familiar with alchemy through the extensive writings of Swiss psychologist Carl Gustav Jung. Jung was attracted to alchemy through a series of dreams he experienced, as well as those of his patients, and their resemblance to alchemical symbols representing the stages of self-development, or individuation. However, for Jung, the entire alchemical work, or opus, was viewed from a strictly psychoanalytic perspective. Transmutation was the changing not of physical matter, but of psychological matter, from destructive problems into life-enhancing attributes.

Some of Jung's seminal works outlining the process of human individuation, or self-becoming, are found in his *Alchemical Studies,* in which he interprets the meaning of the key stages and symbols of alchemy to explain the internal stages of human evolution, or what alchemists call "interior initiation."

Laboratory alchemists cautiously point out that, despite his contributions, and the critical aspect of psychological work in alchemy, Jung is not considered a real alchemist.

According to Dubuis and others, for alchemy to be real alchemy, it must work on all levels of creation—spiritual, mental, emotional, and physical. While one or more can be left out and a transmutation of some sort effected, the results are not considered to be alchemical.

It is true that Jung made some additions to symbolism and gave people a means to look at their interior life. "As regards to alchemy, Jungian psychology shows that alchemy is a universal art and science, and can lend itself to anything, but to reduce alchemy to a theraputic allegory is a mistake," stated Russell House, of Winfield, Illinois. House is the current president of the Philosophers of Nature, and has studied alchemy with Jean Dubuis, Orval Graves, "Frater Albertus," and Manfred Junius, several of this century's leading laboratory alchemists. From 1989 to 1993, House also co-instructed the alchemy classes taught at Rose-Croix University, sponsored by the Rosicrucian Order, AMORC, in San Jose, California.

ALTERNATIVE MEDICINE

Along with psycho-spiritual growth and physical transmutation, alchemy has long been associated with creating near-physical immortality as well as cures for "incurable" diseases. Dubuis has suggested that a carefully prepared tincture, or an alchemically prepared medicine extracted with purified alcohol, made from acorns might prove useful in fighting cancer and some auto-immune diseases.

However, at least one of the major contributions of alchemy to alternative medicine is a little more accessible than either of these: that is, homeopathy. Available in most drugstores and supermarkets, homeopathic medicines are based on the alchemical practices of the Swiss sixteenth-century alchemist Paracelsus. However, it was not Paracelsus who created homeopathy; he only supplied the theory that "like cures like" and that smaller doses of medicine could cure more easily and quickly than larger doses. Alchemical tinctures, like homeopathic medicines, are created from plants, minerals, and metals. Homeopathic treatment was formulated in 1796 and introduced to the United States in 1825. In Europe, alchemically prepared and homeopathic medicines are available to the general public.

According to House, "For the genuine alchemists, healing, like alchemy, must be on all levels and treat the whole being or person, and within the context of nature and evolution. The intent of the healer must offer encouragement in the interior world of the patient and not work against nature's plan of evolution. Like homeopathy, Bach Flower Remedies, or aromatherapy, alchemical medicines work on a subtle level and a crude one at the same time."

QUANTUM PHYSICS

Since its inception, alchemy has been associated with the idea of transmutation, or the fundamental changing of one thing, usually a base metal such as lead, into something else, in this case, gold.

But is transmutation possible?

For alchemists past and present, the answer is a resounding yes!

Trojani is quoted as saying that transmutation has taken place and continues to be done. The reason given is that alchemical operations do not take place on the level of the periodic table of elements, but instead on the fabric of time and space itself. This work on the elements of space and time constitutes work directly on oneself.

In fact, Dubuis, Trojani, and their predecessor François Jollivet-Castelot all agree that not only is transmutation possible, but that it might not require much of the high-tech, high-energy equipment that we have come to associate with subatomic physics.

Jollivet-Castelot wrote a book for the aspiring alchemist, *Comment On devient Alchimiste* (How to Become an Alchemist, 1897) outlining the range of Hermetic disciplines required and giving practical advice on purchasing laboratory equipment, as well as on the moral requirements of the alchemist.

Harvey Spencer Lewis, the founder and head of the American Rosicrucian Order, AMORC, was familiar with Jollivet-Castelot and his work.

In 1915, Lewis himself is said to have transmuted a piece of zinc into gold using little more than an open flame and a crucible. The accounts of this public demonstration have been published several times in the organization's magazine, *The Rosicrucian Digest*. In addition, in the August 1926 edition of *The Mystic Triangle,* AMORC published Jollivet-Castelot's account of his own transmutation of base metal into gold, as well as the recipe for carrying it out.

In more recent times, alchemy has been investigated as a means of supplying cheap energy and for the potential creation of "super metals." At the Paladian Academy's conference in January 1997 near Vichenze, Italy, Professor Christopher McIntosh, author of *The Rosicrucians* and member of UNESCO's Educational Office, Hamburg, Germany, mentioned that the United Nations had recently sponsored a conference of its own in which alchemy was considered a possible tool for the creation of new alloys.

Along similar lines, Dubuis offered some insights into the phenomenon of UFOs. "First of all, there are two hypotheses for extraterrestrials. The first hypothesis says that on Earth, if you are close to the North Pole, there is some kind of fraternity of advanced people that checks on the global functioning of humanity, and that the flying saucers are theirs. The second hypothesis is that you cannot come from distant systems to Earth in everyday physical conditions, so I think that things happen thus. In the system that they start from, they put advanced people on board, and the speed of energy is multiplied by a hundred thousand or a million. They can come here rapidly, and when they enter the aura of the Earth, they are brought back level by level and re-materialize.

"I don't know, and don't want to know, if the Roswell [New Mexico] story is true, but the details that have been given lead me to believe it is true, because they found material that go back to the invisible where they should be. They said the brain of the person had no barrier; this means that they are people that have no barrier between the visible and the invisible worlds. I don't know about the other organs. If it is a fake, then the people who have produced it have a very big knowledge of the occult," Dubuis said.

29 Fulcanelli and the Mystery of the Cathedrals

What Is the Connection between the Cross at Hendaye and One of the Most Enigmatic Figures of the Twentieth Century?

Vincent Bridges

In 1926, a mysterious volume, issued in a luxury edition of three hundred copies by a small Paris publishing firm known mostly for artistic reprints rocked the Parisian occult underworld. Its title was *Le Mystère des Cathédrales* (The Mystery of the Cathedrals). The author, "Fulcanelli," claimed that the great secret of alchemy, the queen of Western occult sciences, was plainly displayed on the walls of Paris's own cathedral, Notre Dame de Paris.

Alchemy, by our postmodern lights a quaint and discredited Renaissance pseudo-science, was in the process of being reclaimed and reconditioned in 1926 by two of the most influential movements of the century. Surrealism and psychology stumbled onto alchemy at about the same time, and each attached its own notions of its meaning to the ancient science. Carl Jung spent the twenties teasing out a theory of the archetypal unconscious from the symbolic tapestry of alchemical images and studying how these symbols are expressed in the dream state. The poet-philosopher André Breton and the surrealists made an intuitive leap of faith and proclaimed that the alchemical process could be expressed artistically. Breton, in his 1924 *Surrealist Manifesto,* announced that surrealism was nothing but alchemical art.

Fulcanelli's book would have an indirect effect on both of these intellectual movements: indirect, because the book managed a major literary miracle—it became influential while remaining, apparently, completely unknown outside of French occult and alchemical circles. This is perhaps the strangest of all the mysteries surrounding *The Mystery of the Cathedrals.*

In the fall of 1925, publisher Jean Schémit received a visit from a small man dressed as a prewar bohemian, with a long Asterix-the-Gaul-style mustache. The man wanted to talk about Gothic architecture, the "green argot" of its sculptural symbols, and how slang was a kind of punning code, which he called the "language of the birds." A few weeks later, Schémit was introduced to him again as Jean-Julien Champagne, the illustrator of a proposed book by a mysterious alchemist named Fulcanelli.

Schémit thought that all three, the visitor, the author, and the illustrator, were the same man. Perhaps they were.

This, such as it is, amounts to our most credible Fulcanelli sighting. As such, it sums up the entire problem posed by the question: Who was Fulcanelli? Beyond this ambiguous encounter, he exists as words on a page and, in some occult circles, as a mythic alchemical immortal with the status, or identity, of a St. Germain. There were two things that everyone agreed upon concerning Fulcanelli—he was definitely a mind to be reckoned with and he was a true enigma.

We are left, then, with the mystery of the missing master alchemist. He is a man who does not seem to exist, and yet he is re-created constantly in the imagination of every seeker—a perfect foil for projection. We might even think it was all a joke, some kind of elaborate hoax, except for the material itself. When one turns to *Le Mystère,* one finds a witty intelligence that seems quite sure of the nature and importance of his information.

This Fulcanelli knows something and is trying to communicate his knowledge; of this there can be no doubt. Fulcanelli's message, that there is a secret in the cathedrals, and that this secret was placed there by a group of initiates—of whom Fulcanelli is obviously one—depends upon an abundance of imagery and association that overpowers the intellect, lulling one into an intuitive state of acceptance. Fulcanelli is undoubtedly brilliant, but we are left wondering if his is the brilliance of revelation or dissimulation.

The basic premise of the book—that Gothic cathedrals are Hermetic books in stone—was an idea that made it into print in the nineteenth century in the work of Victor Hugo. In *The Hunchback of Notre Dame,* Hugo spends a whole chapter on the idea that architecture is the great book of humanity, and that the invention of printing and the proliferation of mundane books spelled the end of the sacred book of architecture. He reports that the Gothic era was the sacred architect's greatest achievement, that the cathedrals were expressions of liberty and the emergence of a new sense of freedom.

"This freedom goes to great lengths," Hugo informs us. "Occasionally a portal, a facade, an entire church is presented in a symbolic sense entirely foreign to its creed, and even hostile to the church. In the thirteenth century, Guillaume of Paris, in the fifteenth Nicolas Flamel; both are guilty of these seditious pages."

Essentially, *Le Mystère* is an in-depth examination of those seditious pages

Fig. 29.1. Fulcanelli claimed that cathedrals such as the Cathedral of Notre Dame were Hermetic books in stone, with the mysteries and glories of humanity encoded in their architecture.

in stone. Fulcanelli elaborates on the symbolism of certain images found on the walls and porches of architect Guillaume of Paris's masterpiece, Notre Dame Cathedral, and its close contemporary, Notre Dame of Amiens. To this he adds images from two houses built in the Gothic style from fifteenth-century Bourges. This guided tour of Hermetic symbolism is densely obscure, filled with green language puns and numerous allusions. To the casual reader, and even the dedicated student, this tangled web of scholarship is daunting.

However, to the occult savants of Paris in the late 1920s, Fulcanelli's book was almost intoxicating. Here, finally, was the word of a man who knew, the voice of the last true initiate. His student Eugène Canseliet informs us in the preface to the first edition of *Le Mystère* that Fulcanelli had accomplished the Great Work and then disappeared from the world. "For a long time now the author of this book has not been among us," Canseliet wrote, and he was lamented by a group of "unknown brothers who hoped to obtain from him the solution to the mysterious *Verbum dimissum* [missing word]."

Fig. 29.2. From the north transept of Notre Dame Cathedral, a sermon in stone.

Mystification about the true identity of the alchemist obscured the fact that credible people had seen his visiting card, emblazoned with an aristocratic signature. It was possible to encounter people at the Chat Noir nightclub in Paris who claimed to have met Fulcanelli right through World War II. Between 1926 and 1929, his legend grew, fueled by café gossip and a few articles and reviews in obscure Parisian occult journals. Canseliet contributed more information: The master had indeed accomplished transmutation; Fulcanelli hadn't really disappeared; another book or two was planned; and so on.

After the war, Fulcanelli's legend, and Canseliet's career, profited from an upsurge of interest in all things metaphysical. By the mid-1950s, conditions were right to reprint both *Le Mystère des Cathédrales* and *Dwellings of the Philosophers*. Simply by having been the mysterious Fulcanelli's student, Canseliet had become the grand old man of French alchemy and esotericism. But the fifties were not the twenties, and many things had changed. One of those things was the text of *Le Mystère* itself.

The Fulcanelli affair would be of interest only to specialists of occult history and abnormal psychology, except for the singular mystery of the extra chapter added to the 1957 edition of *Le Mystère*. This second edition included a new chapter entitled "The Cyclic Cross of Hendaye," and a few changes in its

Fig. 29.3. Left: Do strange symbolic inscriptions carved on the base of the cross at Hendaye contain an alchemical prophecy of the Apocalypse? Above: The images on the four sides of the base of the pedestal are the shieldlike design facing south, the star facing east, the sun facing west, and the moon facing north.

illustrations. No mention of these changes appeared in Canseliet's preface to the second edition.

With Canseliet's use of everything else by Fulcanelli, how are we to account for the complete absence of reference to Hendaye in Canseliet's works prior to the mid-1950s? If the chapter is the work of the illustrator Champagne, then Canseliet must have known about it. This is not a trivial question. The Hendaye chapter is perhaps the single most astounding esoteric work in Western history. It offers proof that alchemy is somehow connected to eschatology, or the timing of the end of the world. And it offers the conclusion that a "double catastrophe" is imminent. If Canseliet had known of this, he would surely have used it, or at least mentioned it. Yet the silence is complete and compelling.

"The Cyclic Cross at Hendaye" is the next to last, or penultimate, chapter of Fulcanelli's masterpiece. After wading through thickets of erudition and punning slang in the rest of *Le Mystère,* this chapter feels awash with the bright sunlight of its Basque setting. The description of the monument and its location is seemingly clear and direct. Even the explanation of the monument's apparent meaning is simple and virtually free of the green language code used throughout the rest of the book. Or so it appears on the surface . . .

We can date Fulcanelli's visit to Hendaye to the early 1920s because of his comment on the "special attraction of a new beach, bristling with proud villas." H. G. Wells, Aldous Huxley, and the smart young London set discovered nearby St. Jean de Luz in 1920, and by 1926 or so the tourist villas had spread as far south as Hendaye. Today, Hendaye Plage, Hendaye's beachfront addition, bustles with boutiques, dive shops, and surfboard emporiums, having become a popular stopover for the young international backpack-nomad crowd.

Although Fulcanelli declares, somewhat disingenuously: "Hendaye has nothing to hold the interest of the tourist, the archaeologist, or the artist," the region does have a rather curious history. A young Louis XIV met his bride on an island in the bay below Hendaye, along the boundary between Spain and France. Wellington passed through, making nearby St. Jean de Luz his base of operation against Toulouse at the close of the Napoleonic Wars. Hitler also paid a visit, during World War II; in 1940, he parked his train car within walking distance of the cross at Hendaye.

"Whatever its age, the Hendaye cross shows by the decoration of its pedestal that it is the strangest monument of primitive millenarism, the rarest symbolical translation of Chilaism, which I have ever met." Coming from Fulcanelli, this is high praise indeed. He goes on to tell us that "the unknown workman, who made these images, possessed real and profound knowledge of the universe."

The cross sits today in a very small courtyard just to the south of the church. There is a tiny garden with a park bench nearby. Standing about twelve feet tall, the Cyclic Cross at Hendaye looms over the courtyard, a mysterious apparition in the clear Basque sunlight. The monument is brown and discolored from its three-hundred-plus years. The stone is starting to crumble and it is obvious that air pollution—the cross sits a few yards from a busy street on the main square—is speeding its dissolution. The images and the Latin inscription on the cross have no more than a generation left before pollution wipes the images clean and the message disappears forever.

The base of local sandstone sits on a broad but irregular three-step platform and is roughly cubic. Measurement reveals that it is a little taller than it is wide. On each face are curious symbols: a sun face glaring like some ancient American sun god; a strange shieldlike arrangement of *A*'s in the arms of a cross; an eight-rayed starburst; and, most curious of all, an old-fashioned man-in-the-moon face with a prominent eye. Rising from this is a fluted column, with a suggestion of Greek classicism, on top of which stands a very rudely done Greek cross with Latin inscriptions. Above the sun face on the western side can be seen a double-X figure on the top portion of the cross. Below that, on the transverse arm, is the common inscription, *O Crux Aves/ Pes Unica,* "Hail, O Cross, the Only Hope." On the reverse side of the upper cross, above the starburst, is the Christian symbol INRI.

In "The Cyclic Cross at Hendaye," Fulcanelli gives us a guided tour of this monument to the alchemy of time. He begins with the Latin inscription, which he interprets in French (translated here to English), from the Latin letters of the original, as: "It is written that life takes refuge in a single space." Following this rendering, he casually suggests that the phrase means that "a country exists, where death cannot reach man at the terrible time of the double cataclysm." What is more, only the elite will be able to find "this promised land."

Fulcanelli moves on to the INRI, concluding: ". . . we have two symbolic crosses, both instruments of the same torture. Above is the divine cross, exemplifying the chosen means of expiation; below is the global cross, fixing the pole of the *northern hemisphere* and locating in time the fatal period of this expiation." His esoteric interpretation of INRI, "by fire is nature renewed whole," goes directly to the issue of chiliasm and a cleansing destruction as a prelude to a re-created and Edenic world. Alchemy, according to Fulcanelli, is the very heart of eschatology. Just as gold is refined, so will our age be refined—by fire.

Fulcanelli concludes the chapter with a series of metaphors: "The *age of iron* has no other seal than that of *Death*. Its hieroglyph is the skeleton, bearing the attributes of Saturn: the empty hourglass, symbol of time run out, and the scythe, reproduced in the figure seven, which is the number of transformation, of destruction, of annihilation," Fulcanelli instructs us. "The gospel of this fatal age is the one written under the inspiration of St. Matthew. . . . It is the gospel according to science, the last of all but for us the first, because it teaches us that, save for a small number of the elite, we must all perish. For this reason, the angel was made the attribute of St. Matthew, because science, which alone is capable of penetrating the mystery of things, of beings and their destiny, can give man wings to raise him to knowledge of the highest truths, and finally to God."

Because Fulcanelli so openly connected alchemy and the Apocalypse, the true nature of a very specific Gnostic astro-alchemical meme emerged into public consciousness. This meant that the secret was no longer contained among the elect societies. For the first time since the age of the Gothic cathedrals, the meme had broken out of its incubational structures.

In a way, the cross and its message serve as proof that there are such things as secret societies. Found throughout history, these societies preserve and present the secret of the cross in various ways. The Kabbalah in Judaism, Sufic Islam, esoteric Christianity, Gnosticism, and the Hermetic tradition have been the keepers of these ideas. The central message of the three main Western religions, that of an eschatological moment in time, is the secret that also lies at the heart of the cross at Hendaye. The meme, the ability to understand the myth and its metaphors, seems to have survived only through the actions of these secret and insular groups.

The cross at Hendaye stands today at the southwest corner of Saint Vincent's Church, the busiest street corner in town. No one notices the ordinary-looking monument with its message of catastrophe; perhaps it was intended to be that way. The secret hides in plain sight . . .

30 Isaac Newton and the Occult

How Important Was the Great Scientist's Hidden Side?

John Chambers

The great mathematician/scientist Sir Isaac Newton lived from 1642 to 1727, and his towering *Principia Mathematica* paved the way for the Industrial Revolution. This work, together with other seminal works of his, seems to be the very antithesis of New Age lore. The visionary poet William Blake, who claimed to see and talk to angels daily, was only one of a long line of mystics—stretching up to the present—who despised Newton as the symbol of every kind of evil, superstition, and tyranny. In another expression of our times, the Wicca/goddess/feminist movement has long regarded the Englishman who invented calculus and discovered gravity as the embodiment of the patriarchal, male scientist who is intent on controlling nature in much the same way as a master controls a slave.

But it is becoming increasingly clear that Isaac Newton, whose formulations still provide the basis for virtually all practical science today, regularly drank deep at some of the same arcane sources as today's farther-out New Age theorists. Chief among these wellsprings was the ancient art of alchemy. It is now generally known that Newton, with Galileo the very founder and paragon of modern exact science, was a deeply interested student of alchemy and an active laboratory worker for a large part of his life, leaving a mass of manuscripts on the subject still extant but not yet thoroughly described.

Joseph Needham, in discussing Chinese alchemy in his monumental *Science and Civilization in China,* summarizes Newton's involvement in alchemy as follows: "Already in 1667, before his election as a Fellow of Trinity College, and soon after the time when at the height of his powers he had conceived the theory of universal gravitation, he was making chemical experiments privately; and between 1678 and 1696, after he had become (as quite a young man) Lucasian Professor of Mathematics (1669), he spent a great deal of time in his own laboratory at the College. This was the period when he composed his comprehensive work on the motion of bodies (*De Motu Corporum,* 1685); and the *Principia* itself appeared in 1687."

Needham cites the testimony of Newton's distant relative and assistant Humphrey Newton to the effect that the scientist rarely went to bed before two or three in the morning, sometimes not till five or six:

> . . . at spring and fall of the leaf, at which time he used to employ about six weeks in his elaboratory, the fire scarce going out either night or day, he sitting up one night and I another, till he had finished his chemical experiments, in the performance of which he was most accurate, strict and exact. He would sometimes, tho' very seldom, look into an old mouldy book wch. lay in his elaboratory, I think it was titled *Agricola de Metallis,* the transmuting of metals being his chief design, for which purpose antimony was a great ingredient.

Researchers have even suggested that Newton's obsessive delving into alchemy (he was not necessarily a true believer in the efficacy of the ancient art, but lived in a time when that art had not yet been discredited) was the cause of his mental breakdown, bordering on madness, which darkened further his so-called Black Year of 1693. Carrying out tests in the late 1970s on samples of Newton's hair, two researchers, P. E. Spargo and C. A. Pounds, concluded that unusually high levels of lead and mercury—the stock-in-trade of practicing alchemists—might have been responsible for this mental breakdown. It may well be that Newton's alchemical researches had a far more beneficial—even an indispensable—effect on his scientific work than the conclusions of Spargo and Pounds suggest.

In a new book of unusual interest, *Isaac Newton: The Last Sorcerer,* British science writer Michael White—while not skimping on the more orthodox details of Newton's life—seeks to bring together many of the threads of the newest findings concerning the more unorthodox pursuits that were an integral part of Newton's multifaceted career. Not the least of White's often arresting assertions is that the scientist's huge knowledge and lengthy practice of alchemy may have planted in his imagination the seeds of a new way of looking at the universe that, growing to maturity, helped him to make the revolutionary leap to the wholly new idea of universal gravitation.

White argues that the alchemical notion of "'active principles,' [which are] rooted in Hermetic tradition" may have had this crucial influence on Newton's mind. Such ideas, writes White—for example, positing that "matter and spirit were interchangeable and [possessed what the early alchemists]

Fig. 30.1. A statue of Isaac Newton by Roubiliac at Trinity College, Cambridge, England.

called a 'Universal Spirit'"—may have subtly conditioned the scientist eventually to be able to "perceive gravity as operating by action at a distance, made possible by a form of active principle."

White points in particular to Newton's long years of labor at his preferred alchemical procedure, the purification of the metal antimony with iron to produce an amalgam—or regulus—called the Star Regulus of Antimony. White states that this specific regulus "does look like a star, and its radiating shard-like crystals may be imagined as lines of light radiating from a star-like center. But the crystal may just as easily be visualized as representing shards or lines of light pointing inwards—a star at the center with lines of light, or force, traveling towards its center." The British science writer contends that Newton's long contemplation of the form of the Star Regulus of Antimony worked on the scientist's mind, guiding him to the hitherto unheard-of visualization of a gravitational force.

Alchemy was not the only instance where the great scientist peered deeply into some aspect of ancient lore, or what was then called the occult. Like the early Renaissance Neoplatonists Marsilio Ficino and Pico della Mirandola (and, a century later, Giordano Bruno), Newton believed that all present-day knowledge was the corrupted descendant of a higher, even a perfected, knowledge dating back to the days of the ancient Egyptians and beyond—the *prisca sapientia* ("pristine wisdom") that sages and prophets like Pythagoras, Democritus, Solomon, Moses, and Moschus the Phoenician had possessed but had hidden in parable and symbol. Remnants of this perfected knowledge (or so it was believed) had been delivered to the court of Cosimo de Médici, in Italy, in 1460, in the form of the Corpus Hermeticum, a work thought to be from the hand of the god/seer and inventor of writing, Hermes Trismegistus, and dating back to many millennia before Christ.

It would not be until around the time of Newton's birth that savants began to realize that this supposed sacred text had been composed no earlier than the second and third centuries A.D. But the author of the *Principia* believed all his life that the very first religion in the world—he thought it was Judaism—had been "the most rational of all others until the nations corrupted it. For there is no way without revelation to come to the knowledge of a deity but by the frame of nature."

Newton sought to discover just what that early, unsullied "frame of nature" was. To that end, he was occupied throughout most of his life with deep if unorthodox studies in theology, the interpretation of the Hebrew prophetic books, biblical archaeology, and ancient chronology. Central to his studies was the belief that, in the words of White, the ancients had "constructed temples and monuments as Earthly representations of the universe (examples of those still in existence may include stone circles found throughout Europe, and the Great Pyramid at Giza)."

This belief drove Newton to an enterprise not dissimilar to that of the modern-day Robert Bauval, who seeks to demonstrate that the arrangement and location of certain Egyptian pyramids were intended to mirror the location of certain stars. Believing that King Solomon was "the greatest philosopher in the world," through the years and by drawing upon all the ancient sources at his disposal, Newton sought to re-create the floor plan of the Temple of Solomon, originally built around 1000 B.C.

According to White, the great English mathematician/scientist "described the heart of the ancient temple as 'a fire for offering sacrifices [that] burned perpetually in the middle of a sacred place.'" Newton imagined the fire as one around which the believers assembled, calling this arrangement a *prytaneum,* and describing the way in which the prytaneum mirrored the cosmos in the following words: "The whole heavens they reckoned to be the true and real temple of God and therefore [so] that a prytaneum might deserve the name of his temple they framed it so as in the fittest manner to represent the whole system of the heavens."

White believes that Newton's contemplation of the re-created shape of the prytaneum may have stoked the powers of his creative imagination in much the same way as did his absorption in the occult pattern of the Star Regulus of Antimony. The British author asserts that, in studying the image of a fire at the center of the prytaneum, with disciples arranged around its flames, "instead of simply seeing the rays of light as radiating outwards from the fire, Newton might instead have visualized them as a force attracting the disciples towards the center."

If this is so, then, amazingly, Sir Isaac Newton actually did manage to discern the pattern of the real heavens as mirrored by the ancients, in veiled fashion, in the sacred architectural design of the Temple of Solomon.

This immense preoccupation with discovering the true shape of the universe as encoded in the works of the ancients may not have been the final expression of Newton's obsessive researches into the occult. White asserts there is some slight reason to believe the scientist also dabbled for a brief period in the so-called black arts.

White bases his assertion on the suspicious burning of a manuscript that had been carried out by Newton, his devoted nephew-in-law John Conduitt, and a helper named Crell only a few months before the scientist's death on March 20, 1727.

The author connects this event with Newton's highly emotional, perhaps sexual, and certainly mysterious relationship, from 1690 to 1693, with the much younger scientist Nicolas Fatio de Duillier. Newton and de Duillier's correspondence during this period suggests that Newton and the younger scientist may have been involved in alchemical research of so forbidden a nature that they hardly dared speak of it to anyone.

Though he didn't believe in evil spirits or demons, Newton probably understood very well the darker sides of the human mind. As author White puts it, "He may even have understood the potential of ritual—not because it could conjure up devils or demons, but because it could focus energies in a way not dissimilar to the ritualistic element of alchemy." Since "the concept of ritualistic concentration of psychic energy" was probably known to Newton's alchemist predecessors, says White, it is "quite possible that Fatio tried to persuade Newton to experiment simply to learn what would happen, to explore another avenue of rediscovery at a time when Newton was desperate to elucidate a unified theory [of the *Principia Mathematica* and the *Opticks*]."

Whether or not these experiments bore fruit, of however twisted a nature, it is likely that they—and not merely Newton's daily exposure to lead and mercury—contributed significantly to his nervous breakdown of 1693. The breaking off of his relationship with de Duillier, which took place in that same year, probably also played a major role.

There were deeper causes: As an infant, Newton had been traumatized by both the death of his father before he was born (on Christmas Day!) and the necessity of his mother to give him over, when he was only three, to his grandparents for raising. In 1693, the hypersensitive Newton, long under intense pressure to produce, may have begun to suffer the long-suppressed, and therefore all the more explosive, effects of that emotionally impoverished childhood. His foray into the black arts, if it actually took place, may have been both a long-delayed outcome of and an attempt to deal with the resurgent memories of those early, barren years.

There are other ways in which Newton seems to have come close to bursting the bonds of his own Newtonian universe. Astonishingly—perhaps prompted in part by the Hermetic dictum "As above, so below"—he wondered if there might exist a realm of subatomic particles, obeying the same laws of universal attraction as the macro-bodies of the celestial sphere. Since the scientist had no way of proving this theory—such methods did not come along until the middle of our century!—he confined himself to merely suggesting the existence of such particles in the list of Queries included at the end of his *Opticks.*

As Joseph Needham explains, Newton carried the explanatory possibilities of his theory of light as invisible "corpuscles" so far that "he came very near to stating what today we should call the levels of subatomic particles (protons, electrons, etc.), atoms themselves, and the molecules which they form. His aim was certainly to compass the extremes of size in the universe, from the minutest particle to the galactic scale, even though it was not possible for him to achieve it."

By the time Newton composed his great *Principia Mathematica,* the scientist had come to the momentous conclusion that gravity was a force that

Fig. 30.2. Isaac Newton experiments with the qualities of light.

seemed to act at a distance by some unknown mechanism, and that universal gravitation resulted in all the matter in the universe being attracted to all the other matter in the universe. But one point continued to trouble him: He had determined that if there were an ether to facilitate gravitation, then this ether must be almost a vacuum by nature, and incorporeal in form. But then, he pondered, what was the exact nature of this incorporeal ether? And how was it able to facilitate gravitation?

Newton was a Christian all his life, a believer in the sometimes (depending on the regime in power) dangerously heretical doctrine of Arianism, which held that there was no Holy Trinity—that God and Jesus Christ were separate, with Jesus standing in his essence midway between God and man. Based on this belief, Newton came to the conclusion—hardly an acceptable one to most modern thinkers—that the incorporeal ether that facilitated the phenomenon of gravitation (and perhaps other forces) was actually made up of the body or spiritual form of Jesus Christ.

Einstein's theory of general relativity represents, along with much else, a complete revisualization of the notion of gravity, and renders all the more irrelevant the question of the existence and nature of the ether. But when we combine Newton's idea of spirit as both permeating and enabling the functions of time and space with his own probings into the possibilities of subatomic matter, we begin to move close to the contemporary notion of a zero-point energy field underlying all physical reality—and much more.

Newton's achievement, then, in both touching upon the realms of the occult and appearing to anticipate quantum theory, seems not only colossal; it seems incommensurable. And it is perhaps best summed up in the words of the great British economist John Maynard Keynes, who was one of the first researchers to examine the records of Newton's alchemical pursuits, and who, in an address in which he introduced those findings to the public in 1942, said:

> Newton was not the first of the age of reason. He was the last of the magicians, the last of the Babylonians and Sumerians, the last great mind which looked out on the visible and intellectual world with the same eyes as those who began to build our intellectual inheritance rather less than 10,000 years ago. Isaac Newton, a posthumous child born with no father, on Christmas Day, 1642, was the last wonder-child to whom the Magi could do sincere and appropriate homage.

31 Newton, Alchemy, and the Rise of the British Empire

The Mystical Foundation of Empirical Science

Peter Bros

Casual observers locate the origin of the British Empire in Elizabethan England because the period appears to have wealth and military glory, the twin marks of empire. Elizabethan glory, however, was short-lived. The wealth came from privateers—the Sir Francis Drakes who raided gold-carrying Spanish galleons—and victory over the vengeful Spanish Armada in 1588 resulted as much from England's weather as from her military genius.

The gold was quickly depleted by Elizabeth's successor, James I, who, resorting to merciless taxation to maintain the Crown's splendor, set the stage for a revolt that took the head of his son, Charles I. Charles II, wary of following in his father's footsteps, borrowed money from the goldsmiths, the bankers of the day, to support his indulgences, but he soon defaulted.

William of Orange landed in 1688 to claim the throne on behalf of his wife, Mary, the daughter of the deposed James II, Charles's younger brother. Parliament restricted the Crown's taxing power, leaving William without funds to defend England against James, who had aligned himself with Catholic France. These events did not augur empire. William needed money to defend his crown; he couldn't raise money by taxation and the Crown's credit was nonexistent. William's only hope lay in persuading the English Parliament to adopt a banking system similar to that of his native Netherlands, a fading empire that had inherited the mantle of reserve banking from Venice.

Reserve banking is the practice of making loans in multiples of the gold deposits on hand in the hope that depositors won't make a run on the bank, all claiming their deposits at the same time. William Patterson, a Scot, studied reserve banking and worked up an ingenious proposal for an English reserve bank.

Fig. 31.1. Epicenter of the British Empire, Parliament House, London (engraving by Thomas Hosmer Shepherd).

Noting that currency circulates as an integral part of commerce, Patterson reasoned that the panic—resulting from the loss of confidence that drove depositors to demand their gold—would not infect currency holders. He proposed creating a bank that would lend money to the Crown in exchange for a note. The Crown's note would then be used to back paper currency that the bank would lend into existence. In effect, the Crown would receive the value of all monies the bank lent into existence, with the bank receiving interest from both the Crown and the loans created by its currency issuance. The currency holders could not run the bank because the currency would be in perpetual circulation.

The English goldsmiths accepted gold deposits, earning money on the difference between what they paid for the gold and what they could get by lending it to borrowers. The proposed bank would compete with their operations and, if given the power to deal in gold on behalf of the Crown, eliminate their profession altogether. The goldsmiths were understandably opposed to financing William's wars with debt-created currency. By allying with the Tories who controlled Parliament, they presented a formidable obstacle to the bank's establishment.

The survival of William's sovereignty therefore depended on a formidable task, the implementation of Patterson's proposed Bank of England over the active opposition of Parliament and the existing banking establishment. Charles Montagu, a member of William's landing party, tackled the task.

Montagu had, while attending Cambridge in the 1680s, befriended Isaac Newton, eventually taking Newton's niece as his lover.

Newton, the second Lucasian Professor of Mathematics, had made a minor stir before the new Royal Society with an ingenious optical invention, the reflecting telescope. His proposal that white light was made up of all colors of the spectrum was met with skepticism by society members, but in 1684, a discussion of gravity by members Edmund Halley, Christopher Wren, and Robert Hooke led to Newton's ideas forming the foundation upon which all scientific thought rests.

The discussion involved Kepler's recently published laws, specifically that a planet sweeps out equal areas in equal times as it travels around the Sun. Hooke wondered if that law, the product of the square of the distance of a planet from the Sun, might be correlated to Galileo's discovery that objects accelerate with the square of the distance over which they fall. If the two could be mathematically related, Hooke reasoned, the same gravity that made objects fall could be seen as affecting the orbits of the planets, demonstrating that gravity was a property of the matter making up the planets.

The three decided to offer a modest prize on behalf of the Royal Society to anyone who could mathematically show a relationship between a planet's motion and the rate an object fell. Halley related the offer to Newton the next time he visited Cambridge. Notoriously cold, arrogant, and intolerant of criticism, Newton said that he had already demonstrated that relationship by applying his recently invented calculus to the orbit of the Moon.

Newton's calculations, however, didn't work. He had characteristically jumped the gun and—although his equations never did successfully balance—by hectoring Halley for more-favorable measurements of the Moon's orbit, he was able, by 1687, to express the gist of his ideas in the *Principia,* a treatise he was obliged to revise for the rest of his life.

Montagu was interested in Newton's attempts to demonstrate that gravity was a property of matter, but his reasons were unrelated to the motion of the Moon. He was interested in Newton for his practice of alchemy. Alchemy was the physics of the time and generated the same fascination as stories of atom-smashing do today. The public held claims of alchemical accomplishments, like current claims of quarks and wormholes, in awe.

Alchemy involved mixing three substances, an impure metal such as iron ore, a pure metal such as lead or mercury, and an organic acid together in a mortar. The mixing could take months. The finished compound was slowly heated in a crucible and then dissolved in an acid under polarized light, the source of Newton's interest in optics and the spectrum. The solvent was evaporated in a process that took years, its completion signaled by an occult sign known only to the initiated.

The distillate was oxidized using potassium nitrate, producing a rough form of gunpowder. To practice alchemy was a crime punishable by death, and the danger of explosion limited the number of alchemists who reached its final stages. Those who survived hermetically sealed the distillate in a special container, the sealing stage giving rise to the practice of referring to "the body of ancient alchemical knowledge" as "the Hermetic tradition."

The sealed container was heated, and when cooled reportedly produced a powder known as the White Stone. The White Stone could be used to transmute base metals into silver, allowing alchemists to stock their pantry with silverware made from iron. Applying their knowledge of the hidden secrets of the universe, alchemists could then distill the White Stone into the Philosopher's Stone, which could transmute base metals into pure gold.

Charles Montagu was interested in the Philosopher's Stone because of its reputed power to turn base metals into gold. He knew that the success of a reserve bank depended on its ability to withstand a run on its assets. He was aware that the ability to withstand a run would depend on the confidence the bank's depositors had that their deposits were safe. He understood that this confidence in the safety of a bank's deposits depended solely on perception, that depositors would not run a bank if their deposits appeared safe.

Montagu set out to exploit the widespread public belief in alchemy and its claim that the Philosopher's Stone could turn base metals into gold to establish the Bank of England, whose paper currency—purportedly representing an equal amount of silver on deposit—would be backed by nothing. He wanted Newton close in case his alchemical reputation was needed to give the bank the appearance of having unlimited supplies of silver to back its paper currency.

Montagu didn't care whether Newton could turn base metals into gold and silver as long as the public believed he could. The first step in making the public believe that Newton was, in fact, capable of such a feat was to promote Newton's universal gravitation as the discovery of the heretofore hidden secrets of the universe, the secrets the alchemist needed to produce the Philosopher's Stone.

Montagu became the president of the Royal Society and used its influence to promote the *Principia,* with Newton's ideas of universal gravitation becoming drawing room talk throughout London. Montagu also tackled Tory control of Parliament, successfully unseating the Tories in favor of William's Whigs in 1694. Montagu immediately tacked a provision onto the annual Ways and Means bill securing legislative authorization for the Bank of England. The bank was organized with a loan of £1,200,000 to William—equal to £120,000,000 (nearly $220,000,000 U.S.) at today's values. William returned a note to the bank, which then lent pound sterling notes into public circulation.

The goldsmiths, however, countered with a provision in the Recoinage Act requiring that old coins be surrendered for their face value rather than for the value of the silver remaining after clipping. England had introduced the milled coins invented by Pierre Blondeau in 1662, but failed to make any provision for retiring clipped coins.

The legislation that created the Bank of England empowered it to handle bullion transactions for England. Because the bank was now responsible for recoinage, it would be forced to pay for retiring all of England's debased coinage at face value.

The recoinage was ordered to take effect February 1, 1697. In the summer of 1695, Montagu discovered that the goldsmiths were collecting clipped coins and cashing them in for their full value in the pound sterling notes the bank had been issuing. He realized that when the goldsmiths controlled enough of the pound sterling notes, they would demand their full value in silver, causing a public panic and a general rush on the bank to redeem all of its paper notes for silver the bank didn't have.

Montagu immediately started rumors that Newton would be made master of the mint in charge of the recoinage. With the master alchemist, the man who had demonstrated intimate knowledge of the secrets of the universe, serving as master of the mint, the bank would give the appearance of holding unlimited amounts of silver bullion. The appearance of unlimited wealth would eliminate the public's fear of collapse and stop a run on the bank's assets.

Montagu, however, discovered that Thomas Neale, installed as master of the mint for life, had no intention of giving up his job. The remainder of 1695 turned into a horse race. Would Montagu be able to install Newton at the mint before the goldsmiths ran the bank?

Montagu gave up trying to install Newton as master, instead moving the warden of the mint to Customs and installing Newton as the new warden on March 19, 1696—not a moment too soon. The goldsmiths, having amassed £30,000 (more than $500,000 U.S. in today's currency) in paper notes, made their run on the bank the week of May 4.

Sir John Houblon was the lord mayor of London, a large stockholder in the bank, and the bank's governor. In 1994, the Bank of England honored

Houblon by placing his likeness on the fifty-pound note. Questions circulated about why the bank would choose a total unknown to honor its three hundredth anniversary. It did so because Sir John was the official who, on that May morning in 1696, met the angry mobs demanding their paper pound notes be traded for silver.

History doesn't record what Sir John told the angry mob on the steps of the bank that day, but we can assume it had something to do with the new man at the mint whose genius put the Philosopher's Stone at the beck and call of the bank, for what else would have sent the angry crowds home, never again to question the liquidity of the Bank of England?

England's enemies would never again question her ability to finance wars on the world stage.

The bank's reputed possession of the Philosopher's Stone became irrelevant as the world came to realize that reserve banking is the money machine that buys empire. Adopting a flexible reserve banking system on the eve of the First World War, the United States used the Federal Reserve System to finance the Second World War, the most expensive, and arguably the most successful, war in history.

Newton took over as master of the Bank of England when Neale finally died several years after the run on the bank. His new job gave him the power of life and death over counterfeiters. Prosecuting his duties with vigor, Newton enjoyed disguising himself in rough garb to carouse sordid bars in search of counterfeiters. With armed men close by, hapless rogues attempting to pass counterfeit coins were arrested. With Newton as the sole judge and jury, these men were slowly drawn and quartered, a practice Newton indulged in for the rest of his life.

Montagu maintained control of the moribund Royal Society until the succession of Queen Anne temporarily dimmed his political fortunes. Together with his hand-picked successor, Lord Somers, he chaired only four society meetings in eight years. Newton stepped in and had himself elected president in 1703, filling the post until his death a quarter of a century later.

During the intervening years, he elevated the society to the position of arbiter of what was and was not science. Just as Montagu had promoted Newton's theory of universal gravitation to give the Bank of England the appearance of infallibility, Newton promoted the Royal Society as the sole source of all knowledge in order to give British science the appearance of infallibility.

Along the way, Newton institutionalized his own ideas as central to British science. When it came to practical applications, however, Newton's infallibility fell in the face of reality. His claims to calculus, the subject of a bitter battle with Leibniz over precedence during Newton's lifetime, was settled by practice in favor of Leibniz, whose notation is now universally used.

With regard to the realm of ideas, though, Newton's infallibility remains unchallenged. Hooke, who went to his deathbed claiming precedence for the ideas in Newton's *Principia,* was figuratively drawn and quartered by the band of intellectual sycophants with whom Newton stocked the Royal Society. Newton actually displayed a "ceremonial" mace on the table in front of him at Royal Society meetings to underscore his authority. The implications of a counterfeit coin surreptitiously slipped into one's waistcoat wouldn't be lost on potential dissenters.

Newton never succeeded in his proof of universal gravitation. Subsequent attempts by his intellectual heirs had to be abandoned when the orbits of planets were found to present greater discrepancies than existed with Newton's use of the Moon's orbit.

The failure has left an unproven proposition at the heart of modern science. Instead of abandoning a failed hypothesis, however, science now assumes Newton's universal gravitation as fact. Science then uses this to predict the mass of planets and stars, predictive facts that are not independently verifiable, perpetuating a proposition that has never been, and never can be, tested. Newton's ideas that white light is made up of all colors and that colors are specific wavelengths that emerge from the prism in descending order are propositions—like mass/gravity—as incapable of proof today as they were in his day.

The British Empire Newton helped create collapsed in the twentieth century, but Newton's ideas—which Montagu promoted as infallible in order to establish the monetary basis of empire and which Newton viciously perpetuated by bludgeoning all dissent, remain both omnipresent and baseless—the invisible, unquestioned, and ultimately nonexistent pillars upon which all scientific thought rests.

32 Newton and the Bible

What Did the Great Scientist Foresee for the Year 2060?

John Chambers

On February 22, 2003, the *Daily Telegraph* of London, England, published a front-page story that began with the words: "Sir Isaac Newton, Britain's greatest scientist, predicted the date of the end of the world—and it is only 57 years away."

The *Telegraph* somewhat softened its horrific first paragraph—that Newton had predicted the end of the world for 2060—by declaring in a fourth paragraph: "Newton, who was also a theologian and alchemist, predicted that the Second Coming of Christ would follow plagues and war and would precede a 1,000-year reign by the saints on Earth—of which he would be one."

But the damage was done. Over the next few days, the news was disseminated to every corner of the globe, getting much play in newspapers, on radio, on TV, and on a vast number of Internet news sites—many of which played the story for laughs, showing, for example, a graphic illustration of a mushroom cloud along with the words, "Party like it's 2060!"

Although the 2060 date came as a shock to the general public, which was not even aware of Newton's theological interests, it wasn't news to the small group of scholars who regularly study the theology of Sir Isaac Newton. One of those scholars, Assistant Professor Stephen D. Snobelen of the University of King's College in Halifax, Nova Scotia, had broached it in the course of the *Daily Telegraph* interview, some nine days prior to the airing on Britain's BBC 2 of a documentary, *Newton: The Dark Heretic*. One of the historical consultants for the BBC documentary, Professor Snobelen is shown in a closing sequence handling and commenting on the manuscript bearing the 2060 date at the Jewish National and University Library in Jerusalem.

The explosive date of A.D. 2060 had been known to Newton scholars since the early 1970s. The scientist's theological and alchemical papers remained out of sight in the house of the earl of Portsmouth (a descendant of Newton's niece) for 250 years until, in 1936, the eccentric Jewish scholar Abraham Shalom Ezekiel Yahuda acquired the largest single collection of the theological papers at an auction at Sotheby's in London. Yahuda bequeathed the documents to the State of Israel, but it wasn't until 1967 that they finally ended up in the Jewish Library in Jerusalem. Even so, they remained difficult to access by scholars until 1991, when the majority of Newton's scientific, administrative, theological, and alchemical manuscripts were released on microfilm.

Sir Isaac Newton (1642–1727) was one of the two or three most influential scientists who ever lived. He discovered the three laws of motion; the concepts of mass, force, and universal gravitation; and the true nature of light. In addition, he independently invented (along with Gottfried Leibniz) the differential calculus.

However, he was also one of the most thoroughgoing and perspicacious researchers into theology and alchemy that the world has ever known. This renowned mathematician/scientist believed that the Word of God was writ large both in the natural world—he had done much to uncover those words—and in the Bible, and Newton was just as driven to discover the Word in the latter as in the former. Further powering his drive to plumb the depths of the scriptures, and of all other noteworthy classical texts as well, was his conviction that the ancients had discovered the same laws of the universe as he had discovered. In setting them forth in the three volumes of the *Principia mathematica,* he was merely dressing up—in modern garb—truths that the great thinkers of the past had known since the beginning of time, truths that they had called the *prisca sapientia* ("pristine wisdom").

Newton's announcement, unearthed three centuries after the publication of the *Principia,* that the world would end—or, more accurately, would transition to a very different state—in 2060 was an announcement uniquely destined to arouse passionate interest and anxiety in the year 2003. After all, 2003 was the year the United States invaded Iraq (the land of ancient Babylon), stirring up to no predictable end the international wasp's nest of radical Muslim terrorism. It was the year that North Korea, Pakistan, and India rattled their nuclear sabers. It was a year in which AIDS, a plague of biblical proportions, continued to ravage the world—and when the SARS epidemic leapt out of nowhere as if to give us all a bitter foretaste of apocalyptic doom to come.

To top it off, 2060 was a date dangerously close to 2012—the year when, according to many prophets and prophetic texts both ancient and modern, mankind will be engulfed in a final, world-convulsing holocaust. A 2002 History Channel documentary on "the Bible code" erroneously calls Newton an early investigator into the uncanny, accessible-to-computers-only code popularized by Michael Drosnin in his books *The Bible Code* and *The Bible Code II* (1997 and 2003).

But Newton didn't believe God's prophetic words were embedded in an eternally dynamic subtext hidden beneath the literal text of the Bible. Deeply religious, the scientist was a member of the Church of England even while he adhered, in secret, to the belief of the fourth-century heretic Arius that the doctrine of the Trinity (that God, the Holy Spirit, and Christ are one) was a diabolical falsehood imposed by the early Church. Newton believed that, though the Son and the Holy Spirit were divine, only God was God.

The scientist had come to this belief through a painstaking study of the scriptures and of other, contemporaneous texts. He believed that the Bible was an expression of the word of God, but that there were many corrupt and flawed versions of the Bible. Newton had set himself the lifetime task of minutely and rigorously examining the texts to see exactly what God had said.

He went about this in the same way as the modern biblical scholar, by rounding up all of the different versions of a particular text that he could get his hands on, in Latin, Greek, and Hebrew—his chief interest being in the book of Daniel and of Revelation—and subjecting them to a minute comparative linguistic analysis; from this he would determine the true meaning of the words. Newton's interpretations are then hardly fantastical, and not even mystical (he steered clear of those prophets, like Ezekiel, who seemed to him to speak in wildly emotional terms). For example, his interpretation of the provocative word *beast* in the Book of Revelation, based on careful linguistic analysis, is simply "groups of people or organizations" (notably, the churches).

In a forthcoming book, *Isaac Newton, Heretic,* Professor Snobelen writes that, for Newton, "the holy Prophecies" of the scripture were nothing other than "histories of things to come" (Yahuda MS 1.1, folio 16 recto). Crucial to Newton's interpretation of these highly symbolic texts was his belief that the prophetic time periods of 1260, 1290, 1335, and 2300 days actually represent 1260, 1290, 1335, and 2300 years, using the day-for-a-year principle.

How did Newton come by this strange belief? In a special communication to *Atlantis Rising*, Professor Snobelen writes: "[Newton was . . .] following in the tradition of Joseph Mede, the Cambridge polymath and prophetic exegete who died in 1638. But the day-for-a-year principle is based on other scriptural texts, such as: [Nu 14:34] 'After the number of the days in which ye searched the land, even forty days, each day for a year, shall ye bear your iniquities, even forty years, and ye shall know my breach of promise,' and [Eze 4:6] 'And when thou hast accomplished them, lie again on thy right side, and thou shalt bear the iniquity of the house of Judah forty days: I have appointed thee each day for a year.'"

Professor Snobelen sets out the prophetic time periods in this way: "The time period 1260 days appears in Daniel 7:25 (as 'a time and times and the dividing of time' [equal to 'a year, two years and a half year']), Daniel 12:7 (as 'a time, times, and an half' [equal to 'a year, two years and a half year']), Revelation 11:3 (1260 days), Revelation 12:6 (1260 days), and Revelation 13:5 (42 months). The time period 1290 days appears in Daniel 12:11. The time period 1335 days appears in Daniel 12:12. The time period 2300 days occurs in Daniel 8:14."

For Newton, these time periods—especially that of 1,260 years—represent the period during which the corrupted Church (this being, for Newton, the Trinitarian Church, chiefly the Catholics) went into a slow decline: that is, the period of its "apostasy," or abandonment of true beliefs. The problem lay in tracking down the exact date of commencement of the period of apostasy. To this date would be added the figure of 1,260 years, thereby arriving at the exact year when the Church would finally crumble, bringing in the wake of its demise a rash of wars and plagues, following upon which the Second Coming of Christ would usher in the New Millennium.

Newton picked up and discarded many commencement dates, until finally, toward the end of his life, he settled upon the year when the papal church had once and for all gathered up all temporal power. This date for the "formal institution of the apostate, imperial Church"—the beginning of the period of "the Pope's supremacy"—was A.D. 800, "the year Charlemagne was crowned emperor of Rome in the west by Pope Leo III." Adding 1,260 years to 800 brings us to the year 2060, when "Babylon will fall," the apostate Church will cease, and Christ will return to Earth to set up a global 1,000-year kingdom of God.

On page 144 of his *Observations* (1733), Newton cited Daniel 7:26–27 as evidence: "But the judgment shall sit, and they shall take away his dominion to consume and to destroy it unto the end. And the kingdom and dominion, and the greatness of the kingdom under the whole heaven, shall be given to the people of the saints of the most High, whose kingdom is an everlasting kingdom, and all dominions shall serve and obey him."

The Halifax professor is quick to say that Newton did not believe the world would literally end in 2060. Rather, there will be a wholly new beginning. "Before the Second Coming, the Jews would return to Israel according to the predictions made in biblical prophecy," he says. "The Temple would be rebuilt as well. Slightly before, or around the time of Christ's return, the great battle of Armageddon would take place when a series of nations (the 'Gog and Magog' confederacy of Ezekiel's prophecy) invade Israel." Christ and the saints would then intervene to establish the worldwide 1,000-year Kingdom of

God. This would be a time of peace and prosperity; in the *Observations*, Newton quotes Micah 4:3: "[The people will] beat their swords into plowshares, and their spears into pruninghooks," and "nations shall not lift up a sword against nation, neither shall they learn war any more."

One of the most compelling aspects of Newton's predicted date of 2060 is how far in the future, comparatively speaking, he sets the time for the "end of the world." A tiny minority of prophetic exegetes around about Newton's time placed the end time in the twenty-first century, but the trend was to place the end within or not long after one's lifetime. Joseph Mede, setting the commencement date at A.D. 476—the time of the fall of the Roman Empire—concluded that the end would come in 1736; William Lloyd, bishop of Worcester, announced in person to Queen Anne in 1712 that Vatican City would be consumed by a flame of fire from heaven in the year 1716; and "Newton's own prophetic disciple William Whiston set 1736 as the end of the 1260 years and the year 1766 as the beginning of the Millennium."

Newton's mid-twenty-first-century date comes, of course, from his choosing as the commencement date the time when the Roman Catholic Church achieved total hegemony over worldly affairs—A.D. 800. But we may ask ourselves: Did Newton know more? Did one of the greatest thinkers of all time—and the man who read more ancient works of arcane literature than anyone before or since—know something that no one else knew?

Professor Snobelen wonders if Newton, who hated prophetic date-setters, would be infuriated if he knew that the whole world now knows his date of 2060. Or would he simply "have been satisfied that now, as we are moving toward the age in which the true gospel is to be preached, it is time to preach openly?" Concludes the Halifax professor: "We will have to wait until 2060 to ask him."

33 The Remarkable Life of G. I. Gurdjieff

Though His Saga Remains One of Mystery, His Influence Is Difficult to Overstate

John Chambers

Peter Brook's 1979 movie *Meetings with Remarkable Men* remains an admirable introduction to the life of the Russian seeker and teacher of esoteric truths G. I. Gurdjieff (1866?–1949), who taught ascension to the Fourth Way of higher consciousness—with methods that were brilliant, brutal, and wildly controversial. Gurdjieff was born in Alexandropol, in Armenia. The movie (based on Gurdjieff's eponymous autobiography) was filmed in Afghanistan, and opens with the scene of a rocky valley floor streaming with TransCaspian peoples who are about to witness an unusual music competition. The musicians, some playing extremely ancient instruments, compete to produce a sound that will evoke a response from the surrounding mountains—an echo, perhaps, or a boulder tumbling down. It's finally the exotic exultation of a single human voice that draws an answering echo from the rocky peaks. The contest is over, but the life of Gurdjieff, who is seen here as a boy attending the competition, has only just begun to sing its exotic song—of Fourth Way redemption—to a struggling humanity.

The boy returns to his house and an unusual relationship with his father, an *astrokh,* one of a vanishing breed of epic bards. As the film unfolds, we see the old man rouse his son with cold showers, slip snakes into his bed and hands, and impart strange knowledge to him. Gurdjieff asks, "Is there life after death?" The father replies, "Only for the few whose exceptional lives have created in them a certain substance that survives death." The old man's belief will become a source of the mature Gurdjieff's conviction that we must vigorously "make" our own souls to ensure a life in the afterworld—and of his belief in our making a concomitant substance, Askokin, with which we "feed the moon."

Brook's movie takes the young Gurdjieff through a series of encounters with the occult. A man rises, zombie-like, from the grave; a demon must be responsible, and a village elder cuts the dead man's throat. Placed in a trance by dervishes, a boy struggles unsuccessfully to break out of a magic circle drawn on the ground; Gurdjieff himself steps forward to yank the boy to safety. The future teacher/guru witnesses "table-turning," sees simple potions cure lethal, violent diseases. His appetite for the esoteric grows.

Brook's movie goes on to focus upon the burning desire of the adult Gurdjieff to discover the secret Brotherhood of the Sarmoung, said to possess primordial esoteric knowledge. Gurdjieff progresses through a succession of encounters with "remarkable men." At the culmination of these meetings, we find Gurdjieff, with a companion, traveling blindfolded on horseback, guided by four Kara-Kirghiz tribesman across the rocky plains of Turkestan. Their destination is the secret monastery of the Brotherhood of the Sarmoung.

Arriving at the monastery after twelve days, Gurdjieff soon witnesses sacred dances that, preserved through the millennia, encode the motions of the planets and the basic forms of arcane knowledge in their movements. These dances, properly executed, serve to evoke this knowledge in the dancers' souls. Soon afterward, the young Gurdjieff, still at the secret monastery of the Sarmoung Brotherhood, sadly bids farewell to his dearest friend, who is departing for the Himalayas and another monastery. On this note, Peter Brook's movie ends.

Gurdjieff's life still had a long and spectacular way to go. After innumerable and unchronicled travels through the Middle and Far East in search of occult knowledge, the Armenian esotericist/adventurer returned to Russia and began the classes in Sacred Dance and the Fourth Way that P. D. Ouspensky describes so meticulously and brilliantly in *In Search of the Miraculous*. The year was 1915. Soon, World War I and the Russian Revolution forced Gurdjieff to flee eastward, under extraordinarily difficult circumstances, with his tiny band of (sometimes eminent) students. The tattered crew of seekers crossed the Caucasus, settled briefly in Tiflis, Georgia, then went on to Constantinople, Berlin, and finally Paris.

In 1922, Gurdjieff rented the Prieuré des Basses Loges, near Fontainebleau. Thus began in earnest Gurdjieff's immensely controversial (and well-documented) Institute for the Harmonious Development of Man, which might have continued indefinitely had not a disastrous car accident in 1924 forced Gurdjieff to close it down. The weakened teacher then turned to writing. *Meetings with Remarkable Men* (the first of his three books) was not to be published until 1960. From 1934 until his death in 1949, Gurdjieff lived in Paris, continuing to receive and teach the occasional student. His work, of course, did not die with him; it continues today, in various schools and countries.

Gurdjieff's teachings and methodology—thought to come from the Sarmoung Brotherhoods that the teacher plumbed in the early decades of his life—are not only actively taught today but sound a subtle note in the cultural consciousness of our time as well. To grossly oversimplify: Gurdjieff taught that humanity dwells in four states of consciousness, with the vast majority occupying the first, a brutish, unaware, animal "sleep." In the second, "waking-consciousness," man is sporadically aware he is asleep. In the third, "self-consciousness," or "self-remembering," man actively fights his way toward a higher awareness by attempting to align his three centers—the physical, the emotional, and the intellectual. The fourth state is the ascension to objective consciousness—establishment in the Fourth Way.

Gurdjieff's classroom techniques, aimed at achieving objective consciousness, often seem brutal; certainly, there can no longer be any doubt that he was the progenitor of "tough love." Gurdjieff believed that we are so frozen in our conditioning—our three centers are so hopelessly, mechanically, uncontrollably out of whack with one another—that we need to be shocked, surprised, and/or practically abused in order to let go of their ordinary, set configurations.

In teaching the Stop exercises, a student was required to stop dead no matter what he was doing. Thus frustrated in following through with his normal conditioning, the student would be forced to cast about for new reactions. Voluntary Suffering kept the student engaged in activities long past the time when he began to feel pain and would normally have stopped; thus he was forced to forge new, unprogrammed—and possibly promising—connections between the three centers. Sacred Movements and Dances that introduced the student to new (or, Gurdjieff would have said, ancient and forgotten), exacting physical and consequently emotional and intellectual patterns of behavior further broke down ossification of old habits and opened the way for a renewed harmony between the centers.

Fig. 33.1. The incomparable G. I. Gurdjieff, whose teachings broke new ground in the field of consciousness studies.

There were many other exercises. Over them all loomed Gurdjieff's magisterial concept of self-remembering. To attempt to describe it (albeit at a great injustice): We must at every moment strive mightily not to let the body respond merely according to old and established patterns of behavior. We must continuously split our attention between the doing of a thing and the watching of the doing of it. In this way, we can monitor it, perhaps change it—and, by never ceasing to maintain a distance between our objective consciousness and the actions that were carried out in its name, we might hope to escape the Terror of the Moment and take another step in the direction of the Fourth Way.

The past decades have not seen a significant increase in the number of practitioners of the Gurdjieffian Way. Even in its heyday—at the time of the Prieuré—critics were quick to point out that students didn't seem to change very quickly and many seemed addicted to the Work and to Gurdjieff himself. This has led not a few critics to conclude that the many exercises in self-remembering do not really conduce to a state of objective consciousness. Or that objective consciousness, whatever it is, has little to do with the annihilation of the ego, nirvana, or the "establishment in the Self" of Siddha Yoga (to describe this much desired state in somewhat more classical terms).

The self-remembering of Gurdjieff, while also intended to underline the non-identity between the self and its actions, called for continuous attention to every one of an individual's worldly acts in such a way as to also continuously draw attention to the ego; the classical meditation of the yogi entailed, rather, continuous attention upon the higher Self within. At a luncheon at the Prieuré in the summer of 1926 or 1927, Gurdjieff criticized, in racial terms, the celebrated essayist/philosopher Waldo Frank's choice of a new wife. Frank never forgave the teacher of esotericism, and his comments in a much later work, *Rediscovery,* seem to many to accurately sum up the shortcomings of self-remembering.

Admitting the necessity of unburdening ourselves of the barrier to truth that the ego constitutes, Frank nonetheless contended that "the value axioms of the original method were never discussed. . . . A method aimed at freeing the self from its ego center became an instrument for developing the ego. . . . The 'I' that observes the body and the world remains unchallengedly ego." Frank unabashedly associated Gurdjieff's "power-ego" with that of Mussolini.

Some wonder whether Gurdjieff's scandalous personal behavior entitled him to exact from his pupils the degree of personal loyalty and unthinking obedience that he did. In *Gurdjieff: A Biography,* James Moore quotes T. S. Matthews's turning of the witty phrase "'His women followers obviously adored him, and some who had found favor in his sight had visible mementos: swarthy and liquid-eyed children.'"

But Paul Beekman Taylor—whose half sister was Gurdjieff's illegitimate daughter—describes in *Gurdjieff and Orage* the sometimes cruel indifference with which the master treated a number of his mistresses and their (his) illegitimate offspring. One mistress who certainly wasn't cast out was Jeanne de Salzmann, who became Gurdjieff's successor at the Paris Gurdjieff Foundation upon his death in 1949, holding that position till her own death in 1990 at the age of 101. De Salzmann bore Gurdjieff a son, Michel, in 1926; that son, "swarthy and liquid-eyed," is now the head of the Paris institute.

Critics wonder whether Gurdjieff's many couplings with his (sometimes) married students really make him any different from Rajneesh, the notorious guru who, residing in the United States, regularly slept with his students and owned ninty-nine Cadillacs (Gurdjieff, too, had a huge predilection for cars).

Gurdjieffians reply that, in effect, "[w]hat does a foible or two matter for somebody established in objective consciousness?" But it may be a question, not of morality, but of Being (a word of which Gurdjieff was fond, and which holds a high place in his eschatology): Can the philanderer really be so completely separate from the teacher/philosopher, especially in the case of a man like Gurdjieff who considered himself to be "established" in objective consciousness, and totally integrated? By integrated, we mean that he did not consider himself to be a "collection of I's" like most of the human race, but a single "I."

Will not one area seriously affect the other?

In recent years, there has been renewed interest in Gurdjieff's bizarre, 1,238-page novel, *Beelzebub's Tales to His Grandson,* especially through the annual *All and Everything* International Humanities conferences coordinated by Seymour B. Ginsburg of Miami and Chicago. These researches have suggested that the novel—and its author also—may be more complexly profound than was previously thought. Gurdjieff wrote the novel over many years, often freely employing the talents of his multilingual students. The deliberate obfuscation of its style (which he did, he said, to prevent the reader from grasping its meaning too quickly—calling this stratagem "burying the dog") masks what the old-time sci-fi pulp magazines called a "space opera." However, it's a space opera with two astounding differences: The major character is Beelzebub, or Satan; and the book aims at being nothing less than an allegorical account of the whole history of mankind, from the birth of our planet, to humankind's fall, to its possible redemption.

Still, even some mainstream scholars recognize that *Beelzebub's Tales to His Grandson* falls into the great tradition of epic accounts of the Fall of Man, including *Paradise Lost,* the later poems of William Blake (e.g., *The Four Zoas*), and James Joyce's *Finnegan's Wake.*

Asked why Gurdjieff's novel has to be quite so weird and impenetrable, Gurdjieffians reply that it's because *Beelzebub's Tales* is woven out of Gurdjieff's unique and comprehensive knowledge of ancient, esoteric, and lost learning. Asked why, if it's so innately difficult, then, Gurdjieff had to go on and deliberately obfuscate the style, they say that this strategy is consonant with Gurdjieff's overall strategy of voluntary suffering. They quote the master's words about his early life: "I wished to create around myself conditions in which a man would be continuously reminded of the sense and aim of his existence, by an avoidable friction between his conscience and the automatic manifestations of his nature."

Adds Sy Ginsburg: "Gurdjieff wanted the book to be read twice silently and a third time out loud. It's speculated that this reading aloud allows the content to bypass the intellect and impact the emotions much more powerfully. Crucial to this is the reading aloud of the 500 plus special words which Gurdjieff constructed from a very wide variety of languages, which 'universal' sounds presumably have an even vaster effect on the emotional center."

Ginsburg, who writes extensively on *Beelzebub's Tales,* believes the book may be a recapitulation of the actual last six reincarnations of Gurdjieff. He also believes Gurdjieff may be the "dancing master" who Theosophical Society founder Helena Blavatsky predicted would be the great teacher of esotericism of the early twentieth century.

However strange G. I. Gurdjieff's intellectual doctrines may seem, however unpleasant his personal behavior and some of his teaching methods, there's little doubt that the thought and teaching techniques of this remarkable esotericist and first proponent of tough love continue to exert a subtle influence. Perhaps, with the growing attention paid to Gurdjieff's *Beelzebub's Tales to His Grandson* by groups such as the All and Everything conferences—and increasingly by universities—the influence may become considerably more than that.

PART SIX

THE SPIRIT AND THE SOUL

34 The Casting Out of Evil Spirits

A Pioneering Psychotherapist Points Her Profession Back to Its Roots

Cynthia Logan

Remember *The Exorcist* and its chilling scenes that caused various reactions among audiences? Whereas some enjoyed the intense effects and dismissed the film as mere entertainment, many experienced an uncomfortable encounter with energies we would like to relegate to Hollywood's active imagination, but can't. Indeed, there is ample evidence that evil manifests on Earth, acting through humans, animals, and nature itself. From swine trapped in the body of a demented man (cast out by Jesus) to heartless, senseless murder and twisted tortures all over the globe, Satan shows his face. And it's not just the gross deviations that constitute evil.

A growing number of people say they are experiencing demonic possession in subtle ways that manifest as various physical, mental, and emotional symptoms and conditions. For them, phrases such as "The devil made me do it," "He's wrestling with his demons," and "What possessed you to do that?" are more than mere adages. These people are sure they are being influenced by demons and, after trying conventional means, many are turning to Dr. Shakuntala Modi for "spirit releasement."

Modi, a board-certified psychiatrist practicing in Wheeling, West Virginia, notes that while seemingly New Age spirit releasement has a significant history, "[t]he earliest evidence of the need to deal with spirits is the work of primitive medicine men, or shamans. . . . Later, the medicine man emerged, using prayers, herbs, drinks, and music to induce the spiritual awareness necessary to ward off evil spirits. The Greeks and Romans believed mania to be possession by evil spirits who represented 'the cult of the dead.'" (Interestingly, by contrast, the Arabs believed the insane to be sent by God to tell the truth and worshipped them as saints.)

According to Modi, the history of psychiatry traces a backward movement. "Over the years, psychiatrists have wandered down countless blind alleys, looking for alternative, 'more scientific' answers to mental illness than those purported by the ancients," she says. "Today, the mental health community is coming full circle, back to the understandings of their early counterparts, such as Plato, who described madness as a state in which 'the wanting soul loses the thinking soul,' causing people to act against their rational natures."

Dr. Modi's own history began in central India. As a child, she lost her father and was raised by an uncle, along with her siblings and cousins. She wanted to become a doctor for as long as she could remember. When family finances became such that only she or her brother could become a doctor, her brother sacrificed his own ambition so that she could achieve hers, an astounding act considering the country's gender prejudice.

Modi became an obstetrician/gynecologist and married a general surgeon. Their son, Raju, was born in India. When they moved to America, Modi realized that, without the extended family system they had enjoyed in India, either she or her husband would have to make a career change. "I had been interested in psychiatry and thought it would be a way I could be a working mother," she says. After graduate school, she practiced traditional psychiatry; using hypnotherapy as an adjunct, she earned an excellent reputation among her peers and enjoyed hospital admittance privileges.

In 1988, her practice began a radical evolution. She became aware of the concept of past-life regression when a patient suffering with claustrophobia instantly regressed to another life in which she was being buried alive. After the session, the patient was relieved of her long-standing and disabling condition.

These results are what keep Dr. Modi pursuing what she often calls God's Work, which forms the collection of case studies in her popular book, *Remarkable Healings*. Replete with case histories, the book details the stories of patient after patient describing similar phenomena. "The results speak for themselves," she says. "People are getting well, their symptoms are clearing, and they are able to resume normal lives." According to Modi, relief is often immediate and dramatic, with patients reporting that they feel more alive and energetic than ever before, or light and empty, as if a great weight had been lifted from them. Others say they can breathe more easily, and that relationships have improved.

Modi emphasizes that hypnotism is not the dramatic, induced state we stereotypically think of. It is, rather, a "parallel awareness" achieved when we focus our concentration deeply and slip into fantasy, or become so absorbed in conversation that we tune out those around us. "The subconscious contains the soul memories of every lifetime," says Modi, adding, "Everything we have

Fig. 34.1. The author and healer Dr. Shakuntala Modi, whose therapeutic work assists in exorcising negative energies from the patient.

ever touched, sensed, smelled, felt, heard, experienced, and done is recorded—not only from our current lifetime, but from all past lives, the time between incarnations, and even from the time of our soul's creation and the creation of the Universe."

While the subconscious can bring up these memories, Modi feels it is vital to include the conscious mind as well. She deliberately avoids using classic relaxation techniques associated with hypnotism (such as counting backwards and suggestions that the patient is becoming sleepy). "Learning takes place consciously," she says emphatically. "We need to be consciously aware of what's going on, not push the memories back into the subconscious!"

According to hypnotized patients, some people have firm boundaries around their energy field, or aura, as if they are heavily armored. This boundary prevents outside spirits from entering them. Other people have soft, porous, fuzzy boundaries, making it easier for the spirits to penetrate their shields and bodies. Different physical and emotional conditions, behaviors, and situations can open one to psychic possession. "We are most vulnerable when ill, injured, unconscious, sedated, or anesthetized," says Modi. Playing with conjuring games such as Dungeons and Dragons, using a Ouija board, engaging in automatic writing or channeling can also invite unwanted "guests."

It's scary stuff. And as if we don't have plenty to deal with during birth and present-life trauma, Modi says our souls can fragment, leaving a core self, bereft of various parts that took off during past or present life trauma, or left to help or stay with a deceased loved one. We can also be possessed by Earthbound spirits, or by demon entities who can plant false past-life memories within us.

Even worse, they claim to implant mechanical devices that interfere with heavenly guidance and influence us negatively, as Modi's patient Josephine, who had severe bulimia, experienced. According to her, dark beings would project a food commercial through devices implanted over her mind that would cause her to think about those foods and then consume them until she would throw up.

Other patients described devices that pushed, pulled, or applied pressure to various organs and tissues in their bodies. They claimed these devices were either active or passive "physical displacement" devices, each tailored specifically to achieve a particular aim, such as throwing off a joint by a fraction, putting pressure on a nerve, or squeezing two bones tightly so they would grate and scrape together. Other devices discovered were "focusing and amplifying devices," such as a focusing dish or wave machine and "black energy absorbers" that, rather than causing active pain, induced a state of chronic fatigue.

Though demons are deliberate and diabolical, Modi advocates practicing releasement with compassion—"I actually treat the entity as a secondary patient," she says. According to her, even the darkest spirit can be transformed and released into the light. She notes a distinction between exorcism and releasement: "Exorcism is a religious ritual marked by the forceful expulsion of a demon entity. It is confrontational, wrenching, and physically and emotionally exhausting to the exorcist and to the subject. It directs judgment upon the entity itself, damning it and casting it out. It can be grabbed by Satan and brutally punished, it can go to another host, or it can return to the person from whom it was cast out."

Modi cautions that, before considering spirit releasement, potential patients should rule out biochemical causes and organic brain disorders, such as those that have been clearly implicated in schizophrenia.

It's a soft, calm voice that people are turning to to help them cast out demons. Modi's Indian accent adds a melodious quality to a quiet, reverent tone. A typical session involving past-life regression includes the following steps: grounding and identification—during which patients are asked to look at their feet and describe what they are wearing, which leads to a recognition of who they are in that current life; processing the traumatic event that comes up from that life, during which Dr. Modi guides her patients through their event, encouraging them to recall, relive, and release the trauma completely; undergoing the process of death, the transition to heaven, and experiences in the light.

These experiences are commonly reported to consist of being greeted by light beings, "ventilation" (where the person undergoing the therapy may be invited to vent pent-up emotions), soul cleansing, a life review, an opportunity to recognize other people and to make connections between the past and current life, and an opportunity to forgive others as well as oneself. "Forgiving yourself for hurting others is the most difficult step in forgiveness," says Modi. "When I ask patients to look back and see when they were hurting someone, they almost always say they see demon entities telling them and pushing them to do the wrong things."

After these experiences are completed, Modi moves on to locating, retrieving, and integrating fragmented soul parts, integrating the past-life personality. Modi says that her patients often describe heaven as a sphere with two sections: "The outer section is like the porch of a house, where things are in an Earthly form. After cleansing, reviewing, and resting, the soul goes down a pathway into the gate of an inner section, where everything is in spiritual form." Here, patients say that they learn, have discussions with others, and plan for the next life. This planning includes personal and group goals.

Once cleared of past-life trauma or entity/demon possession, patients are counseled to stay in the light through a protection prayer given twice daily. Modi suggests her patients request their angels to "remove all the Earthbound, demon and other entities, dark shields, dark energies, dark devices, and dark connections from my body, aura, soul, and silver cord, and also from my home, workplace, car, and places of recreation; then ask them to fill and shield you in a bubble of light and reflective 'spiritual mirrors.' You, and only you, have a right to live in your body/mind!"

While Modi feels that she enjoys a fully integrated, entity-free soul, she refuses to take on the role of healer, insisting that she is a researcher, simply reporting what her patients tell her. She is careful to make this distinction so that the work is presented objectively and will withstand the rigors of scientific scrutiny. So far, her work hasn't come under the microscope. "Those who are ready to see embrace this work," she says, "while those who are not ready don't understand it." She says that her husband and son, both physicians, "sort of understand."

Her work is a consuming passion and Modi, who doesn't own a computer, spent hundreds of hours writing *Remarkable Healings* in longhand, as she does each of her case studies. "I don't want to entrust this to anyone else to transcribe," she says. Despite what she calls "serious writer's block," she is working on a second book, due out next year, which will consider "the nature of God and Creation itself. It will be very exciting," she promises. Modi cautions that her current book is not a how-to manual for laypeople; she suggests contacting the Association for Past-life Research and Therapies, Incorporated, and gives their address and phone number as a reference. The book, though, is becoming a bible of sorts; passed from hand to hand, it is a catalyst for calls that Modi is getting from all over the world. "People come and stay a week or so for intensive therapy," she says.

Freeing oneself of spirit entities does not come cheap; Modi charges the going rate of one hundred and fifty dollars per hour and sessions usually last from three to six hours. Multiply that by the ten or twelve sessions you're likely to need and you've got a bill of between four and five thousand dollars. But, as Modi points out, that's often much less than what people spend on medical treatments over a longer period without benefit of the clear healing that her shorter, intensive work seems to offer.

Though she hasn't conducted any formal studies of long-term cures, Modi has compiled tables comparing primary and secondary emotional and physical symptoms of patients. After hundreds of "remarkable healings," Modi has concluded: "Every disease is a disease of the soul and, with God's help, we can cure anything."

35 The Paranormal Autobiography of Benvenuto Cellini

Did Cosmic Forces Rescue the Great Renaissance Goldsmith?

John Chambers

On a gloomy day in mid-May 1539, Benvenuto Cellini, Italy's greatest goldsmith, lay on a dank pallet in a dungeon in the Castle of Sant' Angelo in Rome and decided to commit suicide.

He had already escaped from his dungeon once, by lowering himself down the castle wall on a rope made of strips of bedsheets, breaking his leg at the bottom. He'd managed to crawl to the house of an eminent friend, but almost immediately was betrayed and hustled back into prison.

This time he'd been flung into a dungeon far worse than the last, so deep and dark that his mattress was already soaked through with seeping water, where the sunlight filtered down from the slit of a window for only an hour and a half a day. Large spiders and venomous worms were everywhere. Because of his broken leg, he had to crawl to the side of the cell to relieve himself.

For a man of Cellini's active, exuberant, even volcanic temperament, this was a living hell. He decided to end his life. But in this starkly empty cubicle, it was hard to figure out how. He looked around; then, as he later wrote in his *Autobiography:*

> I took and propped a wooden pole I found there, in position like a trap. I meant to make it topple over on my head, and it would certainly have dashed my brains out; but when I had arranged the whole machine, and was approaching to put it in motion, just at the moment of my setting my hand to it, I was seized by an invisible power and flung four cubits [six feet] from the spot, in such a terror that I lay half dead. Like that I remained from dawn until the nineteenth hour, when they brought my food.

When Cellini awoke, priests were standing over him; he had been taken for dead. The prison warden, or castellan, taking pity on Cellini, sent him a new mattress. He tells us that, lying on the mattress that night, "[w]hen I searched my memory to find what could have diverted me from that design of suicide, I came to the conclusion that it must have been power divine and my good guardian angel."

An incredible dream that night seemed to support his conclusion. He encountered "a marvelous being in the form of a most lovely youth, who cried, as though he wanted to reprove me: 'Knowest thou who lent thee that body, which thou wouldst have spoiled before its time?'" Cellini replied that he "'recognized all things pertaining to me as gifts from the God of nature.' The beautiful youth rejoined, 'Thou hast contempt for His handiwork, through this thy will to spoil it? Commit thyself unto His guidance, and lose not hope in His great goodness!'" There was much more, Cellini tells us, "in words of marvelous efficacy, the thousandth part of which I cannot now remember."

This dream encounter galvanized Cellini into a frenzy of creative activity. He mixed crumbled stone with his urine to make ink. He chewed a splinter off the cell door to make a pen. He wrote a long poem in the margins of his Bible, describing his body chastising his soul for wanting to leave too early.

This brought him around to reading his Bible. Cellini became captivated by what he read. "With profound astonishment," he writes, "I dwelt upon the force of God's Spirit in those men of great simplicity, who believed so fervently that He would bring all their heart's desire to pass." The prisoner goldsmith decided to imitate these men. Then, he writes, "[t]here flowed into my soul so powerful a delight from these reflections upon God, that I took no further thought for all the anguish I had suffered, but rather spent the day in singing psalms and divers other compositions on the theme of His divinity."

Cellini's captivity in the Castle of Sant' Angelo was far from over. There would be other desperate situations—but, for each one, there would be another seemingly miraculous intervention. Finally, a frail but fiercely joyous Cellini would stand outside the prison, a free man as well as a celebrated craftsman in the boisterous, brilliant final decades of the great Italian Renaissance.

The presence of divine protection in his life seems to have been announced from the start to Benvenuto Cellini, who was born in Florence in 1500 and died there in 1571. At the age of three, he picked up a deadly scorpion and, unaware of its danger, held it in his hands. Only after his father declawed it in his hands would the little boy, somehow unharmed, let it go. Afterward the family "took the occurrence for a good augury." When Cellini was five, his father spotted a salamander "sporting in the intensest coals" in the fireplace, and called Cellini over to see it. At that time, it was thought that salamanders lived in fire, and it was considered a rare miracle to see one doing so. It's likely Cellini ever after regarded this encounter as symbolic of his own unique ability to pass unscathed through the fire of life's disasters.

Apprenticed to the most illustrious goldsmiths of the day, Cellini acquired a reputation as a gifted and original craftsman. The belligerent goldsmith also acquired a reputation as a brawler. He never stopped quarreling with the rich, the powerful, and anyone who came along. He even committed (for good reason, he told himself) the occasional murder. His defiant, hot-headed, self-righteous, and difficult nature led to his frequent banishment from city after city; throughout his life, he crisscrossed Italy (even spending some time in France) as a sought-after and brilliantly productive craftsman, creating objets d'art—coinage, medals, medallions, and the occasional sculpture—for patrons in both civil and religious arenas.

Fig. 35.1. Cellini's famous gold, ebony, and enamel saltcellar depicting Neptune and a reclining woman.

Always, the supernatural never seemed far off. In the deserted Roman Coliseum one midnight in 1532, he actively solicited the supernatural. With a professional necromancer, two assistants, and a virginal twelve-year-old boy meant to seduce the deceased, the audacious goldsmith tried to summon the spirits of the dead. Cellini only wanted to ask if he would see his girlfriend—the prostitute Angelina—again (he was told he would, in one month, and this came true). For their trouble, the ghost hunters were rewarded with a vision of a million howling demons and the Coliseum in flames. Hallucination or not, the adventurers ran home screaming—or so Cellini tells us in his *Autobiography*.

In 1535, the craftsman/author became deathly ill, hovering between life and death for weeks. During this time, it seemed to him that he was wrestling every night with the actual Charon, the boatman of Greek myth said to ferry the souls of the dead across the River Styx to the afterworld. Cellini wrote: "[T]he terrible old man used to come to my bedside, and make as though he would drag me by force into a huge boat he had with him." Even as Cellini described the apparition to a friend, "the old man took me by the arm and dragged me violently towards him. This made me cry out for aid, because he was going to fling me under hatches in his hideous boat." Cellini finally began to recover his health, and it was only then that "that old man ceased to give so much annoyance, yet sometimes he appeared to me in dreams."

Cellini did not back away from quarreling with the most powerful man in Italy and the goldsmith's employer for awhile, Pope Clement VII. This is probably why, in 1538—most likely on trumped-up charges—he was imprisoned in the Castle of Sant' Angelo. His miraculous rescue from suicide by the intercession of a guardian angel didn't mark the end of his difficulties. The castellan, furious that Cellini was more joyful than the castellan himself, ordered that the prisoner be flung into an even deeper dungeon. So roughly was Cellini carted toward this dungeon (his broken leg having healed, he tells us, because he "had so often dreamed that angels came and ministered to me") that he feared he would be thrown into the infamous oubliette of Sammabo, where men plummeted "to the bottom of a deep pit in the foundations of the castle." Ending up

Fig. 35.2. A portrait of the Renaissance goldsmith Benvenuto Cellini.

in just another dungeon, Cellini became so joyful that "[d]uring the whole of that first day, I kept festival with God, my heart rejoicing ever in the strength of hope and faith."

The castellan was beside himself. He had Cellini carted back to his old cell, and issued an order for Cellini's execution—making sure word got back to Cellini. Hearing this was too much, even for Cellini's mighty spirit; he decided for a second time to kill himself. "At this juncture," he wrote, "the invisible being who had diverted me from my intention of suicide, came to me, being still invisible, but with a clear voice, and shook me, and made me rise, and said to me. 'Ah me! my Benvenuto, quick, quick, betake thyself to God with thy accustomed prayers, and cry out loudly, loudly.' In a sudden consternation," writes Cellini, "I fell upon my knees, and recited several of my prayers in a loud voice; after this I said *Qui habitat in adjutorio;* then I communed a space with God; and in an instant the same clear and open voice said to me: 'Go to rest, and have no further fear!'"

The next day, inexplicably even to the castellan himself, the castellan canceled the order for Cellini's execution.

Cellini rejoiced with even greater fervor now, working himself into a most exalted state of altered consciousness. The stage was set for another encounter with the supernatural. He had been begging his guardian angel, whom he considered to be always present, to give him just one last look at the Sun. Waking up one morning to a particularly dark dungeon, Cellini beseeched God himself to grant him such a favor.

Immediately, his invisible angel "like a whirlwind, caught me up and bore me away into a large room, where he made himself visible to my eyes in human form, appearing like a young man whose beard is just growing, with a face of indescribable beauty, but austere, not wanton." Cellini was led through a "little low door" into a narrow street and told to climb up a huge spiral staircase. As he ascended, the goldsmith found himself coming "within the region of the sunlight . . . until I discovered the whole sphere of the Sun. The strength of his rays, as is their wont, first made me close my eyes; but becoming aware of my misdoing, I opened them wide, and gazing steadfastly at the Sun, exclaimed: 'Oh, my Sun, for whom I have so passionately yearned! Albeit your rays may blind me, I do not wish to look on anything again but this!'"

The rays spread to one side, and, as Cellini watched, "a Christ upon the cross formed itself out of the same substance as the Sun." Next, a Madonna appeared, holding a child and escorted by two "indescribably beautiful" angels. "The marvelous apparition remained before me little more than half a quarter of an hour: then it dissolved, and I was carried back to my dark lair," writes

Cellini. He had brought back with him a souvenir from this marvelous out-of-body journey to the Sun: a permanent halo around his head. This "aureole of glory," Cellini declared, "is visible to every sort of [man] to whom I have chosen to point it out; but those have been very few."

Perhaps the castellan saw the halo, and was rebuked. Very soon afterward, Cellini was released.

The goldsmith/author continued to be borne up by the supernatural. But his angelic guardians never showed themselves to greater advantage than when they rescued his greatest work of art from certain disaster.

Cellini's finest artistic achievement is arguably his *Perseus Holding the Head of Medusa* (1545–54), a larger-than-life-sized bronze statue, which still stands today in the Loggia dei Lanzi in Florence.

No one thought that Cellini would be able to cast a bronze statue of such enormous size (eigthteen feet in height, including the pedestal). Not only did the technology for such a feat scarcely exist in sixteenth-century Italy, but also Cellini's enemies were actively scheming to sabotage the work. In the final weeks of this great endeavor, with the aid of ten assistants, Cellini constructed a huge and highly innovative furnace around the baked-clay-and-wax prototype of the *Perseus*. In the final hours of casting, after the most strenuous exertions and just as the casting furnace was starting to liquefy the bronze, Cellini felt himself seized by a fever "of the utmost possible intensity." Certain he'd be dead by morning, he dragged himself to bed, reluctantly leaving the hugely difficult final stage in the hands of his assistants.

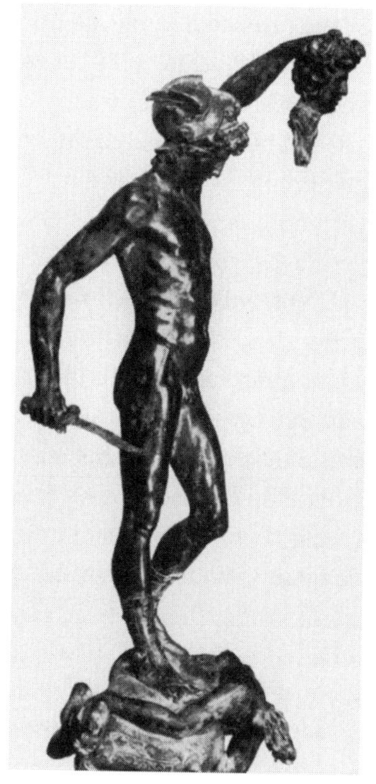

Fig. 35.3. A triumphant Perseus holds up the severed head of Medusa in this eighteen-foot-high statue by Cellini.

Cellini spent the next two hours "battling with the fever, which steadily increased, and calling out continually, 'I feel that I am dying!'" while his despairing housekeeper fought to hide her tears. Suddenly, Cellini writes, "I beheld the figure of a man enter my chamber, twisted in his body into the form of a capital S. He raised a lamentable, doleful voice, like one who announces their last hour to men condemned to die upon the scaffold, and spoke these words: 'O Benvenuto! Your statue is spoiled, and there is no hope whatever of saving it.'"

Howling with rage at these words, Cellini leapt out of bed, pulled on his clothes, and raced for the workshop. He found his assistants standing around morosely; through some disaster, the molten bronze was beginning to coagulate in the furnace.

Cellini was certain one of the assistants was trying to sabotage his masterpiece. He seized control of events with Herculean force. Loads of highly combustible oakwood were rushed from across the street and tossed into the furnace. The furnace blazed up again and the bronze began to melt. Icy rain from a storm outside threatened to cool the furnace again; Cellini had all the doors, windows, chinks, and crannies in the house blocked up with rugs and curtains.

There was a sudden explosion and a tremendous burst of flame; the cap of the furnace had blown off and the molten bronze bubbled out! All seemed lost—until Cellini, in a furious burst of inspiration, had his assistants throw every one of his two hundred pewter pots, pans, and plates into the furnace. The stratagem worked; the bronze began to liquefy and soon the entire statue had been cast to perfection! Amazingly, every ounce of bronze had been used, with nothing left, and the entire statue had been formed—all except the tip of Perseus's right big toe.

Not only had Cellini not succumbed to the fever, but he had never felt better. Had the apparition of the S-shaped man been one more manifestation of his guardian angel? Had it been Cellini's endlessly powerful creative imagination? Or—as his housekeeper suggested happily to Cellini—had the kicks and blows rained on his staff while, in a towering rage, he raced back to his workshop frightened away the lethal fever? Whatever the explanation, Cellini would write in commemoration of that frenzied hour: "I cannot remember a day in my whole life when I dined with greater gladness or a better appetite."

36 Dostoyevsky and Spiritualism

Did the Author of *Crime and Punishment* Have Personal Knowledge of Another World?

John Chambers

In *The Brothers Karamazov*—the masterpiece of the towering nineteenth-century Russian novelist and short-story writer Fyodor Dostoyevsky—Ivan Karamazov tells the story of an atheist who didn't believe in life after death and who, after he died, was sentenced by God to walk a billion miles in penance. Colin Wilson summarizes this story in *The Occult:* "The atheist lay on the road and refused to move for a million years; however, he eventually dragged himself to his feet and unwillingly walked the billion miles. And when he was finally admitted to heaven, he immediately declared that it would have been worth walking ten times as far just for five minutes of heaven."

Dostoyevsky himself experienced visions of heaven that were almost as ecstatic. They came to him in the form of "ecstatic auras"—sudden discharges of electrochemical energy that signal the start of an epileptic seizure. One such ecstatic aura (Dostoyevsky had hundreds of them in his lifetime) came to him the night between Easter Sunday and Easter Monday; he described it in his secret diary as follows: "I felt . . . that heaven had come down to Earth and absorbed me. I really perceived God and was imbued with Him. Yes, God exists . . . I cried. And I can recall no more. . . . I do not know whether that blessedness lasts seconds, hours, or minutes, yet, take my word, I would not exchange it for all the joys which life can give."

More than one hundred years earlier, on April 5 and 6, 1743—strangely enough, also an Easter weekend—another world-famous writer, and one of an even more spectacularly mystical bent than Dostoyevsky, confided to his secret diary a description of the ecstatic aura he had just experienced. This was Emanuel Swedenborg (1688–1772), the Swedish seer, psychic, and scientist who claimed there was direct mystical communication between our world and the spiritual realm and who affirmed Christ as the true God.

Medical researchers Elizabeth Foote-Smith and Timothy J. Smith write: "Fortunately, Swedenborg kept a record of his dreams (which was not intended for publication) during the critical years from 1743 to 1744, and for twenty

Fig. 36.1. The Russian author Fyodor Dostoyevsky, whose intense spiritual experiences informed his work.

years he kept his *Spiritual Diary,* consisting of five volumes. . . . Based on his own testimony, Swedenborg had multiple symptoms of temporal lobe epilepsy, including a characteristic aura, falling, loss of consciousness, convulsions, visual and auditory hallucinations, and trance states."

Swedenborg described his pre-epileptic seizure somewhat as Dostoyevsky described his: "Had also in my mind and my body a kind of consciousness of an indescribable bliss, so that if it had been in a higher degree, the body would have been as it were dissolved in mere bliss. This was the night between Easter Sunday and Easter Monday, also the whole of Easter Monday."

Swedenborg's visions of heaven, dictated to him by the angels and gathered in the course of numerous astral voyages, fill numerous volumes and were taken with the utmost seriousness during the nineteenth century by Blake, Emerson, Coleridge, Carlyle, Henry James Sr., Tennyson, the Brownings, Oliver Wendell Holmes, Thoreau, Goethe, and many others.

Could Swedenborg's admittedly unorthodox descriptions of a higher reality really have been merely the product of maverick and uncontrolled electro-

Fig. 36.2. The eighteenth-century Swedish scientist, philosopher, and spiritual explorer Emanuel Swedenborg had visions not unlike Dostoyevsky's.

chemical charges rampaging through his brain (according to the literature, ecstatic auras are characterized by "intense elation and ineffable all-pervading bliss, a feeling that the secrets of the universe [are] about to be revealed")? Or, if Swedenborg's visions were really visions, or only in part electrochemical, does that then mean that the epileptic fits of Fyodor Dostoyevsky also provided the Russian writer with a gateway through which he could glimpse, like Blake, "an immense world of delight, clos'd by your senses five"?

And do Dostoyevsky's swift but ecstatic visions of other realms peek out here and there in his novels and short stories?

But first of all: Just who was Fyodor Dostoyevsky?

He was a man whose life was almost terrifying in its steady progression of shattering events and unheard-of personal woes. All of these made him stronger; they also drove him daily to distraction.

Dostoyevsky's father was an impoverished doctor in a Moscow charity hospital who tyrannized his little family. When Fyodor was fifteen, his father was murdered by three of his serfs, in circumstances that still remain obscure.

Dostoyevsky hated his father, and felt vaguely responsible for his death. The theme of patricide runs through much of his writing.

Far worse awaited. He attended military engineering college—which he hated—graduated, fulfilled his duties, then threw himself into his great love: literature. He scored an early success with his first novel, *Poor Folk*. But he became attracted to radical politics and frequented a secret society promoting the socialism of Saint-Simon and Fourier. In 1848, he was arrested with friends and found guilty of disseminating antigovernment literature.

His sentence was severe—eight years at hard labor in Siberia (later commuted to four by the czar)—but, in the words of Vladimir Nabokov, "A monstrously cruel procedure was followed before the actual sentence was read to the condemned men." Dostoyevsky and his friends were sentenced to death and brought to the place of execution before a firing squad. They were tied to posts. Dostoyevsky and his companions thought they had only minutes left to live. Then an official stepped forward and commuted the sentences to penal servitude. Nabokov writes that after this horrendous experience of sham execution, "[o]ne of the men went mad. A deep scar was left in Dostoyevsky's soul by the experience of that day."

Dostoyevsky spent the next four years as a convict at hard labor in Siberia. In 1854 he was forced to serve in the army in Semipalatinsk, an Asiatic hell-hole. In 1858, he married and returned to St. Petersburg, beginning a life of incessant activity as a novelist, journalist, and editor. His first wife died and he married his stenographer. In the '60s and '70s, he published his great novels, *The Humiliated and Wronged* (1861), *Notes from the Underground* (1864), *Crime and Punishment* (1866), *The Idiot* (1868), *The Possessed* (1871), *A Raw Youth* [or, *The Adolescent*] (1875), *The Diary of a Writer* (1876–80), and *The Brothers Karamazov* (1880).

He had fame now, but not much fortune. Imprisonment had broken his health; ever afterward he was subject to epileptic seizures. He was addicted to gambling, periodically losing every cent he owned. The great writer fought with everyone. "Over and above all this," writes Marc Slonim, were "his ecstatic flights, his carnal temptations, and the rambling of his tormented soul in search of God, harmony and truth." He died at age sixty.

Given such a life, it is hardly surprising that Dostoyevsky's novels are populated with tormented, desperate, driven, and divided souls. Still, the light of the spirit—for good and for ill—flickers spasmodically in these tattered people. They know they have free will, and they cannot bear the knowledge. George Steiner writes: "They stand at the outermost limits of freedom; their next step must lead either to God or to the pit of hell." The natures of Dostoyevsky's protagonists are torn; it is as if their souls are partially atomized, as if they live in an incessant, mild epileptic state that leaves them at every moment open to God—and to the devil. Steiner writes that

> Dostoyevsky's multiple vision of the soul allowed for the likelihood of occasional fragmentation . . . "ghosts" could be manifestations of the human spirit when the spirit acts as pure energy, divorcing itself from the coherence of reason or faith in order to sharpen the dialogue between different facets of consciousness. . . . What counts is the intensity and quality of the experience, the shaping impact of the apparition upon our understanding. . . . Dostoyevsky surrounded his personages with a zone of occult energies; forces are attracted towards them and grow luminous in their vicinity, and corresponding energies erupt from within and take palpable form. . . . Correspondingly, he drew no firm barrier between the world of ordinary sense-perception and other, potential worlds.

Steiner quotes Merezhkovsky: "'To Dostoyevsky, the plurality of worlds was a manifest truth.'"

For all that, Dostoyevsky did not believe in spiritualism. For him, spiritualism was a form of "isolation" that trivialized religion through mysticism, when what was needed was more faith in true orthodoxy. Perhaps channeled spirits existed, but proof of their existence proved only that the spirits existed; it did not prove that *God* existed. The spirits were, finally, trivial and irrelevant. In 1875, the great Russian chemist D. I. Mendeleev (1834–1907), best known as the formulator of the periodic system of chemical elements, set up a commission in St. Petersburg to investigate the claims of spiritualism. Dostoyevsky waged war against spiritualism in his newspaper columns while also waging war against Mendeleev's methods, which he found high-handed and manipulative. The commission's final report roundly rejected spiritualism as anything but a conscious or unconscious fraud, effectively quashing its popularity for decades.

Still, Dostoyevsky was fascinated by the imagery of spiritualism—was he fascinated by more than that?—and that imagery sometimes peeps through in his works. Professor Ilya Vinitsky, of the University of Pennsylvania, has found strong evidence of Swedenborg's influence in Dostoyevsky's 1873 short story "Bobok." The anti-hero of "Bobok" is an alcoholic literary man named Ivan Ivanovich who attends the funeral of a distant relative and then, as Professor Vinitsky writes, "remains in the cemetery, where he unexpectedly 'overhears' the cynical, frivolous conversations of the dead. He discovers from these exchanges that human consciousness goes on for some time after the death of the physical body, lasting until total decomposition."

The deceased persons end up communicating only with the single, unpleasant, gurgling, onomatopoetic word *bobok*. Then, says Dr. Vinitsky, "the dead, realizing their complete freedom from Earthly conditions, decide to entertain themselves by telling tales of their existence 'on the top floor'—that is, during their lives. But Ivan Ivanovich suddenly sneezes, and the dead fall silent (more, as the narrator suggests, from their reluctance to share such an important secret with a living man than from embarrassment or fear of police)."

Professor Vinitsky believes this short story is a semi-satirical representation of the afterlife as described by Emanuel Swedenborg in his *On Heaven, the World of Spirits and on Hell, as They Were Seen and Heard by Swedenborg* (1758). Swedenborg asserts that "[a]fter death the human soul goes through several stages of purification of its internal content (good or evil) and as a result finds its deserved eternal reward: paradise or hell." The first two states of man, after death, take place in the grave and last "for some several days, for others months or even an entire year." In the second state, man's exterior disappears—putrefaction sets in—and the spirits of the dead become "visibly just what they had been in themselves while in the world, what they then did and said secretly being now made manifest, for they are now restrained by no outward considerations, and therefore what they have said and done secretly, they now say and endeavor to do openly, having no longer any fear of loss of reputation, such as they had when they were alive."

There is evidence in Dostoyevsky's other works—both great and small—of the influence of Swedenborg. In the short story "The Dream of a Ridiculous Man," the much belittled narrator astral-travels to another world that is actually an alternative and Edenic Earth. Swedenborgianism also influenced Dostoyevsky's vision of evil in *Crime and Punishment*. According to the Nobel Prize–winning poet Czeslaw Milosz, Svidrigailov's dreadful image of an eternity in a bathhouse infested with spiders resembles some visions of hell described by Swedenborg.

The influence of Swedenborg is seen most powerfully, however—when it is playing over the contorted, visionary faces of so many of Dostoyevsky's characters—in the wonderful depiction of Father Zosima in *The Brothers Karamazov*, for instance. The discourses of Zosima contain clear Swedenborgian teaching about the spiritual world, particularly that hell is always a voluntary spiritual state.

But in creating the character of Zosima, Dostoyevsky does far more than find a spokesman for Swedenborg. In all his works, Dostoyevsky's abiding and tormenting concern is whether God exists. In his portrayal of Zosima—the utterly good man, and the beloved mentor of the one good Karamazov brother, the priest Alyosha—he seems to be telling us that his answer is yes.

37 Victor Hugo and the Spirits

Did the Author of *Les Misérables* and *The Hunchback of Notre Dame* Draw Inspiration from Different Dimensions?

John Chambers

A glut of books on the market today present supposedly spirit-channeled guidance on everything from ancient mysteries to contemporary social behavior. The goal, ostensibly, is to warn us that if our species continues its self-centered, destructive march and does not make a determined effort to shift upward to a more spiritual level, then we cannot hope to survive. The non-material Light Beings who deliver these messages usually say they are here to help us make the leap.

For anyone who delves intellectually into Earth's mysteries, this can be pretty hard to swallow. Not only are the assertions of the channeled sources impossible to prove, but it's difficult not to impute to them a hugely subjective quality as well—particularly when even the best contradict each other. For example, the guides of the Pulitzer Prize–winning poet James Merrill and those of Ken Carey claim that ours is the only planet in our entire galaxy to be inhabited by intelligent, physical beings.

However, the disembodied beings who speak through popular channels like Barbara Marciniak and Patricia Pereira insist that the galaxy swarms with billions of intelligent life-forms, and that, though the majority of these are non-physical, that leaves several billion who are physical. Moreover, the spirits, who should know better, often play fast and loose with physical sciences such as astronomy. Many, for example, represent themselves as coming from an entire constellation. But when we consider that a constellation is an arbitrary grouping of stars, which, though being of equal apparent brightness, may be thousands of light-years apart, this assertion seems like errant nonsense.

Nevertheless, what some would accept as corroboration of the reality and mission of such disembodied spirits has recently emerged from an unexpected quarter—no less respected a figure than the author of the world-famous novels *Les Misérables* (made into the hit Broadway musical *Les Miz*) and *The Hunchback of Notre Dame* (made into a full-length Disney animated feature).

From 1853 to 1855, the great French writer Victor Hugo, while in political exile on Jersey Island in the English Channel, participated with family and friends in numerous spiritistic séances during which at least 115 different "discarnate entities" held forth on a vast variety of topics. The communications from the spirit world, transmitted by a table leg that tapped out letters (the precursor of the Ouija board), allegedly came from deceased historical and literary personages, including Galileo, Shakespeare, Hannibal, Christ, Muhammad, and Mozart; mythical beasts, such as Balaam's Ass, the Lion of Androcles, and the Dove of the Ark; abstractions, like Idea, Drama, India, and Russia; creatures of the spirit world who said they had never taken life, including the Shadow of the Sepulcher, Death, and Archangel Love; extraterrestrials from the planets Mercury and Jupiter; and the occasional Jersey Island ghost, including the Woman in White, the Headless Man, and the Grim Gatekeeper.

This wasn't an isolated experience. Beginning in 1853, a wave of interest in channeling had swept across France. It held the upper classes in such thrall that the bishop of Paris (France's highest-ranking cleric) warned from the pulpit that eternal damnation awaited those who consorted with the spirit world. Hugo might not have become interested at all had not a close friend, the playwright Delphine de Girardin, arrived from the mainland on a visit and talked the Hugo family into trying to "do the tables."

Fig. 37.1. Victor Hugo, the most influential Romantic writer of the nineteenth century and France's greatest poet.

After two or three attempts, there suddenly appeared the seeming spirit of Hugo's eldest daughter, Léopoldine, who had drowned ten years before, along with her husband; the girl was nineteen years old and pregnant when she died. Hugo's attention was caught, and would not let go for another two years. Finally, in October 1855, upon the failure of every one of the spirits' predictions to come true, and an episode of madness during which participant Jules Allix threatened to shoot everybody at the séance and then went into a catatonic trance, the séances came to a halt.

Hugo was certain a spirit world existed, but equally certain we could never know much about it. He was never tepid about the numerous séances he was now to attend, but at times he was more enthusiastic than at others. In December 1853, Hugo predicted the séance transcripts would become "one of the Bibles of the Future." But in his lifetime he said little about these experiences, fearing derision and negative effects on his political and literary work. The transcripts (of which about two-fifths are lost) weren't published until 1923, and then only partially. In 1968, a more expanded collection was published in volume nine of editor Jean Massin's monumental eighteen-volume *Oeuvres Complètes de Victor Hugo*.

It's easy to be skeptical about these séances. Most scholars believe their contents came entirely, if unconsciously, from the mind of Victor Hugo, a man of huge genius, or from the minds of one or another—or all of the other—usually talented and often well-educated participants at the séances. This being said, it's difficult not to marvel at the originality and imaginative richness of all of the ostensibly spirit-borne messages, the contents of which apparently came as a surprise to the participants. Here is a cross section:

- The attendees had veritable "close encounters of the third kind," communicating with an alien named Tyatafia who was from the planet Jupiter, as well as with the inhabitants of the planet Mercury. The Mercurians were half physical and half spirit and floated, like living beams of light, in the atmosphere of their planet.
- The participants watched as the "talking tables" not only tapped out messages but also drew pictures (with a pencil attached to the table leg), notably of the inhabitants of Mercury but also based on mental images of loved ones that the participants projected onto the table. The spirit control/spirit draftsman of the channeled Mercurian pictures claimed to be the fifteenth-century alchemist Nicolas Flamel—and, strangely enough, the drawings contain ancient alchemical formulae that help describe the Mercurians.
- French poet André Chénier, guillotined in 1794 during the bloodiest part of the French Revolution, appeared and dictated the final verses of the poem he had been working on the day he was executed. The verses, exactly matching the style of the living Chénier, were channeled when Victor Hugo was not at the séance, somewhat disconcerting critics who insist that the contents of the Jersey island séances came solely from the unconscious mind of the great French poet. "Chénier" also described his beheading and what came afterward.
- The table composed music, its leg tapping on a piano keyboard. One of the spirit composers was, supposedly, the spirit of "the Ocean"; another was Wolfgang Amadeus Mozart.

- A number of spirits claimed to be the shades of beasts who, in myth and legend, have helped mankind: the Lion of Androcles, who spared the life of Androcles in the Roman Forum because the Christian had earlier removed a thorn from the lion's paw; Balaam's Ass, who, momentarily given human speech by God, set Moabite holy man Balaam back on the path of righteousness; and the Dove of Noah's Ark, who guided the ark of the living remnants of our planet to its post-Flood destination. The entities told Hugo that animals "couldn't reason but could glimpse God," and they communicated to the poet a thoroughly modern Animals' Rights and even Plants' Rights Agenda; they claimed that beasts, plants, and even stones all contained souls and therefore should be treated with great love and respect. Hugo wholeheartedly embraced these beliefs, returning crabs to the sea, letting his property be overrun by wild animals, and refusing to snip flowers. He would not even kick stones, which the spirits insisted were also vessels of soul matter.
- The turning table channeled a lion speaking the language of lions and a comet speaking the language of comets, the comet using the table leg to draw a self-portrait.
- The spirits preached a doctrine of reincarnation, or metempsychosis, which included passing through lives as animals, plants, and stones as well as human beings. Through our good acts and successive reincarnations, we can attain angelhood—but a single truly reprehensible act can send us tumbling all the way back down the Great Chain of Being to reincarnation as a stone (sinful Cleopatra, the spirit guides claimed, had been reincarnated as a worm). The personification of Metempsychosis also held forth, summing up the nature of metempsychosis in fourteen gemlike aphorisms.
- The spirit called Death asked Hugo to write a last will and testament authorizing the timed release of the séance transcripts decade by decade; in this way, Death explained, the spirits' words could appear to mankind posthumously, in "periods of human crisis, when some shadow passes over progress, when clouds blot out the ideal." The critical future year when the clouds would begin to darken mankind's destiny was, the spirits said, the year 2000.
- The Carthaginian general Hannibal, who, crossing the Alps with elephants, had come close to conquering the Roman Empire in the third century B.C., described in fantastical terms the imperial city of Carthage as it had been before the Romans razed it to the ground.

- The spirits sometimes seemed to speak from the hearts of stars as they described a universe filled with "gleaming" stars obliged to "help" "weeping" stars, and "worlds of reward" on which dwelt the souls of those who had lived meritorious lives in previous incarnations; these latter worlds were obliged to help punitary planets inhabited by the souls of those who had done badly in previous existences.

As the participants of the séances, reeling from these messages, tried to put it all together, they begrudgingly had to conclude that our universe was a somewhat grim place. Everywhere, entities were in chains, stones, plants, prisons, serving pitiless sentences for reasons they could not know. "Your savage universe is God's convict," says the spirit persona of Hugo's six-hundred-line poem *What the Shadow's Mouth Says,* written in 1854 and inspired by the spirits. Elsewhere in the same poem, Hugo describes Earth in terms that make us think of the "scum of the galaxy" bar, teeming with present, past, and future convicts from all across the universe, seen in the first *Star Wars* movie:

On your planet packed with infamous prisons
There dwell the wicked of all the universe,
The condemned who, come from alien skies diverse,
Brood in your rocks, bend in your bowing trees.

What to do about the bad situation most of us face in the universe? The spirits counseled taking total personal responsibility—and being totally joyful. The Shadow of the Sepulcher declaimed to the séance-goers on December 18, 1854:

> You know what I would do if I were in your place? I'd ask for all or nothing; I'd insist on immensity . . . I'd work up a magnificent hunger, an enormous thirst, and I'd race through the drunken spaces between the spheres, singing the fearsome drinking song of eternity, joyous, radiant, sublime, hands full of bunches of grapes made of stars and my face purple with suns! I wouldn't leave a star unturned, and at the end of the banquet I'd pass out beneath the table of the heavens radiant with light!

If we are to believe Hugo's spirits, many of us are already traveling the astral realms somewhat in this manner. One of the strangest of the theories set forth by the Jersey Island spirits was that of *Homo duplex,* the Double Man. This term, used in Latin Christian scripture to describe man's duplicitous nature, was used by the Jersey spirits referring to man's double nature—as an inhabitant of his physical body in everyday empirical reality during waking hours and as a voyager through nonphysical realms in his astral body while asleep, the point of the trips being to gather up psychic strength for the next day.

The spirits describe the indescribable when they exhort our astral spirits to a nighttime voyage with the words: "Get up! Get on your feet! There's a high wind blowing, dogs and foxes bark, darkness is everywhere, nature shudders and trembles under God's whipcord; toads, snakes, worms, nettles, stones, grains of sand await us: Get on your feet!"

Where did all this weird knowledge come from? Almost every critic replies: Victor Hugo. Hugo admitted that much of the spirits' cosmology was in his head before he came to Jersey Island—but, he insisted, not all of it. We now know Hugo secretly studied the core kabbalist wisdom document, *The Zohar*, in the 1830s, and *The Zohar* does echo the spirits' pantheistic doctrine that all matter is coexistent with varying degrees of spirit (the amount of spirit determining how "good" or "bad" matter is). And when Death speaks of coursing joyously through the heavens, he sounds like the heretical Dominican monk Giordano Bruno (burned at the stake in 1600), who insisted we could attain transcendence and personal redemption only through frenzied heroic action, a sort of reaching out to be God himself in everything we do.

It is Victor Hugo's absorption in occult philosophies like the Kabbalah, not to mention the poet's equally intense interest in mesmerism and Hinduism, that today makes people think he may have been, along with Leonardo da Vinci, a grand master of the Priory of Sion. There never was a Priory of Sion; but an even more fascinating subject of inquiry might be just where the immense learning and genius of Victor Hugo leaves off and the strangely compelling (and perhaps in some way objectively real) universe of the Jersey Island spirits takes over.

38 Sound and Pictures from the Other Side

Pioneering the New Science of Instrumental Transcommunication

Bill Eigles

The issue of whether human consciousness survives beyond physical death and if so, in what way, has intrigued our species since time immemorial. Nor has the matter been one of mere academic or theological interest. Rather, human beings have long and diligently sought to communicate with those who have made the transition from Earthly life to whatever realm follows death—in order to gain, among other things, meaningful solace and psychological closure, worldly advice, and/or spiritual wisdom.

Indeed, so impassioned has been the ongoing drive to contact deceased loved ones and friends that history is filled with the lore of contact-seeking through such means as exalted oracles, spirit mediums, journeying shamans, Ouija boards, and automatic writing.

However, Western materialist science has traditionally maintained a dismissive, even cynical, attitude to all notions of communicating with the dead, and for several reasons: the wholly subjective nature of such experiences; the innate susceptibility to charlatanry, imagination, and overriding personal desire; and the difficulties involved in conducting any truly scientific investigation to obtain independent verification. Science has therefore, in effect, held "beyond the veil" to mean "beyond the ability, and hence the desirability, of being investigated."

As far as mainstream culture is concerned, the image of séances held in darkened parlors by exotic mediums during the late nineteenth and early twentieth centuries still serves as a visual emblem for the practice of bamboozling well-meaning but emotionally overwrought or greedy, and thus gullible, common folk.

Nevertheless, the advent of modern-day phenomena such as telepathic channeling of discarnate sentient entities, near-death experiences, and past-life and spirit-releasement therapies has served to renew the debate about the post-death survival of consciousness. This is true for people who have experienced such phenomena firsthand, for conventionally trained researchers who choose to investigate the question seriously, and for those whose New Age mind-set predisposes them to believe in the legitimacy of such phenomena. The rest of the population, it may be postulated, continues to await the arrival of more tangible, observable evidence for the survival hypothesis before seriously entertaining the matter.

That day may have arrived.

Since the mid-1980s, a small, multinational network of private experimenters and researchers, now known as the International Network for Instrumental Transcommunication (INIT), has used conventional electronic equipment such as radios, televisions, telephones, and personal computers to receive and record intelligent signals in the form of voices, images, and text from self-identifying deceased individuals whose consciousness appears to persist on nonphysical planes of existence. These individuals, or transpartners, appear to be former colleagues, loved ones, and others who have made the transition from Earth to the spirit world.

The cofounder of INIT and leading American researcher Mark Macy, of Boulder, Colorado, coauthored a book in 1995 entitled *Conversations Beyond the Light* and now publishes a thrice-yearly newsletter on the subject. A for-

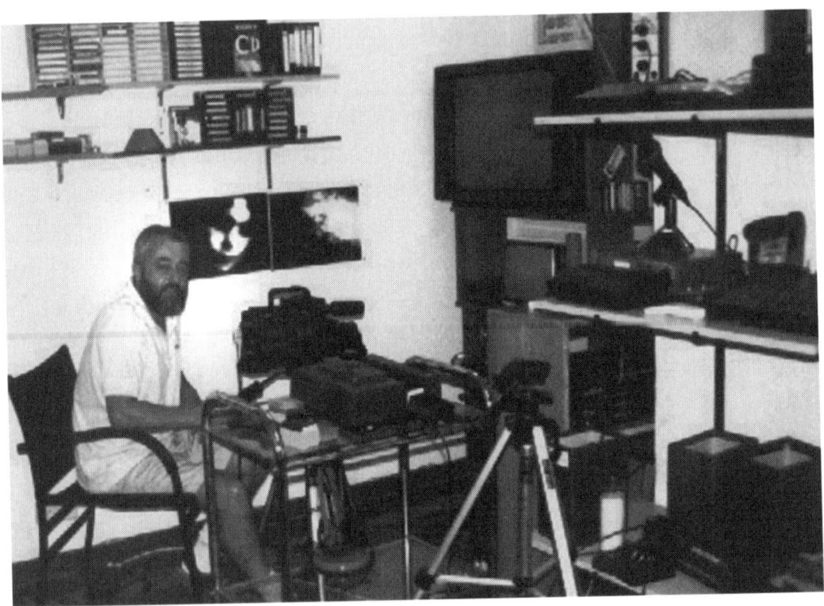

Fig. 38.1. A research office at the International Network for Instrumental Transcommunication.

mer technical writer and the author of anthologies on global problem solving, Macy survived a bout of colon cancer in 1988, coming through with his life intact but his belief system about God (agnostic) and death (fearful) severely challenged. Inspired as a result of his experience to learn what happens when we die, he encountered researcher and former industrialist George Meek, who showed him a personal letter from Meek's wife that was received through a computer after she died in 1991.

This startling hard evidence of life after death overwhelmed Macy and led him to explore with Meek the young field of instrumental transcommunication (ITC), an area in which Meek was already active. From Meek, Macy learned of a spiritual communication device called Spiricom—a set of tone generators that emit a buzzing sound comprising thirteen tones that span the range of the adult male voice—developed in 1980 by a technical wizard named Bill O'Neil under Meek's patronage.

Spiricom reputedly enabled O'Neil to conduct a dialogue with the voice of a NASA (National Aeronautics and Space Administration) scientist, Dr. George Mueller, who died in 1967. O'Neil and Mueller were apparently able to use their collective minds to modulate the unstable buzzing sound of the Spiricom device into a facsimile reminiscent of the voice Mueller had used while alive. After a time, the facsimile became sufficiently clear that an intelligible dialogue between O'Neil and the spirit of Mueller could be heard through the buzzing sound, with Mueller's voice sounding robotlike but nonetheless infused with a definite, living intelligence.

This experience awakened Macy's spirituality, causing him to acknowledge the existence of God for the first time—as well as the immortality of the human spirit—and to view the physical body as merely the vehicle we use to navigate in the dense physical world for our period of Earthly life. Realizing that physical life is only a transitory phase, he lost his fear of death and came to realize that many more exciting experiences await all of us on the other side of the veil.

Since that time, Macy has progressively devoted his life to experimenting with, and writing and lecturing on, ITC and the information that has been conveyed to him and his fellow researchers around the world by their spirit colleagues. These spirit colleagues are usually former ITC experimenters who have died but continue their work from the other side.

Among the more astonishing results reported by Macy and others is the receipt of actual telephone calls from a deceased former European psychologist and ITC researcher named Dr. Konstantin Raudive, who died in 1974. In the spring of 1996, Macy dialogued with Raudive on the telephone for fifteen minutes, and other researchers in Luxembourg have spoken with Raudive for longer periods of time. Such phone contacts, however, are not limited to professional researchers, but appear to be both a spontaneous and more widely reported phenomenon.

For example, the renowned U.S. medical intuitive Dr. Carolyn Myss has reported that in December 1992, she unexpectedly received a telephone call from her Native American shaman-mentor, during which he asked her to write his life's story for publication. Some weeks later, she discovered that her mentor had died in another city two days before her telephone conversation with him took place.

ITC contacts are not limited to telephone calls, but more often have involved television pictures and computer images and textfiles. Computer contacts, for example, often occur after researchers leave home, having made sure that all of their equipment is turned off. When they return home, sometimes their computers will be running, and new files—either pictures or text—will have been planted on disk: direct communications from an identifiable entity on another plane.

The first color television picture of a spirit entity was reported in October 1995 in association with such a computer contact when a German researcher awoke with a compelling urge to try an experiment with his color TV set. He was accustomed to receiving paranormal video images on his monochrome television, but only after receiving phone notification in advance from his spirit colleagues. This time, the researcher simply turned on his color set and trained his camcorder on the picture tube. At that instant, an image of Swedish ITC pioneer Friedrich Juergenson, deceased since 1987, appeared on the screen and remained there for twenty-four seconds. Hearing a loud, cracking noise coming from the next room, the researcher got up to investigate, but not until he had unsuccessfully attempted voice contact with the televised image on his set. Upon entering the next room, he discovered his computer running—it apparently had been switched on paranormally—and on the screen he found a typed message to him under the name Juergenson.

What does it take to establish contact with deceased persons across the veil? Macy emphasizes that ITC contacts are not so much a result of modern communications technology, but rather derive from the minds of living individuals on Earth linking closely with the consciousness of minds on subtler, nonphysical levels of existence in a positive, loving spirit of cooperation. This harmonious vibration has been coined the "contact field," and represents the pivotal mediumistic bridge that enables interdimensional communication with the spirit world to occur. According to information received during various

Fig. 38.2. Left: photo of Swedish ITC pioneer Friedrich Juergenson. Right: video image of Juergenson as it mysteriously appeared on the television screen of a German researcher after Juergenson had died.

ITC contacts, the phenomenon is strengthened by "work[ing] on the inner life, the eternal center," and results from the "unified cooperation of people who are concerned and whose efforts are supported in ITC circles."

In effect, researchers' spirit colleagues have said that ITC can work only "when the vibrations of those involved are in complete harmony, and when their aims and intentions are pure."

Macy's personal work to date suggests that several factors have a hand in promoting successful contact with those on the other side. These include a maintaining passionate desire for contact; constantly, favorably holding thoughts of a deceased person with whom there was a strong emotional attachment; and making steady efforts over time to improve the living individual's mental focus and clarity through prayer, meditation, and other forms of psychic attunement. As Macy says, however, ITC has thus far been provided no user's guide or start-up manual for establishing dependable receiving stations.

Contact work is still very much a case of trial and error, although Macy is confident that he will be able to develop a strong contact field in the future among colleagues on both sides of the veil, and thus create a reliable receiving station in Colorado. Thus far, however, the contact field in Western Europe remains the strongest, as evidenced by the plethora of contacts received by the research teams there from a variety of sources.

The question inevitably arises as to what has been learned substantively as a result of ITC contacts with the spirit world. Evidently, quite a lot. For example, the spirit colleagues of ITC experimenters report that a multidimensional structure of nonphysical reality exists beyond the Earth plane, with the multiplicity of dimensions superimposed and interacting in a complexity impossible to readily convey, or even comprehend, in human language and three-dimensional constructs.

The immediate stage following death, however, appears fairly simple to understand. When most people die, they emerge onto the third, or mid-astral, plane—a world of energy that shares the same space as the Earth, but where individuals are regenerated from their wounds and illnesses and are eventually able to create their desired image of themselves and their surroundings through the power of their thoughts.

One German boy, Ezra Braun, who died of leukemia at the age of twelve in 1986, had a picture of himself sent to the personal computer of a European ITC researcher in 1992. The picture showed a smiling young man in his late teens or early twenties, his arm raised in a wave, his face easily recognizable as that of the boy, only older. His ecstatic, still Earthbound parents confirmed the boy's identity, as well as many other details concerning the boy's pre-death interests and possessions that were revealed in the transmitted picture and in an accompanying written transmission.

In addition to providing a clear view of what life is like on the other side of the veil, and occasionally providing communications from departed loved ones and missed friends, ITC transmissions have also provided spiritual insights from higher levels of consciousness through angelic beings who have never assumed human form. Via letters sent to researchers' computers, these beings have also provided a significant quantity of hitherto unknown information on the prehistory of the Earth, information that conventional sources have been unable to provide.

These beings state, for example, that a planet once existed between Mars and Jupiter, known as either Maldek or Marduk. Although its inhabitants were highly advanced technologically and space travel was routine for them, their technical ability exceeded their better sense, and their planet exploded, creating the asteroid belt that exists today. Before the final detonation, however, some of the Mardukians traveled to Earth and seeded a civilization that eventually became Atlantis. When these former denizens of Marduk interbred with the primitive beings that existed on the Earth of that time, they began the heritage of our own species approximately 20,000 years ago.

Although reminiscent of the theories of researcher Zecharia Sitchin as to the origins of humanity, these revelations are distinctive in that Marduk is claimed to have been destroyed as a planet and now continues to exist only on the astral plane. This subtle world is where many people on Earth go after their demise, to continue living an Earth-like existence in their astral bodies.

Interestingly, people on Marduk apparently have a limited vision of themselves; like the physical Earthlings they once were, they believe that their astral planet is the full extent of reality. Many Mardukians do not acknowledge the existence of life on the physical Earth; rather, many believe that their notions of an earlier existence in physical form are just bad dreams! (What a disappointment to realize that spiritual myopia seems to persist, at least for some of us, even after leaving Earthly life.)

According to Macy, those on the other side of the veil decide who among them will communicate with living ITC researchers. While there is evidence of an overall plan for the work of ITC, few details have been forthcoming thus far. Well-known personages have been known to communicate, such as nineteenth-century English explorer Richard Francis Burton, French author Jules Verne, and American composer Scott Joplin.

Transmissions are more likely to originate from deceased ITC researchers, however, presumably because of a need to foster the energy of the contact field among people who have been involved in the ITC endeavor for some time, both those living on Earth and those existing on the other side. Still, as in the case of little Ezra Braun, deceased loved ones of the experimenters or their friends are sometimes permitted to communicate to ease the hurt and loss of the survivors. In any event, a close emotional attachment that preexisted on Earth apparently strengthens the contact field.

The modern scientific community has not, to date, had incentive to explore the ITC phenomenon in any meaningful way. Despite some rigorous and clearly validating tests by leading sound engineers in England—involving ITC pioneer Konstantin Raudive's results with taped spirit voices in the early 1970s—the limitations of the current scientific paradigm may be too great to be surmounted by simple curiosity despite the receipt of even more profoundly anomalous, inexplicable transmissions via television, telephone, and personal computer in the decades since Raudive's time.

Nonetheless, before his death in 1996, Dr. Willis Harman, the former Stanford engineering professor and president of the Institute of Noetic Sciences (IONS) in California, championed the work of Macy and other ITC researchers and wrote of it as a challenge to modern science. Ironically—perhaps naturally—a recent ITC contact with an angelic being indicated that Harman, having now made his transition, "intends to work closely with the [spirit] group who is trying to contact Mark Macy."

Macy and his fellow INIT researchers are now in the planning stages of a collaborative effort to subject ITC to scientific scrutiny, involving researchers from IONS and the Monroe Institute, both respected U.S. organizations known for their research in the frontier sciences. Will they, with the assistance of their former colleagues beyond the veil, be able to prove once and for all that human consciousness survives death? Time will tell.

For the present, Macy regularly monitors his wide-coverage array of multi-band radio receivers and works at educating as many people as possible about ITC through workshops, presentations, and publications. He believes that should he and others succeed in regularly stimulating clear images, voices, and text from the beyond, ITC could ultimately become a conduit of the love and wisdom from the highest levels of spirit, and thus help transform the world in a rapid and positive way. We hope so, too.

39 Understanding the Near-Death Experience

Why Hasn't Science Gotten It Right?

P. M. H. Atwater

No one can validate a near-death experience except the one who experienced it. The thrust, then, of near-death research is to identify elements and patterns of occurrence, aftereffects, and implications in an attempt to understand how and why the phenomenon happens, what it is, and what can be learned from it—especially as it concerns an examination of existence and the prospect of life after death.

What is passed off today as "the near-death experience" in movies, television talk shows, and popular best-selling books bears little resemblance to the actual phenomenon. Documentary film producers, for instance, have opted for a mythological portrayal of what they think the public wants to see, cast against obligatory detractors (who have never done any actual research in the field and, frankly, don't know what they're talking about), rather than tackling an in-depth examination of core findings—especially those that challenge the standard "amazing grace" scenario. Hundreds now claim to be experts on the subject, yet they have precious little to back up their claim except for a few dozen near-death survivor interviews, lunch with their favorite researcher, and a literature search. The frenzy of trendy books and charismatic speakers that has resulted feeds on itself,

Fig. 39.1. A detail of Ascent in the Empyrean, *painted by Hieronymus Bosch in the late fifteenth or early sixteenth century. It appears to anticipate some modern accounts of near-death experience.*

never once addressing the most important question of all: What if the original findings about the near-death experience are incomplete or misleading?

To address this question, we must reevaluate the premise of near-death studies and the methodology used to arrive at this premise.

Research on the phenomenon goes back more than 150 years, but the work didn't take root as a discrete scientific discipline until after Dr. Raymond A. Moody Jr. coined the term "near-death experience" and published his first book, *Life After Life,* in 1975. Kenneth Ring, Ph.D., opened wide the floodgates for serious inquiry by scientifically verifying Moody's work in 1980 and publishing his book *Life At Death.*

The classical model of the near-death experience was established by this effort. Its eight basic elements follow (descriptions are my own):

1. *A sensation of floating out of one's body* often followed by an out-of-body experience during which all that goes on around the vacated body is both seen and heard.
2. *Passing through a dark tunnel or black hole,* or encountering some type of darkness, often accompanied by a feeling or sensation of movement or acceleration. "Wind" may be heard or felt.
3. *Ascending toward a light at the end of the darkness*—a light of incredible brilliance that emits loving peacefulness—and possibly seeing deceased individuals, animals, plants, lush outdoors, and even cities within that light.
4. *Receiving greetings from friendly voices, people, or beings,* who may be strangers, loved ones, or religious figures. Conversation can ensue; information or a message may be given.
5. *Seeing a panoramic review of the life just lived,* from birth to death or in reverse order, sometimes in the form of reliving the life rather than a dispassionate review. The person's life may be seen in its entirety or in segments. This is usually accompanied by a feeling or need to assess losses or gains during the life and determine what was learned or not learned. Other beings can take part in this judgmentlike process or offer advice.
6. *An altered sense of time and space,* discovering time and space do not exist, losing the need to recognize either of these measurements of life as valid or necessary.
7. *A reluctance to return to the Earth plane,* but invariably realizing that either one's job on Earth is not finished or a mission must yet be accomplished before one can leave the Earth plane.

8. *Disappointment at being revived,* often feeling a need to shrink or somehow squeeze down to fit back into the physical body. There can be unpleasantness, even anger or tears, at the realization that one is now back in one's body and no longer on the Other Side.

Since the average near-death experience contains about five of these elements, people who may have had such an episode become confused. This has given rise to a major complaint voiced by those who attend either local meetings of the International Association for Near-Death Studies (IANDS) or their Friends of IANDS affiliates in the United States, Canada, and internationally. The complaint? *What happened to them doesn't match the "classical model."* Common experiences more closely match the model I developed, explained below.

Knowing nothing about near-death studies when I began my own research in 1978, I isolated four distinct types of near-death experience. The elements were similar to those that comprise the classical model, but the patterning was different, and there were subtle psychological factors that seemed somehow to undergird each type—as if other forces were at work besides the prospect of life after death.

What I found has held up during the years since then, regardless of one's age, education, gender, culture, or religion. In *Beyond The Light,* I discuss this at length, with a separate chapter for each of the four types, plus the near-death experience, anomalies, and the profile of psychological and physiological aftereffects that was revealed in my work.

What follows is a brief version of the four types of near-death experience I discovered.

- *Initial Experience (an introduction to other realities):* Involves elements such as a loving nothingness, the living dark, a friendly voice, a brief out-of-body experience and/or visitation of some kind. Usually experienced by those who seem to need the least amount of evidence for proof of survival, or who can tolerate the least amount of shakeup in their lives at that point in time. Often, this becomes a seed experience or an introduction to other ways of perceiving and recognizing reality.
- *Unpleasant and/or Hell-like Experience (an opportunity for inner cleansing and self-confrontation):* An encounter with a threatening void, or stark limbo, or fearful creatures of darkness or hellish purgatory, or scenes of a startling and unexpected indifference, even "hauntings" from one's own past. Usually experienced by those who seem to have deeply

suppressed or repressed guilts, fears, and anger and/or those who expect some kind of punishment or discomfort after death.

- *Pleasant and/or Heaven-like Experience (an opportunity for reassurance and self-validation):* Pleasurable scenes of loving family reunions with those who have died previously; reassuring images of religious figures/ light beings/angels; validation that life counts; affirmative and inspiring dialogue. Can include a review of the life; personal advice given and/or family secrets revealed. Usually experienced by those who most need to know how loved they are and how important life is and how every effort has a purpose in the overall scheme of things.
- *Transcendent Experience (an introduction to alternate realities and to expansive states of greater insight):* Exposure to otherworldly dimensions and scenes beyond the individual's frame of reference; often includes revelations of grander truths. Seldom follows any particular pattern of imagery. Geared toward societal and evolutionary issues, not personal concerns, per se. Usually experienced by those who are ready for a mind-stretching challenge and/or individuals who are most apt to utilize (to whatever degree) the truths imparted to them.

For any given person, it is possible for all four types to occur during the same experience, or for two or more to occur in varying combinations, or for all four types to spread out across a series of episodes in a particular individual's life. Generally speaking, however, each represents a distinctive type of experience occurring but once to a given person.

In addition to my own attempts to clarify the nature of the near-death experience, there has been, in recent years, a concerted effort made by other researchers of near-death states to "set the record straight" as to *percentages of occurrence* of this phenomenon. Most surveys conducted by various magazines and organizations in the past were not scientific or even reliable. The problem is ambiguous questions that slant answers. The result: overestimates based more on wishful thinking than on anything close to verifiable facts.

The poll used today, giving an estimate of 15 million near-death experiencers in the United States (or 5 percent of the population), was conducted by *U.S. News & World Report* in 1997. However, the figure more in keeping with actual case reportings in the United States, Holland, and Germany is 4 percent (which makes 11 million in the United States). What is of keen interest to researchers is that the 4 percent figure for general populations is showing up in other countries worldwide. Because of this, researchers are downscaling the percentages they quote. Some references: random inquiry in Germany (Schmied, et al.) conducted in 1999 and the original Gallup Poll done in 1982.

For those people who were near death, nearly died, or who did die but later revived or were resuscitated, the estimate of one-third that was previously used to indicate how many would have a near-death experience is also overinflated. The number is closer to between 12 to 20%.

The real problem here, though, is with children. There has never been any survey of any kind that addresses children who experience a near-death state. A given assumption in poll taking is that an individual's near-death experience occurred in adulthood. Preliminary work by Melvin Morse, M.D., a pediatrician in the state of Washington, suggests that with children the figure is closer to 70%—more than double that of adults. Since Morse's work has yet to be duplicated, especially in other countries, no conclusions can be drawn as to what this discrepancy means. It can be said that near-death cases are on the rise. What cannot be said with any real degree of confidence is by how much.

To better understand why my work deviates from that of other researchers, it might be helpful to know how I fit into the scheme of things. In 1978, Elisabeth Kübler-Ross identified me as a near-death survivor and described the now famous classical model. She never mentioned Raymond Moody or his book, nor did I hear of either of these until 1981, when Kenneth Ring bought my self-published rendering, *I Died Three Times in 1977,* and located me via telephone.

During an overnight visit, he was surprised to learn that I had been independently researching the near-death experience and its aftereffects and had amassed a great deal of material. (My self-published rendering has since been resurrected, and is now available on my web site at Ring's invitation.) I became a columnist for *Vital Signs Magazine,* a publication of the newly formed International Association for Near-Death Studies, where I began to share some of the observations I had made, observations that later became the book *Coming Back to Life.*

Never was it my interest or intent to verify or challenge anyone else's work. My job, as I was shown during my third near-death experience, was to bring clarity and perspective to the phenomenon and to test the validity of its revelation.

Thus, I became a field worker whose specialty is interviews, observation, and analysis. I cross-check everything I do at least four times with different people in different parts of the country as a way to ensure that any bias I may have as a near-death survivor will not cloud my perception. Questionnaires for me are auxiliary, used only to further examine certain aspects of near-death states. All of my work is original. Whenever possible, I also interview significant others as well as experiencers. This work has been a full-time profession for me since 1978, in addition to employment that has helped pay for groceries.

To date, I have interviewed over 3,000 adult experiencers and 277 child experiencers, not counting friends and loved ones. This number doubles if one counts the interviews I conducted between 1966 and 1976 in an effort to understand altered states of consciousness, and mystical and spiritual transformational experiences.

In my research of near-death states, I don't use the standard double-blind/control-group method that most professionals employ because I don't trust it. Initial screening with this style, whether in person or by mail, is dependent upon questions that use terms in advance of the experiencer's response and lead the answers, in the sense that certain questions tend to inspire predictable answers. Most of these questionnaire formats have the same antecedent, geared to proving or disproving a single model—the classical one.

Certainly, when everyone uses the same basic research style and instruments, better and more accurate comparisons can be made. And this is desirable on one level. But what if the original work was incomplete or perhaps biased in the sense of a preference—either the researcher's or that of the experiencer—consciously or subconsciously?

I mean to impart no criticism here, for I know how sincere and diligent most experiencers and researchers are, and how difficult it is to maintain objectivity. Nevertheless, it is time for us to admit that:

- No allowance was made during the early years in the field for inquiries about unpleasant and/or hellish experiences.
- Experiencers who had difficulty accepting or integrating their experience were for a long time simply ignored.
- Few people ever reported the tunnel component, yet the tunnel was and still is considered a signature of the phenomenon.
- Seldom was attention paid to episodes devoid of light, even though they were as intense and life-changing as the radiant ones.
- The full spread of psychological and physiological aftereffects went unrecognized for more than a decade.
- Children's scenarios were assumed to be the same as adult scenarios—with similar responses—until recent research indicated otherwise.
- Attempted suicides that occurred after an experience were missed.

- Correlations between life experiences and what was met in the near-death scenario—the sense that what happened was needed—were generally bypassed in favor of the notion that near-death states were a distinctly separate phenomenon.

Both the preference factor (seeing in the experience what we want to see) and the pathological approach (thinking it's something we can dissect like heart disease) fail utterly to address the complex dynamic that is the near-death experience.

Today, in almost every discipline, previous studies are being overturned or revamped, not because past authors were inept, but because their research base was not broad enough to adequately cover their field of inquiry. Since I've already mentioned heart disease, let me use it as an example. We now know that the original model for the treatment of heart disease was faulty—its primary source came from work done on men. When women were finally studied separately, vast differences were uncovered in how each sex reacts—which led to the creation of a more effective model.

I am not suggesting that near-death states are in any way a pathology, but I *am* saying that the same premise applies . . . we need to broaden our research base. Few people realize that Sigmund Freud, the founder of psychoanalysis, formulated his theories while treating twenty-two people. That humankind is ennobled and spiritual by nature was lost in his investigation of the dark, animalistic urges that these twenty-two people exhibited. Exactly like the situation with heart disease, a model of limited parameters was accepted as true for all. Over the years, more people have been hurt than helped by the distortions in Freud's theory.

Near-death studies have been caught in the same situation, a tendency to over-rely on a single methodology. Empirical research can be conducted utilizing a number of different approaches, and I count mine as one of them. Past discoveries in the field of near-death studies are praiseworthy, but observer/analysts like myself are needed to track a myriad of details control-group studies cannot address. If we are ever to understand the near-death phenomenon, we must examine it from 360 degrees. Anything less is unacceptable.

For instance, why do we keep relying on medical investigators in surgical wards for verification of the phenomenon when with neither adults nor children is the principle venue "death during surgery"? This was a reasonable choice during the early years of research, but modern hospitals are turning more and more to the use of a new drug that causes amnesia in patients. Are near-death cases on the decline, as a recent study suggests? Or are the patients simply unable to remember the experience because of the new drug? If we're serious about seeking subjects within the confines of a hospital, why don't we "hang out" in emergency wards? The majority of cases of children in my study, for instance, came from drownings and suffocation, not surgery.

To be fair, the control-group method of research developed about one hundred years ago was a reliable way to study the effect of a single agent acting on a single illness that had a single cause. But that method becomes ineffectual when exploring complex issues like transformations of consciousness.

Charles Tart, Ph.D., terms such abuse "scientism." Tart, internationally known for his experiments with altered states of consciousness—and one of the founders of the field of transpersonal psychology—is the author of two classics in the field of consciousness studies: *Altered States of Consciousness* and *Transpersonal Psychologies.* According to Tart, the job of science is to give us information so we can make sense of life experiences. Scientism, on the other hand, states in rigid and dogmatic terms what reality is and should be.

Tart identifies a true skeptic as one who searches for truth—withholding the temptation to establish finality—and pseudo-skeptics as those who insist on one path to truth, and one reality. Tart reminds us that science evolved from philosophy and depends on open inquiry.

In the spring of 1999, Three Rivers Press of New York City brought out my book *Children of the New Millennium*. Because of problems in publishing, it was replaced in 2003 by *The New Children and Near-Death Experiences.* I want people to know about the change because the book is a major study of children's near-death states, including those of infants and toddlers, and of how such experiences affect the young, especially during critical junctures in brain development.

This is important information. The book also covers the "new child" currently being born—our "global village" babies who are quite unlike those of previous generations. *The New Children and Near-Death Experiences* entices the public to think and rethink not just about near death studies, but also about ourselves as human beings, what we think we are and where we think we're headed—as evolution continues to play leap-frog with our futures. It is a book filled with surprises.

40 The Case for Reincarnation

Is Religion the Only Reason to Believe, or Is There Evidence of a More Scientific Nature?

Ian Lawton

Everyone knows that many Eastern religions hold the doctrine of reincarnation at their core. It is not explicitly found in ancient Vedic texts, although their high philosophy can be somewhat obscure at times, and some scholars argue that the idea would have been present in general Vedic thought—the concept is certainly a cornerstone of the Hindu religion that sprang from that philosophy. By contrast, when the Buddha took his teachings outside of the Hindu mainstream, he was deliberately vague about the idea of reincarnation, arguably in an attempt to take his followers away from their reliance on the tight strictures of the Hindu caste system and the assumption that they'd always be reborn into the same caste. Unfortunately, his vagueness became enshrined in the doctrine of *anatta,* or "no self/soul," whereby one's karma was thought to be added to the universal pot after death, while the individual soul did not survive as a distinct entity.

Despite this setback, Western esotericism has a long history of belief in reincarnation—as I discuss in my second book, *Genesis Unveiled.* A belief in reincarnation was fundamental to both Hermeticists and Neoplatonists—although not, interestingly, Gnostics or even the ancient Egyptians from whom much of this later thought was supposedly derived. And to this day, reincarnation continues to thrive as a cornerstone of Kabbalism although again, the Judaism from which this sprang does not explicitly incorporate it, and also of the Rosicrucian movement.

But all of these worldviews effectively rely, just as any of the major religions do, on the revealed wisdom of their sacred texts. I think many people in the modern world have come to realize that revealed wisdom can contain horrible distortions, however much the disciples of any given worldview might insist otherwise. So at the start of the twenty-first century, must we continue to rely on such ancient revealed wisdom in our search for spiritual truths? The answer is an emphatic no.

There are two major sources of modern research into reincarnation. The first is past-life regression; the second is children who spontaneously remember past lives. And before anyone of a more skeptical bent accuses me of spouting New Age nonsense by using this material, I should emphasize that I too had assumed that it would be easily dismissed by proper, rigorous scientific investigation.

But when I investigated myself, I found I could not have been more wrong. In fact, materialist explanations for these phenomena are inadequate and reductionist, and they concentrate on the weak cases without attempting to tackle the stronger ones. I should also emphasise that the professionals who pioneered research in these areas during the 1960s and '70s were scientifically trained psychologists and psychiatrists, most of whom were initially of a skeptical or atheist persuasion.

The key elements in using past-life regression as proof of reincarnation lie in the cases that fall into two categories. The first, and most obvious, are those in which historical details emerge that are not only verifiable, but also so obscure that they could not have been obtained by any normal means—those in which the possibility of deliberate deception, which is about the only materialist explanation that might have held water in these cases, is so remote as to be negligible.

Three examples serve to make my point.

Gwen McDonald, an Australian woman who had never been abroad, was regressed by the pioneering psychologist Peter Ramster. She remembered obscure details in the eighteenth-century life of a girl named Rose Duncan, who lived in Glastonbury. When this was further investigated in England, by an Australian documentary film crew under controlled conditions, the details were all verified by local historians and residents. These details included obscure or obsolete names of places and people, obsolete elements in local dialect, and details of houses and other buildings as they had existed in the eighteenth century.

Most stunning was the woman's insistence that she had been taken to a cottage, the floorstones of which had been stolen from Glastonbury Abbey. One floorstone had an obscure carving on it that she sketched while still in Sydney. She led the crew to what had become a dilapidated chicken shed, and they swept away decades of droppings. There was the carving exactly as she had drawn it.

Another of Ramster's subjects was Cynthia Henderson, who was brought over to France by the same documentary team. She remembered the life of an aristocratic girl named Amelie de Cheville who lived in the eighteenth century. Not only did she lead them to a ruined château in the country outside Flers in

Normandy—which she had accurately described as her home before leaving Australia—but in trance, she spoke in the fluent archaic French of the period, with a perfect accent, as verified by a local man employed specifically to test this hypothesis.

Out of her trance, she was unable to recall more than a few basic words of French gleaned from no more than two months of study at the age of twelve.

The third case involves a Welsh housewife named Jane Evans, who was regressed live on television by Arnall Bloxham. She recalled life as part of a persecuted Jewish community in York in the twelfth century, and circumstances that resulted in a number of Jews, including herself, taking refuge in the crypt of a local church, where they were eventually discovered and massacred.

Professor Barrie Dobson, an expert on Jewish history at York University, was called in to investigate. From descriptions provided by Jane Evans, he established that the church she referred to must have been St. Mary's, Castlegate. But there was one problem—it had no crypt. Some months later, when workmen were renovating the church, they discovered a crypt that had been sealed off. When they broke it open, they discovered human remains dating to the twelfth century.

The other way in which past-life regression provides impressive proof of reincarnation is in those cases that involve dramatic therapeutic benefits. Many pioneering past-life therapists discovered the technique more or less by accident, often when regressing patients back to their childhoods. Imprecise commands are taken literally by those under hypnosis. When asked, for example, to "go back further," they suddenly began describing events that could not have related to their current life.

Intrigued, the pioneers continued their experiments and found that severe psychological and psychosomatic disorders that had often remained virtually untouched by years of conventional therapy were completely alleviated, sometimes after only a few sessions of past-life therapy—and irrespective of whether or not the patient, or for that matter the therapist, believed in reincarnation. It was this universal experience that convinced all of the pioneers that this was no mere placebo effect, and that reincarnation is a reality.

We turn now to children who remember past lives spontaneously, as opposed to under hypnosis. The American psychologist Ian Stevenson, of the University of Virginia, pioneered research on this subject almost single-handedly for several decades; he is only now starting to achieve the recognition he so richly deserves. Many of his cases also involve verifiable details that are so obscure they could not have been obtained by normal means, unless deliberate collusion and deception were involved. Stevenson's methodology has been

Fig. 40.1. Dr. Ian Stevenson, whose groundbreaking work in the field of reincarnation provides astonishing evidence for the immortality of the soul.

deliberately designed to spot this and other suspect patterns.

To focus on just one of his impressive cases, from an early age Swarnlata Mishra spontaneously recalled details of the life of another Indian girl named Biya Pathak, who had lived in a separate town some way away from her present home, and whose family was eventually traced. Stevenson found that, in all, Swarnlata made forty-nine statements about her previous life, only a few of which could be regarded as inaccurate, and eighteen of which were made before there had been any contact whatsoever between the two families.

These statements included identifying former family members, sometimes while being actively misdirected; coming up with little-known nicknames; and even disclosing to her former husband that he had taken twelve hundred rupees from her money box—something known only to the two of them.

There is one potential paranormal explanation for all this evidence that would not involve reincarnation, which is that all these subjects are tapping into some sort of universal memory or consciousness, and that the past lives accessed in this way do not belong to the individuals under study. But there are two extremely strong reasons to doubt this theory. First, therapeutic results could not be obtained if this was the case. And second, most cases of past-life regression show clear karmic linkages between lives that are personal and individual.

Nowhere is this more evident than in the most unusual cases investigated by Stevenson, those of children born with unusual birthmarks and defects. By investigating postmortem reports and so on, he found that a number of these defects corresponded exactly to wounds that killed the previous personality claimed by the child, and for whom other verifiable data had been found.

The other possibility often mentioned—albeit still relying on reincarnation—is that all of these subjects are tapping into ancestral memories passed on in their genes. But again this theory does not hold water, for two good reasons. The first is that many past lives are found to be close together in time and yet to involve different continents or even races, during an era when people were generally not particularly mobile. The second is that many of Stevenson's cases involve lives separated by only a few years, in which the two families involved are demonstrably not genetically linked.

How does all of this modern evidence relate to the revealed wisdom of the past? Of course, the key corollary concept to that of reincarnation is that of karma, and the one thing that all approaches to reincarnation—both ancient and modern—are agreed upon is that we reincarnate repeatedly in order to progress our karma sufficiently to break free from the "Earthly karmic round" and in order to "reunite with the source." In other words, to reach the point where we have learned and experienced everything we can from Earthly life, so we no longer need to incarnate in physical form—although souls who have advanced to this stage can, of course, volunteer to come back again to help humankind, in general, to progress.

One of the interesting things that modern research can tell us about is the nature of the ethereal realms themselves, and what exactly we mean by reuniting with the source. We find that subjects who have been regressed not just into past lives but also into the interlife between incarnations—again, by a number of pioneering psychologists and psychiatrists operating largely independently—have much to offer in terms of consistent spiritual wisdom. And remember that these are ordinary people, drawn from all walks of life, who do not hold themselves out as spiritual gurus, and who have no religious or political ax to grind.

They report that a huge, rich, and varied amount of activity occurs in the ethereal realms. Souls at different levels of advancement are in training for all kinds of specialist work, from learning to be a spirit guide to other souls to experimenting with creating life by adapting existing blueprints to different environments.

Implicit in all of this is that many other inhabited planets exist throughout the universe, some more physical than others. So, for example, we might advance enough to reunite with the Earthly source or logos, but we would still have a massive way to go before we could begin to appreciate, let alone reunite with, the ultimate creative source or power of the universe as a whole. We might also need to gain different types of experience by incarnating on other planets.

This is rather more complex that the relatively simplistic idea, held by most worldviews on reincarnation, that once we have finished with Earth, the ultimate source immediately awaits us. Some esoteric worldviews discuss hierarchies of angels and demons and different layers of heaven and hell and so on, and Kabbalism incorporates brave attempts to show that the ethereal realms are many-layered. But they tend to represent somewhat rigid and hierarchical approaches, whereas the modern evidence is practical and relatively down-to-earth. It removes a great deal of what—at risk of being controversial—is arguably no more than idle speculation from the process.

To be even more practical in our approach, we need to understand what karmic advancement really means, and how we go about achieving it. Again, past approaches to reincarnation have adopted different views of this process. For example, some of the more rigid philosophies have suggested that any sort of karma, whether good or bad, creates a reaction that must be completed—so the trick is to lead a life of such asceticism, and to reject the physical world to such an extent, that one creates no more karma. Fortunately, modern research suggests that this is complete nonsense based on the questionable premise that karma is about "action and reaction."

Nowhere is this principle more in evidence than in the Hindu view that, for example, people who are disabled are being punished for some misdemeanor in their past. But can this be true? If we return to Stevenson's cases of birthmarks and defects, we find they give us a significant clue, even though their importance as pointers to karmic dynamics has not been properly addressed before.

The subjects find themselves with what appears to be a physical punishment in their current life, and yet they were usually innocent victims in the previous life. How does that represent a karmic process of action and reaction? The answer, I have concluded, is that it does not.

Modern interlife research shows that more-advanced souls not only conduct detailed reviews of their past lives, but also plan their next ones. And even when they choose adverse circumstances, such as physical disability or financial or emotional deprivation, they do so to progress their karma as part of a learning experience. But this research also shows that less advanced souls often ignore all review and planning advice in the interlife, and as a result their lives tend to exhibit repetitive patterns.

This means they repeatedly face similar adverse circumstances, but they are given another opportunity to learn the lesson that escaped them in the past—not brought on by some sort of karmic punishment, or dynamic of action and reaction. The most crucial test is to properly assimilate strong negative emotions of hatred, fear, jealousy, revenge, and so on, either during incarnate life or in the interlife, so that they no longer hold their restrictive karmic charge.

The unfortunates in the birthmark and defect cases seem—arguably through having no proper interlife experience—to have retained rather than diffused emotions of such power from their last life that these were imprinted on their next body—although the defects might serve constructively as reminders that they have emotions from the past that need sorting out.

Thus, the strongest conclusion from my analysis of modern evidence is that karma and karmic progression are about learning and experiencing both sides of every coin. There is no karmic law of action and reaction, and in fact this aspect of the revealed wisdom of the past is not just misleading but positively harmful as well.

Another area in which much of the revealed wisdom of the past is brought into question by modern evidence is the latter's revelation of the extent to which we create our own surroundings in the ethereal realms, based on our expectations and level of karmic advancement. And nowhere is this view more controversial than when we turn to ideas of hell and demons. Although a very few of the modern pioneers concentrate specifically on demonic possession, most find that their subjects are unanimous in the following view: that such ideas are merely human psychological constructs.

This does not mean that they are not real to some people, and certainly those with the strong expectation that they will encounter demons and hellish states in the interlife might do so. But these will be psychic manifestations of their own making, with no permanent or underlying validity. The implication is that if, both individually and collectively, we stop feeding these psychic manifestations with psychic energy, they will wither and fade.

I appreciate that some people might suggest that this is all very fine as far as it goes, but that in itself this modern research and analysis is reductionist and fails to capture the real essence of spiritual experience and esoteric wisdom. I accept that, to some extent, this may be true. Certainly more-advanced spiritual practitioners might well be exploring avenues beyond this relatively simple analysis.

But even those who experiment constructively with powerful hallucinogens or are experienced in entering altered states of consciousness by meditation alone would be well advised to remember the extent to which they may be experiencing or even creating psychic constructs based on their own preconceived ideas, which therefore may have limited objective or underlying validity. In addition, in a more practical sense, if they have been working from a false premise about the workings of karma, for example, then I would argue that even these people might want to go back to the drawing board and reevaluate their approach.

I have a strong belief that this new, rational spirituality that modern research has made available to us can have a massively empowering effect on us as individuals, and that if enough of us take its main precepts on board, we have a genuine chance of altering the future of humanity for the better.

Recommended Reading: Selected Bibliography

Introduction

Brown, Dan. *The Da Vinci Code*. New York: Doubleday, 2003.

Burgess, Anthony. *A Clockwork Orange*. New York: Norton, 1967.

Salinger, J. D. *A Catcher in the Rye*. Philadelphia: Chelsea House Publishers, 2000.

Shermer, Michael. *Why People Believe Weird Things: Pseudoscience, Superstition, and Other Confusions of Our Time*. New York: W. H. Freeman, 1997.

Vonnegut, Kurt. *Slaughterhouse Five*. New York: Delacorte, 1969.

Chapter 1. The Mystery of the Christ

Baigent, Michael, Richard Leigh, and Henry Lincoln. *Holy Blood, Holy Grail*. New York: Delacorte Press, 1982.

———. *The Messianic Legacy*. New York: Holt, 1987.

Brown, Dan. *The Da Vinci Code*. New York: Doubleday, 2003.

Campbell, Joseph. *The Hero with a Thousand Faces*. Princeton, N.J.: Princeton University Press, 1949.

Conrad, Joseph. *Lord Jim*. Cambridge, Mass.: R. Bentley, 1920.

Frazer, Sir James. *The Golden Bough*. New York: The Macmillan Company, 1940.

Golb, Norman. *Who Wrote the Dead Sea Scrolls? The Search for the Secret of Qumran*. New York: Scribner, 1995.

The Gospel of Mary Magdalene. Translated by Jean-Yves Leloup. Rochester, Vt.: Inner Traditions, 2002.

The Gospel of Thomas, Annoted and Explained. Translation and Annotation by Stevan Davies. Woodstock, Vt.: Skylight Paths Publishing, 2002.

Kipling, Rudyard. *The Man Who Would Be King*. New York: Farrar, Straus and Giroux, 2005.

Pagels, Elaine. *The Gnostic Gospels*. New York: Vintage, 1989.

Chapter 2. The Osiris Connection

11 Corinthians 5:10.

Cott, Jonathan. *Isis and Osiris: Exploring the Myth.* New York: Doubleday, 1994.

John 11:25.

Chapter 3. East of Qumran

Baigent, Michael, and Richard Leigh. *The Dead Sea Scrolls Deception.* New York: Summit Books, 1991.

Baigent, Michael, Richard Leigh, and Henry Lincoln. *Holy Blood, Holy Grail.* New York: Delacorte Press, 1982.

Brown, Dan. *The Da Vinci Code.* New York: Doubleday, 2003.

Eisenman, Robert, and Michael Wise. *The Dead Sea Scrolls Uncovered: The First Translation and Interpretation of 50 Key Documents Withheld for Over 35 Years.* New York: Penguin Books, 1993.

Gandhi, Vichard R. *The Life of Saint Issa.* Kila, Mont.: Kessinger Publishing, 2003.

Golb, Norman. *Who Wrote the Dead Sea Scrolls? The Search for the Secret of Qumran.* New York: Scribner, 1995.

Notovitch, Nicolas. *The Unknown Life of Jesus Christ: By the Discoverer of the Manuscript, Nicholas Notovich.* New York: Gordon Press, 1974.

Rig Veda. Translated by Wendy Doniger. New York: Penguin Classics, 2005.

Chapter 4. New Light on Christian Origins

Baigent, Michael, Richard Leigh, and Henry Lincoln. *Holy Blood, Holy Grail.* New York: Delacorte Press, 1982.

Acts 15.

Brown, Dan. *The Da Vinci Code.* New York: Doubleday, 2003.

Bütz, Jeffrey. *The Brother of Jesus and the Lost Teachings of Christianity.* Rochester, Vt.: Inner Traditions, 2005.

Emmerich, Anne Catherine. *The Dolorous Passion of Our Lord Jesus Christ.* Mineola, N.Y.: Dover Publications, 2004.

Chapter 5. Spreading the Goddess Gospel

Baigent, Michael, Richard Leigh, and Henry Lincoln. *Holy Blood, Holy Grail.* New York: Delacorte Press, 1982.

Brown, Dan. *The Da Vinci Code.* New York: Doubleday, 2003.

Starbird, Margaret. *The Goddess in the Gospels: Reclaiming the Sacred Feminine.* Rochester, Vt.: Bear & Company, 1998.

———. *The Woman with the Alabaster Jar: Mary Magdalen and the Holy Grail.* Rochester, Vt.: Bear & Company, 1993.

Chapter 6. Searching for the Real Star of Bethlehem

Ezra 10:9, 13.

Luke 2:8–12.

Matthew 2:1–3.

Matthew 2:16.

Song of Solomon 2:11.

Chapter 7. Hidden History

Baigent, Michael, Richard Leigh, and Henry Lincoln. *Holy Blood, Holy Grail.* New York: Delacorte Press, 1982.

Baigent, Michael, and Richard Leigh. *The Temple and the Lodge.* London: J. Cape, 1989.

Brown, Dan. *The Da Vinci Code.* New York: Doubleday, 2003.

Chopra, Deepak. *The Return of Merlin: A Novel.* New York: Harmony Books, 1995.

Hancock, Graham. *The Sign and the Seal: The Quest for the Lost Ark of the Covenant.* New York: Simon and Schuster, 1993.

von Eschenbach, Wolfram. *Wolfram von Eschenbach's* Parzival: *An Attempt at a Total Evaluation.* Bern: Francke, 1973.

Chapter 8. The Templars and the Vatican

Blavatsky, Madame Helena Petrovna. *Isis Unveiled: A Master Key to the Mysteries of Ancient and Modern Science and Theology.* Pasadena, Calif.: Theosophical University Press, 1972.

Knight, Christopher, and Robert Lomas. *The Hiram Key: Pharaohs, Freemasons, and the Discovery of the Secret Scrolls of Jesus.* Rockport, Mass.: Element, 1998.

Levi, Eliphas. *The History of Magic: Including a Clear and Precise Exposition of Its Procedure, Its Rites and Its Mysteries.* London: W. Rider & Sons, 1913.

Chapter 9. The Lost Templar Fleet and the Jolly Roger

Baigent, Michael, and Richard Leigh. *The Temple and the Lodge.* London: J. Cape, 1989.

Bradley, Michael Anderson, and Deanna Theilmann-Bean. *Holy Grail Across the Atlantic.* Toronto: Hounslow Press, 1998.

Chapter 10. The Mystery of the Battle of Bannockburn

Allen, Richard Hinckley. *Star Names: Their Lore and Meaning*. New York and Leipzig: G. E. Stechert, 1899.

Baigent, Michael, Richard Leigh, and Henry Lincoln. *Holy Blood, Holy Grail*. New York: Delacorte Press, 1982.

Barbour, John. *The Bruce, or the Book of the Most Excellent and Nobel Prince Robert De Broyss, King of Scots*. London and New York: Published for the Early English Text Society by the Oxford University Press, 1968.

Bower, Walter. *History Book for Scots: Selections from* Scotichronicon. Edited by D. E. R. Watt. Edinburgh: Mercat Press, 1998.

Burns, Robert. *The Complete Poems and Songs of Robert Burns*. New Lanark, England: Geddes & Grosset, 2002.

Gardner, Laurence. *Bloodline of the Holy Grail: The Hidden Lineage of Jesus Revealed*. Rockport, Mass.: Element, 1996.

Laidler, Keith. *The Head of God: The Lost Treasure of the Templars*. London: Weidenfeld & Nicholson, 1998.

Wallace-Murphy, Tim, and Marilyn Hopkins. *Custodians of Truth: The Continuance of Rex Deus*. York Beach, Maine: Weiser Books, 2005.

Chapter 11. The Pyramids of Scotland

Bower, Walter. *History Book for Scots: Selections from* Scotichronicon. Edited by D. E. R. Watt. Edinburgh: Mercat Press, 1998.

Chapter 12. The Enigma of the Great Lost Sailor's Map

Hapgood, Charles. *Maps of the Ancient Sea Kings, Evidence of Advanced Civilization in the Ice Age*. Philadelphia: Chilton Books, 1966.

Chapter 14. The Lost Treasure of the Knights Templar

Baigent, Michael, Richard Leigh, and Henry Lincoln. *Holy Blood, Holy Grail*. New York: Delacorte Press, 1982.

Sora, Steven. *The Lost Treasure of the Knights Templar: Solving the Oak Island Mystery*. Rochester, Vt.: Destiny Books, 1999.

Chapter 15. The Mysteries of Rosslyn Chapel

Brown, Dan. *The Da Vinci Code*. New York: Doubleday, 2003.

Hall, Manly P. *The Secret Teachings of All Ages: An Encyclopedic Outline of Masonic, Hermetic, Qabbalistic and Rosicrucian Symbolical Philosophy*. Los Angeles: Philosophical Research Society, 1988.

Hermetica: The Greek Corpus Hermeticum and the Latin Asclepius in a New English Translation. Cambridge, England: Cambridge University Press, 1992.

Wallace-Murphy, Tim, and Marilyn Hopkins. *Rosslyn: Guardians of the Secrets of the Holy Grail.* Rockport, Mass.: Element, 1999.

Chapter 16. Further Anomalies of Rosslyn Chapel Unveiled

Kerr, Mark. *Proceedings of the Society of Antiquaries in Scotland,* vol. 12, 1877. onlinebooks.library.upenn.edu/webbin/serial?id=procsascot.

Slezer, John. *Theatrum Scotiae.* Edinburgh: Printed by G. Ramsay for J. Thomson, 1814.

Wallace-Murphy, Tim, and Marilyn Hopkins. *Rosslyn: Guardians of the Secrets of the Holy Grail.* Rockport, Mass.: Element, 1999.

Chapter 17. A Crack in *The Da Vinci Code*

Barbour, John. *The Bruce, or the Book of the Most Excellent and Nobel Prince Robert De Broyss, King of Scots.* London and New York: Published for the Early English Text Society by the Oxford University Press, 1968.

Bentley, James. *Restless Bones: The Story of Relics.* London: Constable, 1985.

Bower, Walter. *History Book for Scots: Selections from* Scotichronicon. Edited by D. E. R. Watt. Edinburgh: Mercat Press, 1998.

Brown, Dan. *The Da Vinci Code.* New York: Doubleday, 2003.

Gardner, Laurence. *Bloodline of the Holy Grail: The Hidden Lineage of Jesus Revealed.* Rockport, Mass: Element, 1998.

The Gospel of Thomas, Annoted and Explained. Translation and Annotation by Stevan Davies. Woodstock, Vt.: Skylight Paths Publishing, 2002.

Kerr, Mark. *Proceedings of the Society of Antiquaries in Scotland,* vol. 12, 1876. onlinebooks.library.upenn.edu/webbin/serial?id=procsascot.

Pistis Sophia: The Gnostic Tradition of Mary Magdalen, Jesus, and His Disciples. Translated by G. R. S. Mead. Mineola, N.Y.: Dover, 2005.

Chapter 18. The Real Secret Society Behind *The Da Vinci Code*

Baigent, Michael, Richard Leigh, and Henry Lincoln. *Holy Blood, Holy Grail.* New York: Delacorte Press, 1982.

Brown, Dan. *The Da Vinci Code.* New York: Doubleday, 2003.

Gower, John. *Confessio Amantis (Medieval Academy Reprints For Teaching).* Toronto: The University of Toronto Press, 1981.

Picknett, Lynn, and Clive Prince. *The Sion Revelation*. New York: Touchstone, 2006.

Waite, Arthur Edward. *The Brotherhood of the Rosy Cross*. Kila, Mont.: Kessinger Publishing, 1992.

Yates, Frances. *The Rosicrucian Enlightenment*. London: Routledge, 2001.

Chapter 19. "The Star-Spangled Banner" and America's Origins

Baigent, Michael, and Richard Leigh. *The Temple and the Lodge*. London: J. Cape, 1989.

Chapter 21. National Secrets

Baigent, Michael, Richard Leigh, and Henry Lincoln. *Holy Blood, Holy Grail*. New York: Delacorte Press, 1982.

Brown, Dan. *The Da Vinci Code*. New York: Doubleday, 2003.

Ovason, David. *The Secret Architecture of Our Nation's Capital: The Masons and the Building of Washington, D.C.* New York: HarperCollins, 2000.

Chapter 22. Bacon, Shakespeare, and the Spear of Athena

Bacon, Francis. *New Atlantis: Begun by Lord Verulam and Continued by R. H.* Los Angeles: Philosophical Research Society, 1985.

———. *Sylva Sylvarum: Or, a Natural Historie*. London: Printed by J. Haviland for W. Lee, 1631.

Shakespeare, William. *Richard II*. New York: Washington Square Press, 1996.

———. *The Tempest*. New York: Washington Square Press, 1994.

Chapter 23. Unlocking the Shakespeare Riddle

Bacon, Francis. *The Advancement of Learning*. New York: Modern Library, 2001.

Shakespeare, William. *Hamlet*. New York: Washington Square Press, 2003.

———. *The Tempest*. New York: Washington Square Press, 1994.

Chapter 24. Francis Bacon and the Sign of the Double A

Bacon, Francis. *New Atlantis: Begun by Lord Verulam and Continued by R. H.* Los Angeles: Philosophical Research Society, 1985.

Bayley, Harold. *The Lost Language of Symbolism*. Mineola, N.Y.: Dover, 2006.

———. *The Tragedy of Sir Francis Bacon: An Appeal for Further Investigation and Research*. New York: Haskell House, 1970.

Budge, E. A. Wallis. *The Egyptian Book of the Dead.* Kila, Mont.: Kessinger Publishing, 2005.

Potts, Mrs. Henry. *Francis Bacon and His Secret Society: An Attempt to Collect and Unite the Lost Links of a Long and Strong Chain.* New York: AMS Press, 1975.

Smith, William Henry. *Bacon and Shakespeare: An Inquiry Touching Players, Playhouses, Play-Writers in the Days of Elizabeth.* London: J. R. Smith, 1857.

Chapter 25. The Nostradamus Perspective

Koke, Steven. *Hidden Millennium, the Doomsday Fallacy.* West Chester, Penn.: Chrysalis Books, 1998.

Nostradamus, Michel, and John Hogue. *Nostradamus, the Complete Prophecies.* London: Thorsons Publishers, 1997.

Spadaro, Patricia, Elizabeth Clare Prophet, and Murray L. Steinman. *Saint Germain's Prophecy for the New Millennium: Includes Dramatic Prophecies from Nostradamus, Edgar Cayce, and Mother Mary.* Corwin Springs, Mont.: Summit University Press, 1999.

Chapter 26. Giordano Bruno

Hermetica: The Greek Corpus Hermeticum and the Latin Asclepius in a New English Translation. Cambridge, England: Cambridge University Press, 1992.

Mendoza, Ramon G. *The Acentric Labyrinth: Giordano Bruno's Prelude to Contemporary Cosmology.* Rockport, Mass.: Element, 1995.

Chapter 27. Joan of Arc Revealed

Baigent, Michael, Richard Leigh, and Henry Lincoln. *Holy Blood, Holy Grail.* New York: Delacorte Press, 1982.

Shakespeare, William. *Henry VI, Parts I, II & III.* Edited by Lawrence V. Ryan. New York: Signet Classics, 1986.

———. *Twelfth Night.* New York: Washington Square Press, 2004.

Chapter 28. The Alchemist's Resurrection

Hermetica: The Greek Corpus Hermeticum and the Latin Asclepius in a New English Translation. Cambridge, England: Cambridge University Press, 1992.

Jollivet-Castelot, François. *Comment On Devient Alchimiste* (1897), or *How to Become an Alchemist.* Paris: Chamuel, 1897.

Jung, Carl. *Alchemical Studies*. Translated by R. F. C. Hull. Princeton, N.J.: Princeton University Press, 1967.

Lewis, Harvey Spencer. *The Mystic Triangle, 1925: A Modern Magazine of Rosicrucian Philosophy*. Kila, Mont.: Kessinger Publishing, 1942.

McIntosh, Christopher. *The Rosicrucians: The History, Mythology and Rituals of an Occult Order*. York Beach, Maine: Weiser Books, 1998.

Rowe, Joseph. *The Quintessence of Alchemy: The Gnosis Interview with François Trojani*. http://www.lumen.org. Summer 1996.

Chapter 29. Fulcanelli and the Mystery of the Cathedrals

Bréton, André. *Manifestos of Surrealism*. Translated by Richard Seaver and Helen R. Lane. Ann Arbor: University of Michigan Press, 1969.

Fulcanelli. *Le Mystère des Cathédrales (The Mystery of the Cathedrals): Esoteric Interpretation of the Hermetic Symbols of the Great Work*. London: Spearman, 1971.

Hugo, Victor. *The Hunchback of Notre Dame*. Adapted by Marc Cerasini. New York: Random House, 2005.

Chapter 30. Isaac Newton and the Occult

Hermetica: The Greek Corpus Hermeticum and the Latin Asclepius in a New English Translation. Cambridge, England: Cambridge University Press, 1992.

Needham, Joseph. *Science and Civilization in China*. Cambridge, England: Cambridge University Press, 2004.

Newton, Isaac. *Opticks: Or a Treatise of the Reflections, Refractions, Inflections & Colours of Light-Based on the Fourth Edition London, 1730*. Mineola, N.Y.: Dover, 1952.

———. *The Principia: Mathematical Principles of Natural Philosophy*. Berkeley: University of California Press, 1999.

White, Michael. *Isaac Newton: The Last Sorcerer*. Reading, Mass.: Perseus Books, 1999.

Chapter 31. Newton, Alchemy, and the Rise of the British Empire

Newton, Isaac. *The Principia: Mathematical Principles of Natural Philosophy*. Berkeley: University of California Press, 1999.

Chapter 32. Newton and the Bible

Daniel 7:26–27.

Drosnin, Michael. *The Bible Code*. New York: Touchstone, 1998.

———. *The Bible Code II*. New York: Penguin. 2003

Newton, Isaac. *The Principia: Mathematical Principles of Natural Philosophy*. Berkeley: University of California Press, 1999.

Newton, Isaac. *Observations Upon the Prophecies of Daniel and the Apocalypse of St. John*. Kila, Mont.: Kessinger Publishing, 2003.

Snobelen, Stephen. *Isaac Newton, Heretic*, available in PDF format at www.isaac-newton.org.

Chapter 33. The Remarkable Life of G. I. Gurdjieff

Beekman Taylor, Paul. *Gurdjieff and Orage: Brothers in Elysium*. York Beach, Maine: Weiser Books, 2001.

Blake, William. *The Complete Poetry and Prose of William Blake*. Berkeley: University of California Press, 1982.

Gurdjieff, G. I. *Beelzebub's Tales to His Grandson*. New York: Penguin Group, 2005.

———. *Meetings with Remarkable Men*. New York: Penguin Books, 1969.

Joyce, James. *Finnegan's Wake*. New York: Penguin Books, 1999.

Milton, John. *Paradise Lost: A Prose Rendition*. Edited by Robert A. Shepherd Jr. New York: Seabury Press, 1983.

Moore, James. *Gurdjieff: A Biography*. Rockport, Mass.: Element Books, 1999.

Ouspensky, P. D. *In Search of the Miraculous: Fragments of an Unknown Teaching*. San Diego: Harcourt, Inc., 2001.

Waldo, David Frank. *The Rediscovery of Man: A Memoir and a Methodology of Modern Life*. New York: G. Braziller, 1958.

Chapter 34. The Casting Out of Evil Spirits

Modi, Dr. Shakuntala. *Remarkable Healings: A Psychiatrist Discovers Unsuspected Roots of Mental and Physical Illness*. Charlottesville, Va.: Hampton Roads Publishing, 1997.

Chapter 35. The Paranormal Autobiography of Benvenuto Cellini

Cellini, Benvenuto. *The Autobiography of Benvenuto Cellini*. Translated by John Addington Symonds. Kila, Mont.: Kessinger Publishing, 2005.

Chapter 36. Dostoyevsky and Spiritualism

Dostoyevsky, Fyodor. *The Best Short Stories of Fyodor Dostoyevsky*. New York: Modern Library, 2001.

———. *The Brothers Karamazov*. New York: Signet Classics, 1999.

———. *Crime and Punishment.* Translated by Richard Pevear and Larissa Volokhonsky. New York: Everyman's Library, 1993.

———. *Writer's Diary, Vol. 1: 1873–1876.* Translated by Kenneth Lantz. Evanston, Ill.: Northwestern University Press, 1997.

———. *The Idiot.* New York: Fine Creative Media, 2004.

———. *Notes from the Underground.* Translated and edited by Michael R. Katz. New York: Norton, 2001.

———. *Poor Folk.* Translated and with an introduction by Richard Pevear and Larissa Volokhonsky. Ann Arbor, Mich.: Ardis, 1982.

———. *The Possessed.* Translated by Constance Garnett. New York: Barnes & Noble Classics, 2005.

———. *A Raw Youth* [or, *The Adolescent*]. New York: Dial Press, 1947.

Swedenborg, Emanuel. *Heaven and Its Wonders Described with an Account of Hell.* Kila, Mont.: Kessinger Publishing, 2004.

———. *The Spiritual Diary of Emanuel Swedenborg.* London: Newbery, Hodson, 1846.

Wilson, Colin. *The Occult.* London: Hodder & Stoughton, 1971.

Chapter 37. Victor Hugo and the Spirits

Hugo, Victor. *The Hunchback of Notre Dame.* Adapted by Marc Cerasini. New York: Random House, 2005.

———. *Les Misérables.* Translated by C. E. Wilbur. Edited by Laurence M. Porter. New York: Barnes & Noble Classics, 2005.

The Zohar. Translated by Daniel C. Matt. Stanford: Stanford University Press, 2003.

Chapter 38. Sound and Pictures from the Other Side

Macy, Mark, and Dr. Pat Kubis. *Conversations Beyond the Light: Communication with Departed Friends & Colleagues by Electronic Means.* Irvine, Calif.: Griffin Publishing Group, 1995.

Chapter 39. Understanding the Near-Death Experience

Atwater, P. M. H. *Coming Back to Life.* New York: Citadel Press, 2001.

———. *The New Children and Near-Death Experiences.* Rochester, Vt.: Bear & Company, 2003.

Moody, Dr. Raymond A. Jr. *Life After Life: The Investigation of a Phenomenon-Survival of Bodily Death.* San Francisco: HarperSanFrancisco, 2001.

Morse, Dr. Melvin, with Paul Perry. *Closer to the Light: Learning from the Near-Death Experiences of Children.* Boston, Mass: Ivy Books, 1991.

Ring, Kenneth. *Life at Death: A Scientific Investigation of the Near-Death Experience.* New York: Quill, 1980.

Tart, Charles. *Altered States of Consciousness.* San Francisco: HarperSanFrancisco, 1990.

———. *Transpersonal Psychologies.* London: Routledge and Keagan Paul, 1975.

Chapter 40. The Case for Reincarnation

Lawton, Ian. *Genesis Unveiled: The Secret Legacy of a Forgotten Race.* Montpelier, Vt.: Invisible Cities Press, 2002.

Contributors

P. M. H. Atwater, L.H.D., is one of the original researchers in the field of near-death studies. Today, her research base extends to nearly four thousand adults and children and some of her work has been verified in clinical studies. Her findings are contained in seven books, listed on her web site at www.pmhatwater.com. *Beyond the Indigo Children,* her latest book, is the first in-depth study of today's children to combine objective research with mystical traditions and prophecy.

Vincent Bridges is the coauthor of *The Mysteries of the Great Cross at Hendaye: Alchemy and the End of Time* (Destiny Books, 2003). He was also the historical consultant and on-camera tour guide for the groundbreaking biography *Nostradamus: 500 Years Later* (first aired in December 2003 and still playing on the History Channel). More of his work is available at http://vincentbridges.com.

Peter Bros is the president of The FAR, a trust that owns over 120,000 Eastern Mediterranean artifacts, including approximately 20,000 manuscripts, some of which are scrolls dating back more than two thousand years. A critic of consensual science (peterbros.com), he is the author of *The Copernican Series* (nine volumes). His latest book is *Let's Talk Flying Saucers: How Crackpot Ideas Are Blinding Us to Reality and Leading Us to Extinction,* the "crackpot ideas" being the dogma of empirical science.

Richard Russell Cassaro is the author of the groundbreaking book *The Deeper Truth: Uncovering the Missing History of Egypt,* which evokes a powerful image of Osiris as the Shepherd, Messiah, and eternal King of ancient Egypt.

John Chambers is the author of *Conversations with Eternity: The Forgotten Masterpiece of Victor Hugo,* which is his translation of Victor Hugo's tapping-table experiences on Jersey Island. A former managing editor of International Thomson Publishing, John is currently the director of New Paradigm Books (http://www.newpara.com), in Boca Raton, Florida.

David H. Childress has studied firsthand the remains of ancient civilizations in Africa, the Middle East, and China. He is a recognized expert on ancient civilizations and their technology and is the author of *The Lost Cities Series* (eight titles) and numerous other books that chronicle his experiences delving into ancient mysteries. He continues to explore, write, and excite people about the possibility of discovery through his magazine *World Explorer* and his publishing company, Adventures Unlimited Press, located in Kempton, Illinois.

Bill Eigles is the managing editor of *Aperture,* the quarterly publication of the International Remote Viewing Association, which promotes scientifically validated paranormal perception. A former attorney and professional engineer, he is a writer, advocate, and noetic adviser.

Virginia Fellows is the author of *The Shakespeare Code,* which explains some of the amazing facts she discovered after years of research about the great and only partially understood philosopher Francis Bacon. Virginia was working on a second book on Bacon and the occult when she passed away in October 2005.

William Henry is an investigative mythologist and a special projects researcher at the Subliminal Research Foundation in Albuquerque, New Mexico. His extensive database of Egyptian and Sumerian symbolism and mythology enables him to detect the startling ways history is repeating itself today. He is interviewed regularly on radio programs and lectures internationally.

J. Douglas Kenyon has spent the last forty years breaking down barriers to paradigm-challenging ideas. Utilizing the media in their various forms, he has consistently pushed points of view largely ignored by the mainstream press. He founded *Atlantis Rising* magazine in 1994, and it has since become a "magazine of record" for ancient mysteries, alternative science, and unexplained anomalies. He is the editor of *Forbidden History,* a thought-provoking book featuring the work of such groundbreaking researchers as Graham Hancock, John Anthony West, and Zecharia Sitchin.

Ian Lawton is a full-time writer-researcher and lecturer specializing in ancient history, esoterica, and spiritual philosophy. His first two books, *Giza: The Truth* and *Genesis Unveiled,* were noted for the scholarly and logical approach to the spiritual aspects of the matters they explored. In 2004 he wrote *The Book of the Soul,* critical acclaim for which led him to found the Rational Spirituality Movement (www.ianlawtom.com and www.rsmovement.org).

David Lewis is a journalist who specializes in alternative scholarship, dealing with the origins of life, civilization, and human existence. He has regularly contributed articles to *Atlantis Rising* that deal with alternative theories of history, science, human origins, and consciousness.

Cynthia Logan has been a staff writer for *Atlantis Rising* magazine since its inception. She has also contributed to other regional and international publications on the subjects of yoga and alternative medicine.

Jeff Nisbet has enjoyed a thirty-year career in the news business, which has given him a ringside seat to the art of "spin," enabling him to see that the "spin doctors" have worked behind the scenes for millennia to cobble together an approved version of the history we are meant to accept blindly. His investigations indicate that subtexts wait to be found, written between and beneath the lines of both "history" and "myth"—subtexts that ring closer to actual truth than does the subject matter we are taught in grade school.

Peter Novak is a researcher on mankind's cultural legends and modern phenomenological reports of life after death. He is the acclaimed author of such groundbreaking books as *The Division of Consciousness* and *The Lost Secret of Death,* and is often heard on syndicated TV and radio shows as well as being a featured speaker at conferences and symposia in America, Canada, and Europe. In addition, he has had several major papers published on the psychology of afterlife phenomena.

Mark Amaru Pinkham is the North American Grand Prior of the International Order of Gnostic Templars (www.GnosticTemplars.org). He is the author of *Guardians of the Holy Grail: The Knights Templar, John the Baptist, and the Water of Life,* and he is often interviewed on national radio and television regarding the Knights Templar mysteries and secret societies. He is also a tour leader to sacred sites around the world that are associated with the Knights Templar and the Holy Grail.

Steven Sora studied history at Long Island University, although his real passion was uncovering the mysteries left *out* of the history books. While he was collecting evidence of pre-Columbian Atlantic crossings, he came across the two-hundred-year-old search for treasure on tiny Oak Island in Nova Scotia. After a decade of study and travel to research the topic, his book *The Lost Treasure of the Knights Templar* was published in 1999.

Mark Stavish studied alchemy with the Philosophers of Nature—a research and educational group in Wheaton, Illinois, whose focus is alchemy and its techniques—from 1995 to 2000, acting as the director of the Occult Research and Applications Project (ORA) during that period. He is the author of several books: *The Path of Alchemy—Energetic Healing and the World of Natural Magic, Healing Paths—Kabbalah and Energetic Healing,* and *Through the Gates—Lucid Dreaming, Astral Projection, and the Body of Light in Western Esotericism.* He is currently the director of studies for the Institute for Hermetic Studies in Wyoming, Pennsylvania.

BOOKS OF RELATED INTEREST

Forbidden History
Prehistoric Technologies, Extraterrestrial Intervention, and the Suppressed Origins of Civilization
Edited by J. Douglas Kenyon

Gnostic Philosophy
From Ancient Persia to Modern Times
by Tobias Churton

Christianity: An Ancient Egyptian Religion
by Ahmed Osman

The Mystery of the Copper Scroll of Qumran
The Essene Record of the Treasure of Akhenaten
by Robert Feather

The Templars and the Assassins
The Militia of Heaven
by James Wasserman

The Secret History of Freemasonry
Its Origins and Connection to the Knights Templar
by Paul Naudon

Secret Societies of America's Elite
From the Knights Templar to Skull and Bones
by Steven Sora

Founding Fathers, Secret Societies
Freemasons, Illuminati, Rosicrucians, and the Decoding of the Great Seal
by Robert Hieronimus, Ph.D., with Laura Cortner

Inner Traditions • Bear & Company
P.O. Box 388
Rochester, VT 05767
1-800-246-8648
www.InnerTraditions.com

Or contact your local bookseller